# Tribal Situation in India

# Tribal Situation in India

*Issues and Development*

SECOND REVISED EDITION

*Edited by*

**Vidyut Joshi**

**Chandrakant Upadhyaya**

Tribal Research and Training Institute
Gujarat Vidyapith, Ahmedabad

**RAWAT PUBLICATIONS**

Jaipur • New Delhi • Bangalore • Guwahati • Kolkata

ISBN 978-81-316-0865-4



*Published under the auspices of Tribal Research and Training Institute, Gujarat Vidyapith.*



*Published by*
Prem Rawat for **Rawat Publications**
Satyam Apts, Sector 3, Jawahar Nagar, Jaipur 302 004 (India)
Phone: 0141 265 1748 / 7006 Fax: 0141 265 1748
E-mail: info@rawatbooks.com
Website: www.rawatbooks.com

*New Delhi Office*
4858/24, Ansari Road, Daryaganj, New Delhi 110 002
Phone: 011 2326 3290

Also at *Bangalore, Guwahati* and *Kolkata*

Typeset by Rawat Computers, Jaipur
Printed at Chaman Enterprises, New Delhi

# Contents

# Preface

Tribal Research and Training Institute (TRTI), Gujarat Vidyapith, celebrated its Golden Jubilee in 2013. Various programmes were carried out as part of the two-year-long celebration. One of the programmes was to organize a regional seminar on 'Issues and Development of Tribal Communities in Western India. Academicians and tribal activists from four states – Rajasthan, Gujarat, Madhya Pradesh and Maharashtra – participated in the seminar and presented their research papers. They were asked to revise their papers based on the discussion held during seminar. Present volume is the collection of these revised papers. It includes two papers on general issues, four papers on tribal situation in four respective states, two papers on land and forest issues, two papers on health issues, three papers on education, two papers on development and identity issues and two papers on tribal administration issues. We had to drop some papers as they did not fulfil the requirement.

The senior editor, Vidyut Joshi, had brought out a book *Tribal Situation in India* around 1998. At that time the impact of liberalization, privatization and globalization were not so clear as they are today. Moreover, tribals world over have been organizing under the banner of UNO to assert their first nation identity. They have a different concept of development, which is going to become important in future. This change has given a paradigm shift to tribal studies world over. This volume incorporates two such papers along with development studies.

Tribals living in western India belt share a common environment. They were not fully isolated, some of them had direct interactions on daily basis with non-tribals living in these four states. Gandhian workers went to this belt and started Ashrams around 1922 which became centres of tribal development activities. One finds more education, more forest co-operatives, better agriculture and almost no violent organizations which can be seen in other tribal areas of the country. In some cases a tribe is found in one pocket spread in three different states. They have marriage relations, common history, common dialect and also a feeling of belongingness to one community. Bhils of Jhabua (MP) and of Panchmahals (Gujarat) and Tadavis of Maharashtra and Gujarat represent such cases. It was because of this that when Tadavis of Maharashtra faced submergence at Saradar Sarovar project, they preferred to rehabilitate in Gujarat with their Tadavi kins.

Since most of the papers presented in this seminar have state bias, commonalities were not consciously brought out in papers. Our objective was to share our experiences and learn from each other. We found that not only the tribals have common life and culture, they also face common problems. Depletion of resources, growing poverty, submergence and rehabilitation and seasonal migration. These commonalities require a common approach in all the four states. The tribal administration is state specific, but there are common and inter-dependent problems.

A reader will find three different undercurrents in this volume: (1) ethnographic studies, (2) development studies, and (3) identity or critical studies. The last trend has appeared strongly after 1980. We have incorporated papers having all the three approaches.

We are thankful to the authorities of Gujarat Vidyapith for allowing us to hold the seminar and also publishing this volume. We are also thankful to various scholars and tribal activists who took out time from their busy schedule to write papers and put their ideas on paper.

**Vidyut Joshi**
**Chandrakant Upadhyay**

# Acknowledgement

This edited volume is an outcome of collective efforts of several individuals and organisation. First of all, we are thankful to Tribal Research and Training Institute, Gujarat Vidyapith and Tribal Development Department, Government of Gujarat for their kind support to organise the Regional Seminar on 'Issues and Development of Tribal Communities in Western India' on 9–10 August 2015. In this seminar we received more than 20 research papers on different topics related to tribal development in the context of Western Indian states. Out of the papers received, we selected 17 papers for this edited volume. We are thankful to Dr Anamik Shah, Vice Chancellor, Gujarat Vidyapith; Dr Rajendra Khimani, Registrar, Gujarat Vidyapith; and Dr Nimisha Shukla, In Charge Director, Tribal Research and Training Institute, Gujarat Vidyapith for their encouragement and support for bringing out this book. We are thankful to Arun Patel, Sarbeswar Sahoo and Pankaj Mahadik of Tribal Research and Training Institute, Gujarat Vidyapith for their support from the beginning of the workshop till completion of final manuscript of the book. We are thankful to Samir Parmar and Ghanshyam Patel for typing and formatting of the manuscript. We are also thankful to Rawat Publications, Jaipur who agreed to be the co-publisher of the book along with Gujarat Vidyapith.

**Vidyut Joshi**
**Chandrakant Upadhyaya**

# Contributors

**Vidyut Joshi**, Ex-Vice-Chancellor of Bhavnagar University, Gujarat.

**Chandrakant Upadhyaya**, Ex-Director, Tribal Research and Training Institute, Gujarat Vidyapith, Ahmedabad.

**Binoy Acharya**, Director, Unnati, Ahmedabad.

**Tattwamasi Paltasingh**, Professor and Head, Department of Sociology, Sambalpur University, Odisha.

**T.K. Vaishnav**, Deputy Secretary, Chhattisgarh Government, Governor House, Raipur.

**Ganesh Patel**, Ex-Faculty, Tribal Research and Training Institute, Bhopal.

**Madhusudan Trivedi**, Retired Professor and Head, Department of Sociology, Rajasthan Vidyapith, Udaipur.

**Binod C. Agrawal**, Ex-Director, Taleem Foundation, Ahmedabad.

**Sarbeswara Sahoo**, Tribal Research and Training Institute, Gujarat Vidyapith, Ahmedabad.

**Satyakam Joshi**, Director, Centre for Social Studies, Surat.

**Mahender Jethmalani**, Patheya Budget Centre, Ahmedabad, Gujarat.

**Ashok Chaudhari**, Social Activist and Chairman, Adivasi Ekata Samiti, Western India, Gujarat.

**Suman Meena**, Department of Economics, JJT University, Jhunjhunu, Rajasthan.

**J.C. Patel**, Professor and Head, Department of Sociology, Gujarat University, Ahmedabad.

**Kanubhai Vasava**, Assistant Professor in Gujarati, Gujarat Vidyapith, Shadra Campus, Shadra.

# 1

# Introduction

**Vidyut Joshi**

The basic features of our Constitution indicate direction of change or modernization, if one wants to say so, of our society. It is supposed to be a casteless, secular, democratic and socialist polity and society. One may question this type of direction itself, but that could be a separate issue for discussion. So far as this paper is concerned, this type of direction provides the point of departure for discussion on how we have formulated the tribal problem.

The point that follows from this is that we have shaped or we are supposed to have shaped our policies and programmes to realize this type of change. We judge failure or success of our policies and programmes from this point of view. But what is more important here is that our Constitution considers, at least formally, every citizen as equal. Legal and administrative framework, institutional network and policies of development in general are also considered suitable for tribals. Of course, tribals are part of the Indian society and general problems of consciously changing or modernizing Indian society are also applicable to them. But they also form a special case in this wider framework and the problem is the nature and type of this special category. Perhaps there is no unanimity among sociologists and anthropologists on this point. So the 'problem that has been exercising in the minds of thinking persons in India, especially after the attainment of independence, is what should be the place of tribal peoples in the framework of the Indian nation and how they should be developed and brought to a level with the rest of the people socially, economically, culturally and politically'. There were several debates on this issue at the dawn of Independence. Three different approaches of isolation, assimilation and integration were put forth. Late Pandit Jawaharlal Nehru took initiative in accepting the approach of integration (Nehru, 1955: 1–8) for tribal development policy. Thus, 'the tribal policy, apart from the constitutional provision, is the contribution of late Prime Minister Shri Jawaharlal Nehru. He (also) advocated five principles, known as the tribal 'Panchshil' (Joshi, 1987: II). Our various policies and programmes of tribal development are supposed to have been based on this approach of integrating tribals with the mainstream and bring them at par with rest of the people. Of course, someone may raise question about this so-called 'mainstream', and that is worth raising issue. However, it does not concern us at this juncture.

Though it must be agreed that 'the Indian experiment of tribal development has been hailed as unique in the Third World perspective of the treatment of the indigenous people, one has to take a balanced view of its processes' (Singh, 1982: 1322). On one side, the tribals have become full citizens. They have, by and large, maintained their identity. They have not gone extinct and have rather maintained their demographic growth rate. If we consider this as a part of the integration process, why again the question of genesis arose after more than four decades of our experience? Tribal development policies and programmes assumed that all the tribals will develop and will 'integrate' themselves with the so-called 'mainstream'. This has happened only in a symbolic way. Most of our researchers agree on this point that as a result of the planned tribal development, stratification on secular lines has taken place among tribals and only a small section has been able to take advantage of our tribal development programmes. This being so, the question arises: where did we go wrong? For sometime people believed that this is because of inefficient and corrupt bureaucracy that the programmes were not implemented well. We created special administrative set-up for tribal development and we know that it has not shown better results. At some places tribals' co-operatives of different types were shaped. They worked well in the beginning. But their benefits did not percolate to the lower strata of tribals. Experiments of tribal development through voluntary efforts have proved successful only in certain cases and in certain pockets. On the other hand, land alienation pushes the pauperized tribals out of their habitats, seasonal migrants move from place to place in search of work. Generally, dams have been constructed in tribal areas by involuntary acquisition of their land. The tribals lose their land, habitat and milieu resulting into pauperization, causalization and psychological stresses and strains. Official and illicit felling of forest trees have benefitted outsiders while tribals face loss of their environment. This would lead us to revisit our basic assumptions about tribal problem. Is tribe a special category? If yes, of what type? What is the nature of tribal-non-tribal relationship? Why they are backward? Is this tribal backwardness a cultural backwardness?

## 'Tribe' and its Indian Context

The word 'tribe' is generally used for a 'socially cohesive unit, associated with a territory, the members of which regard themselves as politically autonomous' (Mitchell, 1972: 232). Often, a tribe possesses a distinct dialect and distinct cultural traits. The term 'primitive tribes' was often used by western anthropologists to denote 'a primary aggregate of peoples living in a primitive or barbarous condition under a headman or chief' (*Encyclopedia of Social Sciences*, Vol. 15). Various anthropologists define tribe as a people at earlier stage of evolution of society. This gave a sort of moral tone that the tribals are yet to develop and become civilized. It is because of this that they were also known as 'primitive', 'barbarous', or 'aboriginal' people. This sort of moralistic overtone was later on reduced by using terms like 'pre-state society', 'pre-literate society', 'folk society' or 'simple society'. All these terms with evolutionary approach indicated that the tribals are backward in comparison to other advanced groups. In this direction, tribal development means a transformation from pre-state to state society, from simple to complex society and like.

An ideal type of tribe can be characterized as a socially homogenous unit having its own dialect, political and cultural institutions and territory which isolate it from the outside influences. This sort of ideal type was constructed by early British anthropologists of evolutionary school and it fitted well to some of the African, American and Australian tribes which they studied in those days. This type of construction suited best to their cultural hegemony and colonial interests. In Indian languages we do not have any synonym for the word tribe. This means that the tribal-non-tribal categorization did not exist in pre-British era. With this background, when British scholars started studying India, they wanted to call Indian society as a society of various tribes. A Ph.D. thesis of Calcutta University was entitled as 'Some Kashatriya Tribes of Ancient India' (Law, 1923). Looking to the cultural diversity of Indian sub-continent and existence of certain highly 'civilized' groups according to their own standards, the British scholars could not describe entire sub-continent as tribal. However, they were not sure about identifying particular groups as 'tribe' or 'caste'. Latham describes certain groups in Punjab and Sindh as tribes. He describes Lepcha and Kirata as Nepalese tribes. But while describing ethnology of Gujarat, he was not sure whether the Memon, the Khoja, the Sidi, the Ahir, the Rabari and several such groups are tribes or not. So he simply describes them (Latham, 1859: 262–271). Even Enthovan, in his acclaimed work, *Tribes and Castes of Bombay Presidency*, does clearly distinguish between caste and tribe.

Nationalists in India charged anthropologists for destroying national identity by creating a category called 'tribe' for which there was no synonym in almost all Indian languages. However, it should be noted that in India it was not the anthropologist but the colonial officer who played the key role as an adviser, researcher and administrator in tribal affairs. Ghurye writes: 'In the Census Report of 1891, Baines arranged the castes according to their traditional occupations. Under the category of agricultural and pastoral castes, he formed a sub-heading and named it 'forest tribes'. In next two censuses, those of 1901 and 1911, Sir Herbert Rieley and Sir E.A. Gait included the so-called animists. Dr Hutton, at the 1931 Census, followed Baines, but substituted the term 'primitive tribes' for 'forest tribes' (Ghurye, 1943: 7). It is necessary to remember here that it was only Ghurye who did not accept the category of 'tribe' as propounded by the British. But most of the Indian academic, under the influence of their British counterparts, accepted the evolutionary definition of tribe (Vidyarthi and Rai, 1976: 167–174). However, when it came to determining elements of tribes for the purpose of naming a group as tribe, there was no unanimity. The degree and range of differences, especially with reference to their relations with the non-tribals, show so much variation that it was extremely difficult, almost impossible, to evolve one single ideal type of Indian tribals. There is so great variations in their ways of life, past and present, that any attempt to classify them would remain arbitrary in absence of its total understanding.

But one thing is certain that except a few groups all the 'tribals' had relations with 'non-tribals'. What is necessary is to define the nature and type of that relationship. We will deal with this issue in the latter part of this paper.

In the absence of a suitable definition of tribals, we have resorted to arbitrary selection of certain social groups living in forests and hills and we have belied them as 'Scheduled Tribes' for the purpose of some special programmes to be given to them as prescribed by the Constitution. The story of how various social groups were included in the schedule is well known and needs no repetition. It was exigency and it was also necessary to immediately select certain groups for providing special programmes. But it was not necessary for our scholars and administrators to forcibly fit the characteristics, described by western anthropologists' notion of a tribe as an isolate, homogenous, autonomous social unit. Now they view tribals in relations to non-tribals (Dube, 1977). This sort of change in perspective changes our entire view towards tribal problem.

India is a very complex society. It is not the best example of plural society, because while pluralism stresses cleavages and discontinuities between the sections of people differentiated by race, ethnicity, religion or culture, there has been an all-pervasive sense of cultural unity, interactions and interdependence and sharing of certain common symbols in spite of multifold diversities. Tribals were not alien, their isolation was only partial and relative, and throughout the history they were part of Indian civilizational universe. They were part of this wider civilization, at the same time they were different. They were not part of caste hierarchy in general. They were also not part of 'Sanatan Dharma'.

## Nature of the Tribal Problem

Tribal problem has a reference to non-tribals. Comparatively, they are considered backward in almost all walks of life. Now, the question is, what is the nature of this backwardness? 'Backwardness' and 'tribal backwardness' have been defined in various ways depending upon the approach that one takes. All the definitions of backwardness are based on arbitrary points of backwardness and development. However, we should take note of some approaches.

The classical anthropological approach defines backwardness in terms of culture. From the evolution of culture point of view, there is obvious distinction between 'primitive' and 'civilized', between 'simple' and 'complex' societies, between 'scattered' and 'dense' population and above all between 'pre-state' (autonomous) society and societies that have 'developed' state.

This kind of evolutionary approach also delineates various stages of economic development on which different civilizations can be placed.

Tribal backwardness is termed as 'primitive' in this parlance, because they are considered to be on lower stage of development. It is also believed that if tribals are put in contact with advanced culture, they will learn and develop. People from the 'civilized world' become a sort of change agent when they come into contact with tribals.

Taking tribals as isolated from the mainstream of Indian culture several people have opined that this isolation should break and cultural contacts with the non-tribals will help them in overcoming their backwardness. Several anthropologists in India have tried to prepare scale of development and placed various tribal communities somewhere on this scale after measurement. All tribal development programmes have a basic assumption that the development administration will help tribals. Not only that but some of the officers believe that they are there to develop tribals. This has happened only partially. On the other hand, the non-tribal intervention has created certain problems like pauperization, land alienation and seasonal migration.

Indian social scientists have found the genesis of backwardness in social situations. The world 'social' has been identified with caste and hence 'defective caste structure' is considered to be the genesis of backwardness. Following paragraphs lucidly describe the genesis of backwardness in terms of caste:

> It has been noted already that the problem of backwardness has arisen on account of the defective Hindu social order. Even Islam and Christianity could not escape the all pervasive influence of castes.

Many representatives who met us, and especially those of younger generation, attributed the present plight of a large number of the backward classes to economic backwardness and suggested with a facile logic that the only way to remove social evils was to improve the economic conditions of the depressed and backward classes. The economic backwardness of a large majority is certainly alarming, and in itself constitutes a colossal problem. But we must recognize that in India economic backwardness is often the result and not the cause of social evils. Our society was not built on an economic structure, but on the medieval ideas of 'varna', caste and social hierarchy (Government of India, 1955: 39).

The idea of attributing backwardness to caste system has relevance in terms of tribal backwardness also. Because it was postulated that the tribes were 'backward Hindus' a part of Hindu society and they were to be absorbed in the larger Hindu system with the help of the process of sanskritization. However, the process of development that started was a secular one of the linking tribal economy with national economy – that started penetrating in tribal region. The very development process has created stratification on secular lines within tribal community.

The British notion of tribal backwardness stems from their notion of cultural backwardness. The British policy tried to separate tribals from the non-tribals. When British entered tribal areas, there were encounters and uprisings. Hence, the administration of such regions was separated from civil administration. This came to be known as 'non-regulation system'. It was believed that this system, with its 'simple methods of administration and avoidance of complicated rules and procedure, was peculiarly suited to aboriginal race' (Sinha, 1970: 6). In 1874, the Scheduled Districts act was passed as a result of which civil and criminal justice, settlement operations and revenue works were given to special officers in this area. The Government of India Act of 1935 provided for 'excluded areas' and 'partially excluded areas' outside the scope of the legislature and under the authority of the Governor. Various such acts were passed to separate tribal areas from the rest of India. Of course, such a separation was arbitrary, because there was no clear demarcation between the tribals and the non-tribals. Verrier Elwin's approach should be evaluated in this context, but unfortunately his British birth came in the way of the better appreciation of his views. Some of his views on tribal problem still have a relevance.

The British policy of isolation was opposed by the nationalists. They were very clear that the tribals were part of Indian Society (or Hindu society as some have put it). The ground for this approach was prepared by A.V. Thakkar, popularly known as Thakkarbapa, and some workers of 'Servants of India Society' (or Hindu society as some have put it), who did pioneering work among the tribes. Many nationalist leaders supported tribal movements against the British. The Congress, under the leadership of Mahatma Gandhi, opposed the segregation of tribals from the rest of India. It asked its workers to go to tribal areas, establish *ashrams* and prepare them for the national struggle. Opposing British policy of isolation of tribals was a part of its anti-British and nationalist ideology. Hence, it naturally considered assimilation of tribals with the non-tribal India.

Until the Independence, the general trend among sociologists and anthropologists was to study the social and cultural aspects of tribal life. The question of what to do with the tribes did not bother them much. For them, it was clear that they were part of the Indian society and they believed that the difference between the tribals and non-tribals would gradually vanish and the tribals will merge in the mainstream. The only problem was to speed up this process with as much ease as possible.

## Tribal-Non-Tribal Relationship

Historically speaking tribals always had relations with the non-tribals. But the formation of princely states by Rajputs in tribal regions led to a sort of relationship between non-tribal kings and tribal subjects. Tribal situation in Gujarat has not been studied from this point of view. This was a 'winner-loser' or 'patronage-exploitation' type of relationship. Apart from the mythological stories of tribal-non-tribal relations, the recorded history narrates that during the Mughal period, the land was in abundance and Bhils were living in forest leading as prosperous life as non-tribal rural folks used to live. It was during this period that the Mughals won over several kingdoms in Rajputana and Rajput chiefs came to Gujarat. Some of them came to forest areas and won the Bhils in fierce battles. The Bhils had to run away and settle in hills. The hill terrains were not that fertile. The economic degeneration and relative isolation took place between the 12th century and the 16th century. Kesrisinh of Gabbargah (near Ambaji) killed a Bhil chief and established his rule in Taranga in 1269 AD. Ashkaran was a well-known king in his line who was named as 'Maharana' by Mughal king Akbar. In Panchmahal, Jalamsinh established 'Jhalod' village as his capital and subjugated Bhils of the surrounding area. One of his descendants named Kumar went further into the interior and established 'Sunth' estate in 1255 AD (Parikh, 1979: 133–147). The states of Baria, Naswati Chhota Udepur, Rajpipla, Vansda and Dharampura in tribal region have similar stories. In almost all cases the Bhil chieftains lost and left the places to settle in interior forests.

These historical records prove that the Bhils (not 'tribe' in modern parlance) were either subjugated or driven away into the interior forests by invading Rajputs. The subjugation or life in forests brought changes in their lifestyle and culture. But it is necessary to remember that this sort of culture is the result of the historical experiences through which they have passed.

In British and Gaikwad territories things took a fairly different shape. Gaikwad won the kingdom from a Bhil chief and established his fort which came to be known as 'Sogandh' (Desai, 1920). Gaikwad invited Patidars from Kheda who cleared forests and settled in tribal areas of Baroda in South Gujarat. Dublas of Valsad and Surat, Vasavas of Bharuch and Rathwas of Baroda were traditionally cultivating land in this zone. The Rathwas were known as Rathwa Koli and Koli is a caste. However, they were not 'owners' of land in legal sense of the term because land settlement was not done in this area. Patidars settled here and became legal owners whereas tribals became their ... labourers.

The Parsis had fled into tribal belt in the 15th and 16th centuries to escape the prosecution at the hands of Sultan of Gujarat (Hardiman, 1985). They settled in rural south Gujarat and gradually became landowners whereas erstwhile owners Dublas became their 'halis' or landless labourers. How they became landless labourers is to be seen in their land relations. Things were not much different in Rajasthan, Madhya Pradesh and Maharashtra.

As a result of the Muslim invasion of Rajasthan, Gujarat and Malwa that occurred during that time, many Rajput warriors fled these areas and came to settle in the Narmada valley. Around 1437 AD, the Rathore (Rajput) chieftain Anand Dev claimed for himself the kingdom of Aliraipur, his kin carving up Phulmal, Sondwa and Jobat as their territory (Baviskar, 1995: 54).

This type of formation of states in tribal regions subjected tribals to the Rajput authority. Thus, when the word 'tribe' was coined for forest dwellers, they were not isolated and politically autonomous people. They were already integrated within the administration of British India or within the Indian states where the British kept a watch. Thus, the backwardness of Indian tribes is because of this subjugation and not because of isolation and autonomy.

Though states were established in tribal regions, there was not much 'administration' by native states in interior tribal villages. Native states invited non-tribal cultivators from plains and settled them in not much interior parts. Compared to native tribals, the non-tribal peasants came with superior agricultural technology and produced surplus with the help of tribal labourers. In almost all cases, non-tribals who came late became landowners whereas the native tribals became landless labourers. In Gujarat, this sort of master-servant relationship developed in some parts having mixed population. Backwardness of landless labourer tribes should be attributed to this relationship. The non-tribal masters were against any sort of social reform among these tribals and they were harassing those tribals who were doing such activities (Joshi, 1980: 21). Around 1922, when Jugatram Dave went to Sarbhon village and started teaching Halpatis, his efforts met with failure because their masters did not allow Halpatis to attend school (Dave, 1975). Not only that, but they were kept as bonded labourers by the landowner masters and they had no freedom to choose their fate (Breman, 1974: 36–45). The disintegration of 'hali' (bonded labour) system was even more painful for erstwhile servants. Now, he is free in a free market but has no job. The question for him was not only that of liberation but also of empowerment so that he gets his dues.

When we talk of land and tribals, land acquisition for development purpose must be kept in mind. Almost all dams are located in tribal areas. This location is important because the irrigation helps non-tribals in plains, while tribals get alienated from their land. The Land Acquisition Act of 1894 provides for cash compensation. It is assumed that with the compensation in form of cash they receive, the tribal oustees would purchase land elsewhere and get resettled. The special situation of the tribals was not taken into consideration and policy for their rehabilitation was not formulated. As a result, several thousand tribal oustees were deprived in such development projects (Joshi, 1987: 21–26).

Same is the case of tribal's relationship with forests. Prior to 1854, forest was not a scarce commodity and tribals were traditionally enjoying forest rights. But then forest wood was required to build battleships in England. It was also required to build railway lines. When the British government started cutting forest for this and such other purposes, there were encounters. By the enactment of the Forest Act of 1864, the government took away all the customary forest rights of the tribals. They were allowed to cultivate forest land only by paying fines.

Thus, tribal backwardness is neither cultural nor social (caste-based) at root. They were not isolated, homogeneous tribals as viewed by some British anthropologists. They had relations with people in plains. But, in this relationship, they have always remained losers and have suffered in terms of forest, land and water resources.

The scenario changed after 1990. After Rio summit, educated tribals established their own organization. This has given rise of identity politics in this region. All four states have their 'Adivasi Ekta Parishad'. It is an identity-based organization which tries to raise awareness for sustainable tribal development, conserve and assent tribal development, making participation of tribals possible in their development programmes, demand autonomy and demand implementation of all the provisions of PESA and Forest Rights Act. In fact, enactment of PESA and FRA were due to the pressure created by this awareness.

## Conclusion

So, the tribals are part of the Indian society, at the same time they are different. Special policy and programmes are required to address and redress these differences. When we plan for tribal development, we have to regard these differences, take a special note of their different situations and capabilities and provide them facilitation to develop on the line they want to take. The very meaning of development is unfolding from within. This means that the tribals have to unfold their capabilities to develop. Outsiders cannot develop tribals, they can become only facilitators if they want to do so. If they have to unfold from within, they must have participation in any development decision. Their felt needs should be transformed in development programmes. Nehru did this in slightly different manner when he proclaimed 'Panchsheel'.

How can tribals participate in their development programmes? They can participate only if they are considered as equals. The command and obey relationship can take place between unequals only. An individual tribal is too weak to stand as equal against a non-tribal. So they have to get organized. The forms of organization could be different depending upon different programmes. The non-tribals have to work as facilitator for organization-building. Once organized on the basis of felt needs, they will develop content and programmes for their participation. When tribals' participation, in different development programmes, is accepted in various departmental documents, it should not remain ceremonial.

## References

Baviskar, Amita. *In the Belly of the River*, Oxford, Delhi, 1995.

Breman, Jan. *Patronage and Exploitation*, Routledge, New Delhi, 1974.

Dave, Jugatram. *Mari Jivankatha*, Navjivan, Ahmedabad, 1975.

Desai, Govindbhai Hathibhai. *Navsari Prant Sarva Sangraha*, Baroda State, 1920.

Dube, S.C. *Tribal Heritage of India: Ethnicity, Identity and Interaction*, Vol. I, Vikas, New Delhi, 1977.

Enthovan, R.E. *Tribes and Castes of Bombay Presidency*, Vols. I and III (Reprint), Government of India.

Ghurye, G.S. *The Aborigines: 'So-called' – And Their Future*, Gokhale Institute, Pune, 1943.

Government of India. Report of the Backward Class Commission, VI, 1955.

Hardiman, David. 'From Custom to Crime: The Politics of the Drinking in Colonial South Gujarat' in Ranajit Guha (ed.), *Subaltern Studies*, Vol. IV, Oxford, New Delhi, 1985.

India, *The Adivasis*, Publication Division, Ministry of Information and Broadcasting, New Delhi, 1955.

Joshi, Vidyut. *Ashramshala: Ek Adhyayan*, Gujarat Sewa Mandal, Ahmedabad, 1980.

Joshi, Vidyut. *Submerging Villages*, Ajanta, New Delhi, 1987.

Latham, R.G. *Ethnology of India*, John Van Voorst, London, 1859.

Law, Bimla, Charan. *Some Kashatriya Tribes of Ancient India*, University of Calcutta, Calcutta, 1923.

Mitchell, Duncan G.A. *New Dictionary of Sociology*, Routledge and Kegan Paul, London, 1972.

Nehru, Jawaharlal. 'The Tribal Folk', in Government of India, *The Adivasis*, Publication Division, Ministry of Information and Broadcasting, New Delhi, 1955.

Parikh, R.C. and Shastri, H.G. *Gujaranto Rajkiya Ane Sanskritic Itihas*, Vol. VI, B.J. Institute, Ahmedabad, 1979.

Pillai, Devdas. *Winners and Losers*, Popular, Bombay, 1972.

Sills, David L. *International Encyclopedia of Social Science*, New York, Macmillan, Reprinted edition, 1972.

Singh, K.S. 'Transformation of Tribal Society', *Economic and Political Weekly*, XVII, 33 and 34 (14 and 21 August, 1982).

Sinha, S.P. 'A Special Deal for Tribals in India: A Historical Appraisal', *Tribe* (VI. 4), March 1970.

# 2

# The Changing Nature of Tribal Studies in Western India

**Vidyut Joshi**

Sociologists and anthropologists associated with Tribal Studies complain that the golden days of Tribal Studies are over. Gone are the days when a participant observer was spending many days in tribal areas to understand tribal society and culture.

Over the years, it has been seen and people also talk that the golden days of tribal research are over. There were times when we used to walk in tribal areas, stay there with them, enjoy the area, enjoy the courtesy of tribal people, talk to them, live with them, be a part of them, and write reports and memories. I have written a Gujarati memoire which is very popular 'Aa Pan Gujarat Chhe Boston'. So, those days are gone. Perhaps, the nature of Tribal Studies has changed.

The issue is to find out what has happened that those days are gone. And what has happened to Anthropology and Sociology and why the feel that they are becoming irrelevant. Is it Sociology as a whole that is becoming irrelevant? Or the Sociology that we practice and Anthropology that we practice are becoming irrelevant? May be we will have to ask the question and I will begin with the Wallerstein Open the Social Science Report. In 1996, an International Commission was appointed. The task was restructuring Social Sciences and they submitted a report, with title the 'Open the Social Science' (Wallerstein, 1997).

The issue is that when we say that the golden days of tribal studies are over, we will have to remember that knowledge is a social construct. This being so, the social research that we conduct in tribal area and the text that emerges out of the research has to be seen in context. The text cannot be viewed in isolation. It has to be viewed in a context. And if we divide the tribal research scenario over a period of time, we can say that there are three different contexts in which tribal research has taken place over a period of time.

## Objective

The objective of this paper is to take a stock of tribal studies in India, with special reference to Western Indian Studies.[1] Tribal studies have also been carried out by scholars of other disciplines like Economics, History and Psychology. But the present paper covers work done mainly by sociologists and anthropologists. By tribal studies we mean research, survey or any kind of academic study, empirical or non-empirical, being carried out where reference point is tribal or scheduled tribe. This paper excludes those works carried out by Census or NSS in tribal areas.

## Text and Context

For all practical as well as academic purposes we mean to say that knowledge being a social construct, any such study should be reviewed in terms of its context. Thus, a text can be understood better in its contexts. This being so, the entire time span of Tribal Studies in India can be easily divided in three phases: First pre-Independence phase or the British Raj phase; second, post-Independence phase or the development studies phase; and third, the globalization phase or the identity studies phase.

## First Phase: Pre-Independence Phase

This phase is marked by beginning of tribal studies in India (and also elsewhere). The phase has three distinct contexts:

1. The British Raj
2. The British anthropologists' notion of tribe,
3. Tribal administration.

### *The British Raj*

The interest of British Raj in India was to understand Indian people in order to rule them. The British had a legacy of evolutionary thesis of Herbert Spencer (1867), where it was believed that like organism, the society has also evolved from a simple society to a complex society. Britain was a complex society or a developed civilization, as various systems like state, church, education had emerged there as separate systems, whereas in other parts of the world separation of systems or institutions had not taken place and hence they were tribal or primitive or simple society. This sort of knowledge of being advanced in evolution satisfied their colonial hegemony. When Britishers came to India, they came with this set of knowledge. Hence, their interest was to understand Indian people, their life and culture to rule them with this perspective.

### *The British Anthropologists' Notion of Tribe*

Prior to the British rule, we had no generic term like tribe to address a set of people. Ours was a complex hierarchical society and we had different names for different people. The British anthropology used to define tribe as a 'socially cohesive unit, associated with a territory, the members of which regard themselves as politically autonomous' (Mitchel, 1979: 232). Often a tribe was marked with a distinct dialect and distinct cultural traits. The term primitive tribe was used by western anthropologists to denote 'a primary group of people living in a primitive or barbarous condition under a headman or a chief (*Encyclopaedia of Social Sciences,* v. 15). Various anthropologists defined tribe as a people at the earlier stage of evolution. This sort of anthropological knowledge gave a moral tone that tribals are yet to develop and become civilized. It is for this that they were also called 'primitive', 'barbarous,' or 'aboriginal' people. This sort of moral tone by anthropology was reduced by using terms like 'pre-state society', 'pre-literate society', 'folk society' or 'simple society'.

### *The Tribal Administration*

When contractors of the Raj went to tribal areas, they were beaten by tribals for entering their region and cutting their forests. This compelled the British administrators to understand tribal society and culture. Moreover, the Raj also assumed the role of tribal transformation which they took as 'Transforming tribal society form a pre-state, to a state society, pre-literate to a literate society, from animistic religion to an organized religious society and from a simple society to a developed complex society. This task was handled more by the missionaries. When the British Raj was established here, Britishers were interested in forest resources. In 1849 or so when the first British contractor went to forest to cut teakwood to say down the railway track, they were beaten by tribals – 'why are you cutting our forest?' So they appointed a commission over how to peacefully clear fealty forest. And the first Forest Act was carried out in 1854 and the objective was to clear fealty forest. Not to regrow the forest. Today forest department claims that the objective at that time was to clear fell forest. So their interest was to peacefully manage tribal area to clear fealty forest and to exploit resources. So they studied tribals, their lifestyles, their behaviour pattern, and did not disturb them much. It was isolation, as practiced by Verrier Elvin, that is to put them in isolation and manage them well.

## Overview of the Literature

### *The Tribal Studies in First Phase*

The Britishers did not want to disturb tribal area because if revolt took place it would be difficult to rule and they wanted forest wealth. So they had a theory of isolation: Let they be kept in reserves, let they be separated from the mainstream of society, let they remain there and we will manage them well. The first school in tribal area was established by the police department in 1856. And many a times, later on, they were managed by the forest department in those days, not by the education department. This was done to keep them isolated. This went on. And in such a context, what sort of studies would emerge? Ethnic Studies.

This sort of notion of tribe gave rise to Ethnic Studies pattern. British anthropologist wanted to call India a tribal society. A Ph.D. thesis of Calcutta University was entitled as 'Some Kshatriya Tribes of Ancient India' (Law, 1923). Latham describes certain groups of Punjab and Sindh as tribes. He describes Lepcha and Kirata as Nepalese tribes. But while describing ethnography of Gujarat, he was not sure whether the Memon, the Khojas, the Sidi, the Ahirs, the Rabaris and several other groups are tribes or not. So he simply describes them (Latham, 1859: 262–271). Even Einthoven, in his acclaimed work, *Tribes and Castes of Bombay Presidency*, does not clearly distinguish between caste and tribe in some cases.

In Indian universities, various departments of sociology and anthropology inherited this sort of evolutionary perspective and started distinguishing between castes and tribes. The trend of ethnic studies was set in. It is not our purpose to list out studies.

That has been done by Survey of Research volumes of ICSSR. What we want to say is only this that studies of life and labour, races and culture, marriage and family and a tribe or tribes of a particular areas became a trend in this pre-Independence phase.

Following this pattern, many Indian anthropologists and sociologists wrote many ethnographic accounts like 'Dublas of Gujarat' (P.G. Shah). Hutton was our census enumerating those days. And he put, first time, some section as animist tribe, to which Ghurye opposed in those days that this cannot be done. The pattern of how different tribe behaves, races and culture, life and living, marriage and family, all sorts of studies were made. Through such studies British Raj succeeded in establishing some people as tribal groups, pre-state, homogenous, dialect-speaking, territorially bound group, which is separate from mainstream India. They wanted to do it and they could successfully do it.

Nationalist scholars like Ghurye opposed to such ethnic studies and isolation approach. In 1922 Chauri-Chaura occurred and Gandhi stopped the Freedom Movement, asserting that we cannot run the Freedom Movement with violence. And he asked his workers to go to tribal areas and train the tribals to be a part of the mainstream.

## Second Phase: The Development Studies

The second phase of studies has to be seen in three different contexts now. First of all, we became a welfare state. It is said that the state was wedded to tribal development. Now research studies are conducted to support state activity of tribal development.

Before Independence, nationalist scholars charged anthropology for destroying national identity by creating a category called tribe, for which there was no synonymous in almost all Indian languages. In administration, this separate category was created by administrator. But most of the Indian academicians accepted this term and its British definition. But independent India had other problems with this set of knowledge of tribes.

### *Tribal Welfare*

The British Raj wanted to rule tribal areas for exploiting forest wealth. Now, the state of India, a welfare state, was wedded to tribal welfare and development. The Indian State put tribal affairs directly under the President. However, the evolutionary and the separatist definition of a tribe, as given by British anthropologists was not accepted. It was difficult to evolve a common definition for Indian tribes. Finally, it was left to the will of the President to identify a group as tribe. We all know many examples where mistakes have been committed.

### *The Development Perspective*

The development perspective was debated a lot in early Independence days. We all know that social scientists readily shifted away from the British notion of separation of tribes from rest of Indians and also did not accept the assimilation approach propagated by Prof. Ghurye. They all accepted the integration approach given by Jawaharlal Nehru (S.K. Singh). This was the new development perspective and it was believed that with education and other development programmes, the tribals will develop and integrate with the so-called mainstream.

### *Institutional Set-Up*

We all know that the Anthropological Survey of India 'started Tribal Studies with the development perspective. The Ethnic Studies got a back seat and Development Studies came in fore front'. Tribal Research and Training Institutes (TRTIs) were specially established to boost development efforts of the governments. Many universities opened Sociology and Anthropology departments which took up Tribal Studies. Research institutes under ICSSR also have carried out many Tribal Development Studies. Various departments of the Central and state governments also gave grants for Tribal Development Studies. All these efforts provided academic inputs in tribal development policy and programmes.

Now with change in political context, the perspective also changed. The State did want to exploit forest resources. But it also wanted to develop tribals as the State was wedded to tribal welfare. So the term changed to Scheduled Tribes, and you all know how difficult it was to prepare a list of Scheduled Tribes. A lot of debate went on in the Constitution Assembly and they could not describe the features of a tribe. So finally, when Constitution was in making, they decided that special groups selected under the 5th Schedule as decided by the President of India. President wrote to all Chief Ministers to enlist the tribes in their areas. It so happened that Gujarat was part of Bombay state and Saurashtra was a separate state, and Nalsarover where there are some 11 villages of Padhar, seven fell in Saurashtra and four fell in Gujarat part of the Bombay state. The Chief Minister of Bombay said that our tribes are in eastern forest belt, so Padhars of four villages were not incorporated in the schedule. Dhebarbhai was the Chief Minister of Saurashtra. He said that there are no tribals in Saurashtra. Manubhai Shah was Commerce Minister and it is said that he talked to Dhebarbhai to find out the tribals in Saurashtra, because of Central grant for tribal development. So they identified Padhars of seven villagers as tribals. So, two real brothers living in different villages acquired different status, one of a tribe and other one of general stream. Many such examples can be given. But what is important here is the fact that the status of 'tribe' was not given either on the basis of anthropological knowledge or anthropometric measures, lent on the basis of general impression. Birth in an ascriptive group become criteria. Mina is a tribe in Rajasthan. They are backward in south Rajasthan, but not so in other parts of the state. But they fall in one category.

So there were several such problems. And again, as British had a clear view of Evolutionary Anthropology, we had a clear exigency of developing people living in forest and hill areas. So we prepared a list and started development programmes. This is where we started the studies to help the programmes. The development perspective changed from isolation to integration. We all know the 'Nehruian Tribal Panchsheel', I need not elaborate those things.

## Studies in Second Phase

We started with Education and Tribal Development Studies. I have seen Udaipur TRTI list of Grants for publication of books.[2] They are mainly education, development, and migration studies. I have also gone through the list of studies of TRTI, Gujarat. There were 15 studies on education and 78 studies on development issues. This would be true for Maharashtra and MP TRTIs also. There are migration books and books on education, etc. It was so much important that ICSSR specially started a cell under G.P. Nayak where Gore, Desai and Chitnis edited three volumes on Education of Scheduled Castes and Scheduled Tribes in India. Several people did several kinds of studies. I am also a part of it, I studied tribal education, ashram schools and I have written some books on it. But that day, there was the belief that people really developed through education. That went on till 1990s. Then health and development, particularly Anthropological Survey of India took up the task of preparing volumes on people of India, their health and nutrition status and all sorts of studies. TRTI took up several studies. In Rajasthan, a TB study was conducted. Area planning studies, micro-planning for particular forest area, particular area planning schemes, integrated rural development plan, tribal development plan, and various sub-plans were made. Indian Institute of Management was given a special grant for Dharampur, a tribal Block development plan. Many tribal area development exercises were carried out in this phase.

Forest and Development Studies were in vogue in this phase. Most of them were survey reports meant to provide inputs in development programmes. What is the relationship between forest and tribals? As they are a part of the forest, they have to depend on the forests. There were studies on Forests Labour Cooperatives. Impact of Forest Labour Corporative on tribal development; Minor Forest Produce, 'bidi patta' and many such studies have been carried out in Rajasthan, Gujarat, MP and other places. If we want, we can make a long bibliography of such works, agriculture and development studies were also conducted. What sort of agriculture suits more in the tribal areas? What sorts of crop suits more? Various experiments were made. There was a scheme of giving buffaloes to tribals under Integrated Rural Development Plan. And in enthusiasm, we have given buffaloes to tribals. I was in Thandala Block of Jhaluna district to study IRDP. I asked them where are the buffaloes given to you. They said they are with the *baniyas*, since buffaloes are not the right animal for undulating terrain. Their preferred animal was cow, but they were given buffaloes without proper enquiry. As a result, all the buffaloes went to the *baniyas* of the region. Another scheme by the Integrated Rural Development Plan for 'primitive tribes' was to give storage bins. Since the primitive tribes do not have storage for grains, aluminum boxes were given to them to store grains.

While travelling in a tribal area known as Rajpeepla in Gujarat, a merchant came up to me, asking if I wanted aluminum grain storage boxes for cheap. On enquiry, I was told that the primitive tribes do not take these boxes, since they don't have grains to store in them. They neither have grains in their houses, nor locks on their doors. They live in huts, and there is no space to store these boxes in their homes. In our enthusiasm, we have carried out many tribal studies which partly suited and partly did not suit the tribals.

When I criticize Tribal Studies, I am criticizing myself as well, as I am a part and parcel of these studies. In western Rajasthan, Dr Doshi started the studies. Dr Doshi, Professor Madhusudan Trivedi, Dr Bargawa, Dr Mridula Trivedi, P.C. Jain, Ambrasht, Ruhela all have been engaged in one or the other aspect of tribal studies. But, in the latter half of the second phase, we started realizing that something is wrong. The vision that tribals will integrate with the mainstream is not coming true. So the larger thesis of modernization that India is a melting pot where all ethnic identities will melt and a pan India identity will emerge did not happen. So in the latter half, stratification studies began. Surat centre had organized a special seminar on this and put an emphasis on stratification studies. Even in Rajasthan, stratification studies were undertaken with questions like why only a small part of the tribals develop and form into an elite group and rest of them remain as they were. This realization was good, but had it been stretched further logically, we would have come to third stage.

The latter half of this phase is marked by stratification studies. CSS, Surat, under the stewardship of I.P. Desai gave impetus to tribal stratification studies. Of course, much earlier Bailey started this trend. S.L. Sharma carried it out in Rajasthan urban setting. This shift came more from universities and autonomous research institutes and less from ASI and TRTIs. Stratification studies clearly suggest that as a result of the development programmes, an elite class has emerged among tribals, as it has happened in non-tribal society. Tribal group, as a whole, could not develop and integrate with the main stream. It remains to be seen whether the elite tribals integrate themselves with the non-tribal elites or not. Another trend was to study development and deprivation. The Narmada Rehabilitation studies carried out by Vidyut Joshi (1986–19) are a pointer here.

## The Third Phase: The Identity Studies

The third stage starts with Rio de Janeiro, 1991. In the United Nations' Conference on Environmental Development (UNCED), there was a special section on Tribal Development. Tribal leaders and activities from world over had come there. Not only tribals, all subaltern groups like women, Dalits, Blacks, LGBT were there.

### *Change in Development Perspective*

By 1990 it was realized that this sort of development programmes will not bring the desired results of integrating tribal society into mainstream. A movement started in US, Canada and other developed countries for tribal voice in development. This was reflected in India also. The UNCED (United Nations' Conference on Environment and Development) held at Rio de Janero had a special section for indigenous people (tribals) where many Indian tribal NGOs participated. Now they have a World Forum of Indigenous People that meets every year and sets agenda for tribal development. Every year they also publish report on 'The Indigenous World'. India is covered in this report. Now they demand self-rule. They want control on their resources. They want a sustainable development. Many young elite tribals hold this view.

Now, this new set of researchers and activists oppose modernization and development, proclaiming that the kind of development being talked about really does not percolate beyond a stratum. It stays on the upper layers and benefits only a few. They opposed this type of development and said that they wanted sustainable tribal development instead. Sustainable development means where all the stakeholders get their share, and the future generation also gets its share, and the resources are not overexploited but regenerated. They also said that there is nothing like linear modernization. This finally broke the modernization myth-that there is only one set of modernism. There can be many kinds of modernism, depending on what is the meaning of being 'modern' for an individual and a group.

### *Emphasis on Human Rights*

After LPG, tribal resources have suffered a lot. Now they oppose any use of their resources that does not have their participation. They demand their rights. This has of course put government administration in some difficulties in administering tribal areas. The Naxal Movement is the extreme form of this approach.

The way development took place was America-centred. And the Wallerstein Open the Social Science Report also criticizes the way Social Sciences are structured to satisfy post-1945 need of Europe and America. Then if that is the case, what about Blacks? What about minorities? What about females? What about Schedule Tribes and Dalits? Schedule Tribes from world over got united. They are meeting every year.

They don't call themselves tribes. They call themselves First Nations, claiming that they are the First Nation and everyone else is the Latter Nation.

Now tribes claimed their rights – Human Rights – to be an integral part of all discussions and decisions taken for their tribes. Human Rights Acts were as such passed in 1949, but this type of rights of other people were specially added to UNO after 1980 with this pressure. Unfortunately, we don't teach these things in anthropology and sociology.

### *Emergence of Tribal Identity*

This is actually a logical corollary of stratification studies. Now those tribals who benefitted from development programmes, did not merge with the mainstream. Instead, they want their own separate identity to be preserved. Kotada in Udaipur District has Adivasi Ekata Samiti. I visited Kotada in 1988 and stayed with them for a week. At state level there is Adivasi Ekata Samiti. This is across party line. They meet once every year and discuss developmental issues. They also want to revive tribal culture in changing circumstances.

So far as Sociology and Anthropology and other Social Sciences are concerned, the days of grand theories and meta narratives are over. This is anti-foundationalism that has come to stay. This has changed our research practices also. The days of hegemony of research institutes are over. The days of an Anthropologist spending days in fieldwork are over. The days of Action research, identity research and participation by tribals in research have come to stay.

Zeenabhai Darji, a non-tribal Gandhian leader who was running several very good institutions in south Gujarat in Vyaara area, was once told by young tribals to leave the area and turn the institution over to the tribals. Harivallabh Parikh, who was running Rangpur Ashram, also faced such opposition. Harivallabh

Parikh was sick and I went to see him. There were some tribals outside the ashram. They refused to come inside the ashram and asked me to accompany them to their village for a discussion. In a conversation that lasted all night, they told me that they will respect Harivallabh Parikh till he is alive, but as soon as he passes away, they will take over the ashram. These kinds of things have started happening. They further argued, what do you call freedom after all? 'My Village, My Rule'. Why did we take back India from the British? So that we will have our rule, our regulations, our justice, our culture in our village and this is how the village will be structured. This is what Nehru said, which did not come true through our development phase.

## Tribal Studies in the Third Phase

The Tribal Studies in this phase has three sub-sets – all known as identity studies. First set is by those anthropologists and sociologists who are critical of mainstream Development Studies. Second sub-set is by tribal elites who want to assert their identity and express themselves through literature. Third sub-set is the certification studies or status enquiry studies by TRTIs. All three sub-sets are qualitatively different.

The pioneer of first sub-set is a Canadian anthropologist, Hugh Broody, with his book *Maps and Dreams*. He came to Gujarat on a World Bank Mission that opposed Narmada Sardar Sarovar Project. He said that you acquire land, build dams and you go through the records prepared by the government. But what is the concept of land among the tribals? There are three layers of land holdings among tribals. First is the 'house' land, second is the 'farm' land, and the third is the 'grazing' land, where their cattle is grazed. When the grazing land is acquired by the government, no kind of compensation is paid to the cattle breeders who are dependent on the land for feeding their cattle. The question is that since they have their own norms of governance, and have been running their affairs for several generations, who are we, as outsiders, to interfere in their affairs, make rules for them and try to run their society? They want to run their own organizations. This kind of identity search is emerging in a big way in tribal areas, even in Rajasthan up to some extent.

After Hue Broody, I came across an anthropologist Felix Padel book *Out of this Earth*. Felix Padel studied Vedanta in

Orissa. He said that to a tribal, their hill alumina (*Dungar*) is their God. We are scratching their God and disturbing them. He asked the Indian anthropologists and sociologists to leave them alone, let them do what they want with their hills. We already know what results have come in Orissa of a movement against Vedanta.

Some of you might know Baburao Baviskar's daughter Amita Baviskar. Amita Baviskar is on the line of tribal rights, and tribal identity, supporting the notion that they should be allowed to run their own affairs. Now, world over, this sort of identity studies have been institutionalized. Their paradigm is not the development paradigm. They also do not follow the usual 'survey' method and do not believe in 'objectivity'. There is a whole range of such studies and one can prepare a bibliography.

All such studies speak clearly in favour of the tribals running and managing their own affairs, preservation of their culture and identity and their active participation in all decision-making. The Government of India took note of these emerging pressures. PESA act, Forest Rights Act. PESA (Panchayati Raj Extension to Schedule Areas) Act lays down rules like acquiring permission from Gram Sabha before taking over land from a village. But these rules are not implemented either. So with the emergence of extensive identity studies, the entire fervour of conducing socio-economic Development Studies and anthropological studies by going to the tribal areas has subsided.

The second sub-set of identity studies are by tribals themselves, and some people helping them. Ganesh Devi established an institute called 'Bhasha' in Gujarat. He did an all India survey of languages, specifically tribal languages, and declared that tribal dialects and languages are dying. It was taken very well. Tribal youth, who have become educated and who are either professors or teachers or bank officers or government officers, have seen these contradictions of development and the other side-deprivation of development, such about their lifestyle, marriage style, what to preserve and what not to preserve, touched by their sensitivity and they started writing stories and poetry. Some tribal elites have started a journal named *Adilok*. Earlier, there was a journal called *Dhol*. At least 50 Tribal elites have by now published. So issue is this various forms of tribal literature. Anthropology, sociology and social sciences have come to a stage where there is a paradigm shift in knowledge. And we all belong to old paradigm, so we find ourselves on defensive. We feel that everything has deteriorated, the people are corrupted now, and tribal area has depreciated too. While, in fact, it has not. The contexts and ethos have changed and now we are not a part of the game, they are part of the game. Rajasthan has a tradition of folklore and has a folk roe society. But it has not kept pace with the new paradigm.

The third type of identity studies are carried out by the TRTI. Although it is not the case in Rajasthan, in most other states, including Gujarat, the TRTI has been given the responsibility of Certification of Scheduled Tribes and Castes. It has carried out at least 30 such studies by the end of 2012. Same is true for MP, CG and Maharashtra TRTIs. TRTI employees are engaged in checking and reporting the validity of Tribal Certification to avoid frauds in education and government jobs based on the certificates. All TRTIs in our country are engaged these days in this certificate verification tasks. Although Tribal Studies can be conducted based on genealogy, they still use governmental documents to carry out their identity studies.

## Notes

1. The paper is a revised text of the lecture delivered as (Late) Prof. S.L. Doshi Memorial Lecture. Author is thankful to the trustees of Prof. S.L. Doshi Memorial Trust.
2. Please refer to TRTI list of grants given for studies. A look at the studies made at other TRTIs (Gujarat, MP, Maharashtra and C.G.) also reveal the same pattern.

## References

*Adilok*, A Gujarati Journal by Tribals, 2012.

Baviskar, Amita. *In the Belly of the River*, Oxford, Delhi, 1995.

Broody, Hugh. *Maps and Dreams*, Douglass and MacIntyre, Vancouver, 1988.

*Dhol*, A Gujarati Journal by Tejagadh Academy, Gujarat.

Doshi, S.L. and Jain, P.C. *Social Anthropology*, Rawat, Jaipur, 2001.

Enthoven, R.E. Tribes and Castes of Bombay Presidency (Reprint), GoI.

*Encyclopaedia of Social Sciences*.

Ghurye, G.S. *The Aborigines: 'So Called' – And Their Future*, D.R. Gadril, Mumbai, 1943.

Joshi, Vidyut. *Aa Pan Gujarat Chhe Dosto* (2nd Ed.) (Gujarati), Parshwa, Ahmedabad, 2002.

Joshi, Vidyut. *Aadivasi Vikas Darshan*, Gujarat Vidyapith, Ahmedabad, 2009.

Joshi, Vidyut, *Ashram Shalao: Ek Adhyayan* (Gujarati), Samajik Seva Mandal, Ahmedabad, 1980.

Joshi, Vidyut. *Organising Unorganised Labour*, Oxford, IBH, New Delhi, 1990.

Joshi, Vidyut. *Rehabilitation: A Promise to Keep*, Tax Publication, Ahmedabad, 1991.

Joshi, Vidyut. *Submerging Villages: Problems and Prospects*, Ajanta, Delhi, 1986.

Joshi, Vidyut. *Tribal Situation in India*, Rawat, Jaipur, 1988.

Latham, R.G. *Ethnology of India*, John Van Voorst, London.

Law, Bimanchandra. *Some Kshatriya Tribes of Ancient India*, Calcutta University, 1923.

Mac, M.F. *A Select Bibliography of Scheduled Tribes*, CSSS, Surat, 1982. (Mimeo) .

Mitchel, Duncan. *New Dictionary of Sociology*, Routledge and Kegan Paul, London, 1972.

Padel, Felix and Das, Samarendra. *Out of this Earth*. Orient Black Swan, Hyderabad, 2010.

Rathod, J.N. *An Enquiry Report of Naika: Naikada of Kadada Village* (mimeo), TRTI, Ahmedabad, 2003.

Shah, P.G. Dublas of Gujarat, Gujarat Research Society, Bombay.

Sharma, S.L. *Ethnicity and Stratification among Tribals in Urban Setting*, Rawat, Jaipur, 1996.

Singh, S.K. 'Transformation of Tribal Society', *EPW*, XVII, 33 and 34.

Spencer, Herbert. *Principles of Sociology* (available online), 1867.

*Survey of Research in Sociology and Social Anthropology*, V. I-III, 1971. ICSSR, New Delhi.

*The Indigenous Word, 2002–2003*, IWGIA, Copenhagen, 2004.

Trivedi, Madhusudan. *Entrepreneurship among Tribals*, Printwell, Jaipur, 1991.

Trivedi, Mridula. *Towards Social Mobility*, Himanshu, Udaipur, 2007.

TRTI – Ahmedabad. *Publication Catalogue* (mimeo), TRTI, Ahmedabad, 2012.

Upadhyay, Chandrakant. *Pomlas of Gujarat* (mimeo), TRTI, Ahmedabad, 1981.

Wallerstein, I. et al., *Open the Social Science Report*, Vistaar, New Delhi, 1997.

# 3

# Tribal Situation in Rajasthan

**Madhusudan Trivedi**

The tribal, as we find in today's independent India, are a different lot of people. Myths about the tribal are many. It was alleged that they are uncivilized and far away from the national mainstream living in the interior parts of the country, i.e. in hills and forests. In case of tribal situation in Rajasthan, it has its roots in feudal system of princely states in Rajasthan, followed by British colonial rule, particularly, before Independence. For the purpose of government, the groups of the tribal are included in the list of Scheduled Tribes, announced by the President of India. Basically, these tribes, thus, are one of those groups that have remained steeped in illiteracy, poverty, and backwardness for centuries during the period of all the ruler communities. They have always been victims of exploitation. Their scheduled status is due to their general backwardness, poverty and exploitation in the past. Recently, their isolation has relatively been reduced with their migration to the plains, towns and cities. They accepted agriculture and many non-traditional occupations.

## Physiographic Scenario

Rajasthan is a 'Land of Kings' or 'Land of Kingdoms'. It is the largest area of 3,42,239 sq km/1,32,139 sq miles or 10.4 per cent of India. It is located on the western side of the country. The geographic features of Rajasthan are the Thar Desert – which shares border with Pakistan along with Sutlej-Indus river valley – and the Aravalli Range, which runs through the state from south-west to north-east, almost from one end to the other, for more than 850 km (530 miles). Mount Abu lies at the south-western end of the range, separated from the main ranges by the west Banas river.

## Land

The land situation of the tribals is in crisis, particularly in south Rajasthan is critical. Agriculture is not their traditional occupation. If the land cultivation is considered as a criterion of peasantry, it could safely be said that very few of them earn major portion of the livelihood from cultivation. In this region, land is rocky, sandy and undulating. There are hardly a few patches in a vast terrain, which are of good quality land. If we take the total land owned by a family, it is found that a little less than the half of the families own the size of 'less than a hectare'. In the land size between 1 to 5 hectares, there are around 55 per cent families but they can take mostly one crop a year.

**Table 1**

*Land-Men Ratio in Tribal Sub-Plan Area*

| *State/ District* | *Average Size of Land in Hectares* | | | | | |
|---|---|---|---|---|---|---|
| | *1970–1971* | *1975–1976* | *1980–1981* | *1985–1986* | *1990–1991* | *2002–2003* |
| Rajasthan | 5.4 | 4.6 | 4.4 | 4.34 | 2.24 | 1.93 |
| Banswara | 2.5 | 2.2 | 1.8 | 1.80 | NA | NA |
| Dungarpur | 2.1 | 1.8 | 1.7 | 1.41 | NA | NA |
| Udaipur | 2.2 | 2.1 | 1.84 | 1.75 | NA | NA |

*Source:* Tribal Area Development Department, Government of Rajasthan (2014–15).

A comparative examination of data shows that the state's average per capita net area is 0.49 hectare. Compared to it, the net agriculture area for tribal sub-plan is much lower. Initially land transfer and now, land alienation (as a result of lack of irrigation facilities) and land fragmentation (after the enactment of 'law of inheritance') caused further decrease in land holding size.

## Minerals

The geological succession of Rajasthan is considered to be the most complex rock structure in solid geography. There are a few formations which may be called as one of the oldest upon the surface of the earth. The state has a large variety of mineral resources. The central Aravalli region, the Delhi series and the Vindhyan systems of rocks contain the bulk of the mineral wealth of the state. Over 30 important minerals, both metallic and non-metallic, and a large variety of building stones are found. In the desert region the Eocene formation yields lignite coal. In the north-west region are found nummulitic limestone, porous sandstones and the region is believed to be potentially rich in oil. Bentonite and gypsum are some of the other minerals of the region. The Vindhyan and the Delhi systems of rock provide a variety of excellent building material, particularly the red and white sand stone and different varieties of marble. Rajasthan has a large potential in metallic mineral deposits. Copper and zinc deposits are worked upon intensively at Khetari and Udaipur, respectively.

The tribal belt, consisting of the state's tribal sub-plan area, is rich in mineral deposits such as manganese, soapstone, limestone, graphite, dolomite, and granite and building stones. The district of Udaipur possesses minerals, such as lead-zinc ore, iron ore, soap stone, fluorite, asbestos, calcite, rock-phosphate, kaolin, marble and building stones.

## The History

The history of ancient India is the history made out by orientalist Sanskrit scholars who have without any exception described the tribal as a sub-human kind of people living at the periphery of the society. R.S. Sharma has discussed about the status of the tribals in ancient India. The epistemological theoretical perspective about the tribals of this period is very clear. It was the time when the Dravidians and Aryans, and at a later stage, the Rajputs, Muthas and Mughals made all efforts to have their hegemony over the tribals.

The Aryans met some of the indigenous people who inhabited this country at the time of their immigration. The early historians do not describe particular tribal groups but refer to Nisadas a number of times. The ethnography of 18th and 19th centuries made by the British and Indian anthropologists very clearly shows that there emerged a definite division among the tribals in general and the Bhils in particular. The tribals do not have any traditional occupations like the Hindus. Certainly, tribals are early settlers in this country. They were followed by immigration of Dravidians, Aryans and other groups. In the earlier periods of history there was enough land. In the course of history, for centuries the tribals took to hills and forest life. They began to be known as *Aadimjati* – oldest residents or aboriginals, *Girijan* – hill dwellers and *Vanvasi* – forest dwellers.

During the epic period, there were two types of society. One, tribal society and the other, a territorial and Varna system based state society. Hopkins also observed that the tribal society did not have any state base. It was only the chief who commanded power. The phenomenon of class was also absent in this society. Even during the Ramayana and the Mahabharata period, the *varna-based* non-tribal society predominated. R.S. Sharma observes:

> Thus, at the initial level, during the epic period, the tribals lived on bootycapture and cattle rearing. They operated in various parts of the land of the seven rivers. Agriculture did not prove to be of any importance to them to lead to a food producing economy. And, therefore, there could not emerge any class and state system in the tribal society till the period of Gupta empire.

The tribal always remained encapsulated within the environs of hills and forests, particularly, after the invasion of the plains of the region by Rajput invaders. It is stated that the tribal practised a pastoral life characterized by animism. They were by and large, a classless and stateless society. Although the notion of an egalitarian society found among the tribal is also contested but the tribal social formation or the development of stratification among them has passed from chiefdom to state and class and not a Varna-based society.

During the medieval period, the tribal began the process of state formation and the discrete ethnic identity. In fact, they emerged as a separate power and ethnic group during this period. While discussing the process of state-formation among the tribal, K.S. Singh provides a broad-based data in support of his thesis. The process can be observed at its peak during the 13th century.

In western India, the erstwhile princely states of Banswara and Dungarpur were founded by Bhil rulers. The popular legend associates Banswara with the killing of a Bhil chieftain Bansia and Kushalgarh with that of Kushala Bhil. It is believed that their heads lie buried in the foundation of the palace gates. The image that arises from such legends is one of the establishment of the kingdom by the Rajput chiefs in the area heavily inhabited by the tribals. In course of time, the Rajputs in Bihar, Madhya Pradesh and Rajasthan established their ascendancy over the tribal hegemony and drove them to forests and hills. It was a watershed in the history of the tribal. At this juncture, a new process of ethnic-transformation began. The tribal, on one hand, took to the acceptance of Rajput ethnic attributes and, on the other, accepted Rajput political subjugation.

If we have to rely on colonial and feudal historians of the kind of Kavi Shyamal Das, Gauri Shanker Ojha, James Tod and a few others, the tribal in the independent India do not need any safeguards and protection. According to these sycophantic colonial-historians, the tribals were a brave and chivalrous people who struggled against the foreign invaders, the Mughals, and lived a very courageous life. Nowhere have the historians described the exploitation and oppression which the tribal had to face from one generation to the other at the cruel hands of their rulers and the elites (*jamindars, jagirdars* and *banias* or *mahajans*) of that time society. The legends and myths vividly given by the historians were created by the people in power.

Singh very interestingly analysed the integrative process of tribes who took to some of the Rajput ethnic characteristics as a model for their imitation. The process of state formation which was initiated in the beginning of the medieval period suffered a setback with the Rajput ascendancy. The tribals got identified as adversaries of the Rajputs. It appears that for a longer period of history beyond the medieval period, the Rajputs indeed, acted as the model of change among many Indian tribes. Whereas the accounts of Gonds, Santhals and Bhils given by Haimendorf, Tod and others for this (medieval) period indicate that the tribal groups enjoyed a lot of freedom, occupied entire tracts and lived as the lords – the masters of valleys, villages and passes. There are also events in medieval history where the tribal fought against the Mughals to help the Rajput rulers to retain their power. The Bhils helped Rana Pratap of Mewar to fight against the Mughals in the battle of Haldighati. Rajput power legitimized as a mark of 'Bhil allegiance' for the years to follow the ritual of Tika. It was performed whenever a prince was crowned by applying an inauguration mark on his forehead.

But when some of them took to settled life and migrated to plains, their mode of shifting cultivation took to low cultivation. At this stage of development little, fertile land was left because the non-tribal peasantry had already owned the most of the fertile and irrigated land. Though, in the last hundred years whatever the land-holding the tribals possessed have been fragmented to the optimum. A large number of the tribal have to give up from land cultivation.

Thus, inequality was caused and increased by the opening of tribal isolation and the administrative intervention made by the colonial and feudal powers. During this period the Bhils who remained in hills and forests were categorized as 'wild Bhil', 'Bhil of forest' or 'kalia or langotia Bhil'. And those who migrated to the plains with the opening of isolation categorized as 'Bhils of plains', 'village Bhil', 'cultivating Bhil' or 'Ujala Bhil'. Both developed social and economic differentiation which can be seen in the institutions or marriage, mode of production and above all the style of life. The tribal struggled hard to regain their political autonomy. The imperialist school of ethnographers had the vested interests to seek conversion of tribals to Christianity or Bhagatism. The opening up of isolation divided the original tribal stock into two endogamous groups of hills and plains. Historically and not traditionally, the tribals all over the country had different modes of cultivation and forest produce as their substantial sources of earning a livelihood.

During British period, as the Christian missionaries made their entry in India, they had their working base in the tribal areas all throughout India. Christianity carried with it an ideology and served in the context of colonial rule. They argued that the roots of de-generation and evil among tribals lied in their religion. They considered tribal institutions as 'degenerate and base'. If the tribal religion was changed, the Christian missionaries argued, they could be reformed. The missionaries attacked the ideological base of the tribal economy. They condemned communal ownership on local resources. They encouraged the concept of private property and land. K.S. Singh very effectively summarizes the role of missionaries in transforming the indigenous tenets of tribal economy:

> They gave a new sense of self-respect to the tribal peasants and to create a separate identity for them.

The impact of colonial rule on Indian tribes and more particularly on the tribal economy has been differential. There were only a few tribal pockets which has massive economic transformation. A large number of them, as a result of tribal policy, lost their land and weakened their access to forest. The loss of land and forest compelled them to take to agricultural wage earning and as a casual worker, and also some had to opt other urban petty occupations. It was during this period that the tribal people came in contact with non-tribals of urban background, persons in villages itself, towns and in cities in increasing frequency.

The founding fathers and the members of constituent assembly unanimously brought on record the fact that the tribal all over the country had to suffer from a number of disabilities. The safeguards in a modest way are gestures of compensation for the earlier tribal neglect and sufferings. The Constitution while providing safeties and securities ensures the fullest participation of tribal in all walks of national life. The Government of India, in pursuit of its tribal policy, has prepared certain development schemes. As a result of tribal policies, plans and programmes for tribal could not upgrade themselves as they should have been.

In post-independent India, more and more tribals have started leaving agriculture and accepted wage earning jobs, such as agriculture labour, daily wage earner as road and building construction worker, service in government, public and private sectors, etc. This is largely due to the fact that whatever land they owned, part of it was lost during the British Raj and still larger part got fragmented owing to 'the law of inheritance' in the family. After Independence, the implementation of protective discriminations are developed for the tribals after the promulgation of Constitution. The Constitution has provided certain privileges to them under Article 275.

## The People and Administrative Divisions

The Bhils, the second largest group of the state of Rajasthan, constitute the third largest group in the country, the first two being Gond and Santhal. According to the Census of 2011, the tribal population of the country is composed of 10,42,81,034 persons constituting about 8.6 per cent of the total population. The population of tribals in the state of Rajasthan consists of 92,38,534, forming 13.5 per cent of the total population of the state. Besides, Mina and Bhils, the other three major tribal groups include Garasia, Damore and Saheria.

**Table 2**

*Percentage of Tribal Population of 2001 and 2011 Census*

| *Year* | *Rajasthan* | *Banswara* | *Dungarpur* | *Pratapgarh* | *Udaipur* |
|---|---|---|---|---|---|
| 2001 | 12.6 | 72.3 | 65.1 | 59.9 | 47.9 |
| 2011 | 13.5 | 76.4 | 70.8 | 63.4 | 49.7 |

The percentage of tribal population in Rajasthan state, Banswara, Dungarpur, Pratapgarh and Udaipur of 2001 and 2011 Census, respectively, are given in Table 2. The Central government sanctions special grants to the state governments for the purpose of promoting the welfare of the scheduled tribes or to raise the level of their living. Since the planned development of the tribals, massive efforts are made by the central and the state governments to improve the quality of their life. In the year 1952, a network of basic extension and development services was established in villages. The Community Development Programme helped in creating awareness in rural communities of the potential means of development which made quicker adoption of major technological advancement in agriculture possible. Special Multipurpose Tribal Blocks were started during the First Five Year Plan. Panchayat Raj Scheme gave a boost to tribal entrepreneurship. Some non-traditional occupations were introduced among tribals through different programmes. It included Integrated Rural Development Programme (IRDP), Special Livestock Production Programme (SLPP), National Rural Employment Programme (NREP), and the new 20-Point Programme. The IRDP was launched in 1978–79 in 2,300 Development Blocks which were earlier covered by special programmes like Small Farmers Development Agency, Drought-Prone Areas Programme, Command Area Development, etc. This programme was extended further to 300 Development Blocks of the country with effect from 2 October 1980. This programme is a part of the new 20-Point Programme.

## Tribal Groups in Rajasthan

Among the Scheduled Tribes, the highest concentration is noticed, according to 1981 Census, in Banswara and Dungarpur districts where their proportion to the total population of the districts comes to 72.63 and 64.44 per cent, respectively. Other districts with higher proportion are Udaipur (34.33%), Sirohi (23.11%), Sawai Madhopur (22.67%), Chittorgarh (18.16%) and Kota (14.83%). According to the Scheduled Castes and Scheduled Tribes Orders Act, 1976, the Scheduled Tribes of the state are shown in Table 3:

**Table 3**

*Tribal Groups of Rajasthan*

| *Sr. No.* | *Tribal Groups* | *Total Tribal Population* | *(%)* |
|---|---|---|---|
| 1. | Bhil, Bhil Garasia, Dholi Bhil, Dungri Bhil, Dungri Garasia, Rawal Bhil, Tadvi Bhil, Bhaglia, Bhilala, Mawasi Bhil, Vasava. | 18,61,502 | 44.50 |
| 2. | Bhil Mina | 18,687 | 0.45 |
| 3. | Damor, Damaria | 30.603 | 0.73 |
| 4. | Dhanka, Tadvi, Tetaria, Valvi | 16,238 | 0.39 |
| 5. | Garasia (excluding Rajput Garasia) | 1,21,939 | 2.92 |
| 6. | Kathodi, Katkari, Son Kathodi, Son Katkari | 2,541 | 0.06 |
| 7. | Konka, Kokni, Kukna | 165 | 0.01 |
| 8. | Koli, Dhan, Tokre Koli, Kolcha, Kolgha | 1,881 | 0.04 |
| 9. | Mina | 20,69,456 | 49.47 |
| 10. | Naikda, Nayaka, Choli Vale, Kapadia, Nayaka, Nana Nayaka | 10,287 | 0.25 |
| 11. | Patelia | 1,724 | 0.04 |
| 12. | Saharia, Seharia, Sahariya | 41,487 | 0.98 |
| 13. | Others (unspecified) | 1,674 | 0.16 |
| | Total | 41,83,124 | 100.00 |

*Source:* Census of India, 1981, Rajasthan.

The 12 Scheduled Tribes groups, along with their sub-groups, Damore, Garasia and Seharia, constitute the major tribal groups of the state. They are major because they have a numerical strength and their concentration is in a definite pocket. As a matter of fact, racially and historically there are two major stocks of tribals, namely, the Minas and the Bhils. In Rajasthan, there is a hierarchy of the tribal groups in terms of socio-cultural and demographic variables. The Mina occupies higher rank followed by the Bhils and then other tribal groups. Table 4 shows the data from 1981 Census.

**Table 4**

*Population of Major Tribal Groups of Rajasthan According to 1981 Census*

| *Tribal Groups* | *Population* | *Percentage to total Tribal population* |
|---|---|---|
| Mina | 2,069,456 | 49.47 |
| Bhil | 1,861,502 | 44.50 |
| Garasia | 121,939 | 2.91 |
| Sahharia | 41,427 | 0.99 |
| Damor | 30,603 | 0.73 |
| Others (Unspecified) | 58,197 | 1.40 |
| Total | 4,183,124 | 100.00 |

## Literacy

In the princely states of erstwhile Rajputana, education was discouraged. Only those belonging to high castes, elites, and the rich class took to moderate education. In exceptional cases, higher education was permitted. The development of literacy and education in the state, therefore, is a post-independent phenomenon. In the first Census taken after Independence in 1951, only about nine persons out of a 100 knew how to read and write. This poor state of literacy increases to 24.05 per cent in 1981 as against the national percentage of 36.17. Their backwardness and exploitation are also due to their low level of literacy. The tribal literacy rate in 1981 was 10.27 per cent, which is most alarming. About 18.85 per cent tribal males and 1.20 in case of female tribals were literate only. The rate of literacy in tribal areas continues to be lower and distressing than the state average.

Table 5 shows the picture of district level literacy rate which is very low in comparison to the state level. If one looks at the percentage of literacy for the tribal population only, the picture is still distressing. In 1961, the literacy level among the tribals was 5.7 per cent only. There was a marginal increase in literacy percentage to 6.5 and 10.3 in 1971 and 1981, respectively. But now Census 2011 indicates that literacy rate is improving fast. The table points out that the literacy rate of the tribals in different districts of tribal sub-plan area is further very low. The literacy situation pushed the tribals to indebtedness. The number of indebted families in tribal belt is very high. It can be seen that maximum of the families took loan from moneylenders, landlords and local businessmen on very high rate of interest.

**Table 5**

*Literacy Rate in Tribal Areas*

| *Year* | *Literacy Rate (in %)* | | | |
|---|---|---|---|---|
| | *Rajasthan* | *Banswara* | *Dungarpur* | *Udaipur* |
| 1951 | 8.96 | 4.63 | 5.21 | 8.20 |
| 1961 | 15.21 | 8.79 | 10.44 | 13.60 |
| 1971 | 19.07 | 12.42 | 14.31 | 17.41 |
| 1981 | 24.38 | 16.78 | 18.20 | 22.01 |
| 1991 | 38.55 | 26.05 | 24.59 | 27.97 |
| 2001 | 60.41 | 45.50 | 48.60 | 59.80 |
| 2011 | 67.06 | 56.30 | 59,50 | 61.80 |

## History of the Tribal Development

The tribal problems vary according to the level of development attained by the tribal. For instance, those living in isolation, amidst hills and forests, have the problem of scarcity of land, lack of irrigation facilities in the hilly terrain and the increasing decay of forests surrounding their villages. For the tribals residing in plains, the nature of problems is different. Here educated unemployment has increased, the need for larger credit to modernize agriculture has become urgent and above all, social change has created a new set of problems. For the tribals living in the regions of heartland, the problems are basically economic. They do not have any political problem. They want security of job, a decent standard of living, easy accessibility to the resources of a civilized life, and acquisition of education.

The history of tribal development programmes goes back to the implementation of Community Development Projects (CDP) in the whole of the country in 1952. After two years of CDP, in 1954 Multipurpose Tribal Development Blocks were set up. This programme gave an experience to development administration that the economic standard of the tribal was generally low and this required special attention. The study team on social welfare and welfare of Backward Classes on Plan projects laid by Renuka Roy reviewed the tribal scene in the late 1950s and recommended the following areas of tribal life for intensive development in its report of July 1959: (i) Economic development and communication, (ii) Development of education, and (iii) Public health, as the overall order of priority.

While planning a strategy for tribal development the objective of the Constitution is always to be kept in view. It is determined by the central government within the provisions given by the Constitution. The mid-term appraisals of tribal development and the study teams constituted from time to time have observed that the state government should formulate an approach for tribal development concentrating on a few essential things such as drinking water, food and the year round employment at least for 300 days in a year on reasonable wages, education, and health and village roads. The Central government has devised certain development programmes which have to be implemented by the state governments in rural and tribal areas. Some of the programmes which are implemented among the tribal all over the country are – Integrated Rural Development Programme (IRDP); Drought Prone Areas Programme (DPAP); Desert Development Programme (DDP); Training of Rural youth for Self Employment (TRYSEM); Jawahar Rojgar Yojana (JRY); Development Programmes at MADA level; Sahariya Development Programme.

State government is responsible to implement development plans among the tribal people. Before the Fifth Plan, tribal development was looked over by different government departments. But in the Fifth Plan, Area Approach was taken for tribal uplift. After discussing practical aspects of policy, it became clear that the tribal area should be divided into three distinct categories: first, those areas where the tribals are in a majority; second, those areas where the tribal are scattered; and third, those areas where the Scheduled Tribes are still leading a primitive life.

For the development of the tribals in the state of Rajasthan, therefore, a three-pronged strategy has been devised since the implementation of Fifth Five Year Plan. This strategy consists of the following approaches:

1. Tribal Sub-Plan Area
2. Modified Area Development Agency
3. Sahariya Project

### *Tribal Sub-Plan Area*

In the first category, the adoption of regional development programmes is feasible. Without regional development, the development of the common people is just not possible. Therefore, the areas having a majority of tribals were demarcated and a definite sub-plan was launched for their development. In Rajasthan, special programme has been devised for tribal sub-plan region. It consists of the districts of Banswara, Dungarpur and Pratapgarh along with some tehsils of Sirohi and Udaipur districts. The areas, where there is less than 50 per cent of tribal population, are excluded from the sub-plan area. Thus, tribal sub-plan area contains 23 blocks of 17 Panchayat Samities. The area constitutes 5.8 per cent of the total area of the state having about 43.7 per cent of the state's tribal population.

### *Modified Area Development Agency*

The second category of programmes is for the development of scattered tribal in the state is known as Modified Area Development Agency (MADA). Outside the tribal sub-plan area, there are pockets of tribal people with a high percentage of concentration.

The MADA programmes are meant for those tribal who are residing in different pockets of the state. The problems of these scattered tribal are more serious than those of the tribal belonging to the first category. In the areas where the tribal are in a large number, they are still the owners of land and forest. Compared to these groups the tribal under the MADA category have to rely heavily on physical labour for their livelihood. In whole of the state, there are 38 pockets distributed over 2,938 villages belonging to the 13 districts. These 38 pockets have been identified as MADA blocks. It covers mostly about 20.6 per cent of the tribal population of the entire state. These selected villages are those which either have a population 'above 10,000' of the tribal or the villages having more than 50 per cent of the tribal.

### *Sahariya Project*

The third category of the tribals is of the population who live in a primitive lifestyle. In this category are Sahariyas, who are found in Baran district. For this primitive tribal group a special project known as Sahariya project has been devised. In this project specific development programmes are prepared for effective administration. Sahariyas are identified only primitive tribe of Rajasthan living in 435 villages in two blocks of Shahabad and Kishanganj of Baran district. Besides the above mentioned categories of tribal, there are, however, tribal groups who are not included in any area or category. There are no special programmes for these groups. They get all benefits under individual beneficiary's schemes.

## Tribal Development Programmes

Above three categories of tribal projects are continuous within development programmes. There are broadly two varieties of programmes. One, 'Regional or Area Development Programme' and the other, 'Individual Beneficiary Programme'. In the First Five Year Plan, emphasis was on tribal development through the additional financial resources for Community Development Approach to solve the problems of the tribal. At the end of the plan (1954), 43 special Multipurpose Tribal Development Projects (MTDPs) were created. This approach continued during the Second Five Year Plan. This effort was ineffective, therefore, in the Third Five Year Plan, a different strategy for tribal development was evolved by converting those Community Development Blocks into Tribal Development Block where the concentration of TDBs in the country became 504. This strategy of development had its limitations. It failed to address the cause of the tribal population of the country living outside the TDBs.

The Tribal Sub-Plan strategy was developed by an expert committee set up by the Ministry of Education and Social Welfare in 1972 under the chairmanship of Professor S.C. Dube for the rapid socio-economic development of tribal people and was adopted for the first time in the Fifth Five Year Plan. The strategy adopted continues till this day. The Planning Commission has issued guidelines for the states to earmark the funds for TSP to be placed under a separate budget head code 796 from total state plan outlay. As per guidelines issued by the Planning Commission, the tribal sub-plan funds are to be non-divertible and non-lapsable. Funds for tribal development under TSP are sourced from State Plans: the specific area programmes of Special Central Assistance (SCA) to Tribal Sub-Plan (TSP) and grants under Article 275(1) of the Constitution and funds under other schemes of the Ministry; special programmes of central ministers/departments; and institutional finances.

## Ethnicity, Ethnic Identity and Class Formation

Ethnicity consists of race, descent, and culture. An ethnic group is broadly defined as a social collectivity which possesses, and is aware of, its distinctiveness by virtue of certain shared historical experiences as well as certain objective attributes such as, race, tribe, language, religion, dress, diet, etc. – a combination of some of which endows it with a differential character vis-à-vis other groups they perceive it and it perceives them. One very ethnic character of the diverse erstwhile 19 princely states of former Rajasthan is the shared experience of living under the feudal regime. Right from the decline of the Mughal empire to the emergence of Rajput states in the 18th century, the people of princely states have suffered together the oppression and exploitation of the feudal regime. Though movements for political awakening in Rajasthan are traced back to 1905, the real thrust was provided by the establishment of Praja Mandal in different states. The first Praja Mandal was established in 1931 at Jaipur. The Mewar Praja Mandal was established in 1934. Along with other people, even the tribal men and women of erstwhile states of Mewar, Dungarpur and Banswara participated in the Freedom Movement.

According to the hypothetical position taken, Sharma considers tribals of ancient India as a class society. Class to him is a 'group of people who either own the means of production or are deprived of these' (Sharma, 1983).

## Tribal Ethnic Identity

Basically, tribal by nature are animists. They believe and enjoy nature. Their gods and goddesses represent the nature. But the tribal are defined and interpreted in the perspectives which are convenient to the non-tribal interventionists or outsiders. Ghurye argues that the tribals are backward class Hindus. Bose talks about the Hindu mode of absorbing the tribal people. Srinivas postulates that both the lower castes as well as the tribal people attempt to move up the societal ladder by adopting the style of life, including rituals of the upper castes. All these suggest that the tribal people are permanently relegated to the receiving end, constantly trying to enter or being inducted into the Hindu mainstream.

It was the genius of the tribal which took them closer to Hindu way of life. The tribal society existed in a social conditioning constituted by the historical forces of the interaction between the two – the tribal society and the Hindu society – in the sphere of religion and socio-cultural ideology. The Christian missionaries made their entry into tribal pockets with the encouragement from the British Raj and the feudals of princely states. The Bhagatism in the form of Hindu conversion movement and the Christian missionaries work to 'civilize' the masses of tribal people began. Yogendra Singh observes:

> The missionary view developed a little later. It saw all the roots of degeneration and evil in Indian society in its religion (Hinduism), and offered avenues for its redemption in conversion to Christianity – the missionaries treated, particularly Hindu Institutions as 'degenerate and base'.

Most of the missionaries were Baptists, 'from lower orders in British society'. They were committed to reforms of their own society as well as Indian society. In India, the Christian missionaries worked among the tribals of Bihar, Madhya Pradesh, Gujarat and Rajasthan. They lived in the remotest villages where the tribals were encapsulated by the hills and forests.

Robert Deliege observed that the Bhils who remained stuck in the hills and forests did not have any change in their ethnic structure. Among those who migrated to plains, there appeared the emergence of Hindu values and practices. Their economy also experienced diversification due to the introduction of monetary system. Malcolm gave three-fold division of Bhils on the basis of their ethnography. First, the Bhils who did not give up their primordial institutional practices (he gave the name 'wild Bhils'). They did not migrate to plains; second, the tribals migrated to plains but retained its habits of arm (he called the cultivating Bhils); and third, 'village Bhils' who took to settled life.

Ethnicity is a sociological construct that may acquire political functions or may be linked or used to nationalist politics by political manipulators but ethnic nationalism is only one kind of mobilization. At present, ethnicity as a multi cultural phenomenon within independent territorial nation-state is common and the issue of nationalism and ethnicity is not of immediate concern. The concept 'ethnicity' is not unknown in India. In last few years, it steadily became a part of public vocabulary. At the popular level, a whole range of things from garments to food, have increasingly been labelled ethnic. Politicians have peppered their speeches with this word while talking about various groups. Ethnicity and ethnic identity have been held responsible for virtually everything, from the break-up of nations to the outcome of elections. Gopa Sabharwal (2006) raises a question whether ethnicity has become a social category in India. Has it become a sociological category? She herself believes 'it has'. She utilizes the concept 'ethnicity' as a framework in explaining social life in a particular urban setting – Belgaum city in Karnataka state.

Most of the Indian research scholars tend to transplant western definition into India without really tailoring them to the Indian context. A few have worked out detailed typologies or approaches to ethnicity and some of the scholars write at a very general level. The scholars who have unhesitatingly used the concepts in the Indian context are mostly western, such as, Das Gupta (1975), Myron Weiner (1978), Schermerhorn (1978), Paul Brass (1985), followed by Indian scholars like Pandian (1987), Kothari (1989), Phadnis (1989), and Baruah (1994) among others. A sociological approach, based on the premise of interconnection of institutions (Beteille, 2002), cannot take an isolationist approach. Instead, the sociological approach to ethnic groups in any society needs to take into account all groups of society based on notions of shared culture, common origins and a sense of distinctiveness, may or may not be politically relevant.

For ethnicity to come about, the groups must have a minimum of contact with each other, and they must entertain idea of each other as being culturally different from themselves. It essentially is an aspect of a relationship and not a property of a group. Social relationships have an ethnic element. It is because ethnicity is an aspect of social relationship between agents who consider themselves as culturally distinctive from members of other groups with whom they have a minimum of regular interaction. Ethnicity is defined as social identity.

Thomas H. Erikson, while discussing ethnicity, describes some empirical ethnic studies:

1. *Urban Ethnic Minorities:* This category includes immigrants in cities as well as migrants to industrial towns. Research on migrants has focused on problems of adaptation, on ethnic discrimination from the host society and issues relating to identity management and cultural change.
2. *Indigenous People:* Aboriginal inhabitants of a territory are relatively powerless and are only partly integrated into the dominant nation-state. These indigenous people are associated with a non-industrial mode of production and a stateless political system.
3. *Proto-Nations:* These groups have political leaders who claim that they are entitled to their own nation-state and should not be 'ruled by others'. These groups may have more substantial characteristics in common with nations than with either urban minorities or indigenous peoples. They are always territorial based. They are differentiated on the basis of their class, status and educational achievements and they are large groups. These groups may be termed as 'nations without a state'.
4. *Ethnic Groups in 'Plural Societies':* Plural Society are usually designated as colonially created states with culturally heterogeneous populations. These groups that make up the plural society, although they are compelled to participate in uniform political and economic systems, are regarded as highly distinctive in other matters.

The definition of ethnicity would include all of these kinds of groups.

Park (1950) regarded the city as a kind of ecological system with its own internal dynamics, creating diverse opportunities and constraints for different individuals and groups. At the same time, it contained several distinct 'social worlds' based on class and race or ethnicity. Park's work highlighted that every society is more or less a successful melting-pot where diverse populations are merged, acculturated and eventually assimilated, at different rates and in different ways, depending on their place in the economic and political systems.

In the Indian context, it is important to note that urbanization preceded colonialism and hence a city is not a new structural type of which local communities have to adapt (Rao, 1991). In this regard Sabharwal (2006) says that any attempt to treat traditional Indian community structures like caste – as being transformed into ethnic groups in urban context – is not valid as such an attempt was made by Hardgrave whereas the link between tribe and ethnicity is well established in Indian Anthropology. Dealing with the concept of ethnicity, Brass (1991) remarked that 'ethnicity is to ethnic category what class consciousness is to classes.' Thus, where there are ethnic groups, the presence of ethnicity is a given. As 'ethnicity' is considered important in the mobilization of ethnic identities and is responsible to insist on the significance of their group distinctiveness and on rights that derived from this identity (Glazer and Moynihan, 1975).

Ethnicity has been a main pre-occupation since the late 1960s and it remains a central focus for research in 1990s. In 1975, Glazer and Moynihan said: 'Ethnicity seems to be a new term'. Its first usage is attributed to the American Sociologist David Riesman in 1953. The word 'ethnic', however, is much older. There are many approaches to ethnicity. All the approaches agree that ethnicity has something to do with the classification of people and group relationships. In day-to-day language, it has a ring of 'minority issues' and race relations. In social anthropology, it refers to the aspects of relationships between groups which consider themselves, and are regarded by others, as being culturally distinct. Banton (1967) says that ethnicity has to do with group identification and is more concerned with the identification of 'us' whereas racism is more oriented to the categorization of 'them' (Banton, 1983; Jenkins, 1986).

## American Approach

It is the belief that industrialization would lead to disappearance of ethnic identities. Vamer and Srole (1965) had written with hope that 'our developing industrial and factory economy with its own hierarchy permits and demands that ethnic members move up and come out of ethnic sub system into the common life of any country' (this was the melting-pot dream of American society never materialized). This never happened and today most nations are multi-ethnic and recognize cultural pluralism as the norm. Both, nation and theorists realized as did the Americans Glazer and Moynihan, in their landmark book, that ethnic groups are 'forms of social life that are capable of renewing and transforming themselves', i.e. these groups do not and will not disappear (1975). And, therefore, suddenly the main concern of American ethnicity switched from assimilation to multi-culturalism or cultural pluralism. Discrimination on ethnic grounds is spoken of as 'racism' in Trinidad and as 'communalism' in Mauritius (Eriksen, 1992) but the forms of imputed discrimination referred are nearly identical. It is true that groups who 'look different' from majorities/dominants groups may be less liable to become assimilated into the majority than the others. And it is difficult for them to escape from their ethnic identity even if they wish to. Therefore, the term ethnicity refers to relationships between groups whose members consider themselves distinctive, and these groups may be ranked hierarchically within a society. It is, therefore, necessary to distinguish clearly between ethnicity and social class.

## Soviet Approach

The Soviet approach constituted a unified body of theory rooted in Marxist philosophy, best seen in the work of Yulian Bromley, implementing, subjective and objective criteria. This approach states that 'consciousness is a fundamental feature characterizing an ethnic community' (Bromley, 1974). Consciousness implies ethnic self-awareness, i.e. ethnic identity is not an isolated phenomenon but one that is articulated in relation to other like groups in society. According to him 'unless an ethnic community is distinguished from other similar communities, it is fiction' (Bromley, 1977). He explained stability and continuity as features of an ethnic group. Stability is not permanent and may change with time. Fundamental features are retained even when the group migrates. Most of them are cultural and include language, folk art, folk lore, customs, rites, etc. Such features preserve their ethnicity even in places of new settlements. Bromley accepts the role of endogamy in maintaining the stability of the ethnicity. Religious beliefs, too, is important for inter-ethnic marriages. Theorists, who had gone in search of the new historical community among the Soviet people, were disappointed to find instead resilient nationalities.

American and Soviet approaches in different ways regarded ethnic assimilation as their main problem. Their view of assimilation did not allow them, despite the use of metaphor of 'melting-pot'. As a result of assimilation it is unpredictable that what will emerge and what new or hybrid will come in existence? Instead, both societies seemed to know in which mould the assimilation process should cast itself. Both the theories of social class always refer to systems of social ranking and distribution of power. On the other hand, ethnicity does not refer to any social ranking. Therefore, ethnic relations are always egalitarian in this context. Although, many poly-ethnic societies are ranked according to ethnic membership.

Frederick Barth (1969) and his associates chose to present ethnicity as being an aspect of social organization and not of culture. He regarded ethnic groups as social constructs that had no priori existence, and not therefore primordial groups. He stated that ethnic groups cannot exist in isolation but only in contrast to other like groups. He concluded that 'ethnic categories provide an organizational vessel that may be given varying amounts and forms of content in different socio-cultural systems. They may be of great relevance to behaviour, but they need not be; they may pervade all social life, or they may be relevant only in limited sectors of ethnicity.

Yet another theoretical perspective in ethnicity comes from Manchester School. Their main concerns were regarding the changes that came in African society as a result of colonization and urbanization Some of the theorists did a terminological shift by using ethnic groups instead of tribe. Among them, the leaders were J. Clyde Mitchell (1956), A.L. Epstein (1958), Max Gluckman (1961) and Abner Cohen (1974). They noted that traditional tribalism was of no use in urban settings and was replaced by ethnic groups. Cohen viewed ethnic groups as constructs which help people to preserve or defend political and economic interests. The emphasis on urbanization and the subsequent emergence of the concept 'ethnicity' marked an important point in African sociology.

There has been a shift in social anthropological terminology concerning the nature of the social units we study. Instead of 'tribe' the term 'ethnic group' nowadays is much more common. Ronald Cohen (1978) remarks, 'Quite suddenly, with little comment or ceremony, ethnicity is an ubiquitous presence'. This switch in terminology implies more than a mere replacement of one word with another. The use of the term 'ethnic group' suggests contact and inter-relationship. It is wrong to say that the ethnic group is in total isolation. Basically, ethnic group remains more or less discrete, but they are aware of and in contact with members of other ethnic groups.

Virtually every human being belongs to an ethnic group, no matter where he or she may be in any country. Anthropologists themselves belong to ethnic groups or nations. The concepts and models used in the study of ethnicity can often be applied to modern as well as non-modern context, to western as well as non-western societies. In this sense, the concept of ethnicity can be said to bridge two important gaps in social anthropology: it entails a focus on dynamics rather than statistics and it relativize the boundaries between 'us' and 'them', between moderns and tribals.

In that, most theories are located between two extreme positions – the primordialists and the circumstantialists. The primordialists dealt with the ascriptive nature of ethnic identity and highlight the emotional and kinship links in group formation. The believers of it stress the presence of strong primordial ties. It is also believed that ethnicity is universally observable and as deep-rooted, as say speech or kinship. The circumstantialists stress the voluntary nature of ethnicity, and define it as an identity based on social acceptance and subjective identification of internal and external social conditions. Ethnicity is, thus, defined by circumstances and constructed to achieve specific goals especially in situations of ethnic competitions (Levinson, 1994).

On the other hand, instrumentalists view ethnic identity as a tool that can be mobilized or manipulated to achieve specific ends usually in the fields of politics and the economy. The work of Paul Brass (1991) and Glazer and Moynihan (1975) are good examples of such an approach. Not all ethnic groups are based on the identity of race; similarly, not all the racial groups form ethnic groups. Racially similar groups may in fact be divided into ethnic groups on the basis of cultural distinctiveness, as has happened between the tribal groups in India. Both are the form of social differentiation, one (race) is based on physical criteria and another (ethnic group) on cultural criteria and are easy to differentiate (Van Den Berghe, 1967). Indian sociology has a sizeable literature on ethnic markers, such as, caste, religion, language, tribe, etc. but it lacks a theory of ethnicity. There is a dearth of literature on caste. In Indian society, there are other groups forming criteria (equally important) such as, region, religion, sect, language, and tribe and these cannot be ignored. But these markers have not received equal treatment in academic terms.

Indian scholars use the term ethnic or ethnicity most frequently while analysing Indian tribes. Indian social anthropologists who not only have regarded tribes as an exclusive field of study for themselves but have also stated time and again that central to their definition of tribe and ethnic group is the concept of race. They have followed the Soviet approach and tried hard to prove that India's North-Eastern tribes equal the Soviet 'ethnos' with a distinct territorial referent (Acharya, 1988; Danda, 1992; Datta, 1992; Kumaran, 1992; and Subba, 1992). Contrary to it, historians have emphasized on religion and sects and neglected other group, forming criteria. Sabharwal markedly says that all the cultural markers must be regarded as valid basis of group formation either singly or in combination.

The earliest recorded Indian usage of the term 'ethnic' was in a paper written by N.K. Bose (1965). While discussing social composition in Calcutta, he describes the diversities with ethnic roots in language, religious faith and historical tradition. He regards the Bengalis as an ethnic group, as also the Rajasthani community, Guajarati, Punjabis, Sikhs, Anglo-Indians, South Indians and Muslims. He linked economic interests with ethnic identity. Bose writes:

> Although Calcutta is a centre of Bengali culture, a Bengali wishes a Rajasthani to remain as he is rather than demand that he confirms to the ways of Bengalis.

His approach, thus, neither advocates assimilation nor homogeneity, nor does it assert the hegemony of the dominant Bengali culture. Bose did not think Calcutta was going to repeat the American example in large part due to the imperfect urbanization. American melting-pot approach did not happen because in all the societies ethnic groups have persisted. The 'Salad bowl' approach as opposed to the melting-pot seems to bear out Bose's concerns. His observations could well have been a starting point for work on ethnic groups in India as he took care of all the criteria for forming ethnic groups. Bose concentrated his attention upon immigrant groups as constituting ethnic groups in Calcutta. These trends have been adopted by Indian sociologists comfortably (Apte, 1978).

The work of American sociologist Schemerhom (1978) reflects the ideas having formulated a theory of ethnicity applicable in India. According to it, he regards ethnic group as minority groups, while consideration of majority group is nonetheless worthy. Therefore, he excludes Hindus from the perview of his classification (Mimer and Srole also omitted the WASPs from their theory), since they are the majority group. Schernerhom defines an ethnic group as a collectivity existing within a larger society; having real or fictional common ancestory; memories of a shared historical past, and a cultural focus on one or more symbolic elements (kinship patterns, physical resemblance, religion, language, nationality or combinations of them) defined as the epitome of people-hood (1978).

Language is one of the main markers of group identity and it is an important means of interaction, communication and socialization. But association between language and ethnic group is neglected. Caste is considered to be another ethnic phenomenon. Some sociologists have commented on the link between caste and ethnicity. Andre Beteille in a series of writings, has linked the role of caste along with language and religion, in a political arena as resembling that of ethnic groups. Srinivas too later said that in the future caste will be conceived in terms of ethnicity (Padgaonkar, 1993).

## Changing Tribal Ethnicity

A tribal group is an ethnic entity. That is why the predominant characteristic of a tribal group is its ethnicity. The members of a tribal group share a common ethnicity. The ethnicity, too, has its own historiography. It is like a cultural stream which passes from generation to generation. For instance, the practice of polygamy and the tradition of living in scattered villages are the traits of a tribal group. It provides a special identity to the group. If the ethnic traits are lost or changed in the process of transformation, it is possible that the group loses its identity.

Therefore, on the one hand, the problem with a tribal group is to retain its ethnic identity and, on the other hand, to integrate it in the national society by accepting technological, secular, democratic and socialistic social system. Here, ethnicity is related to state or political ideology of the nation, as ethnicity has a close linkage with the state and its development packages.

Inequalities among the tribals and with non-tribals are due largely to two processes:

1. Ethnic
2. Class formation

When the tribal accept sanskritization, and the values and practices of great tradition, they undergo the process of ethnic transformation. It leads them to attain the status of caste status but as a result of such efforts, they never could get any place in caste hierarchy. This is one form of social stratification.

The other form of social stratification is the achievement of class status. The tribal groups are likely to develop various forms of classes. The forms of ethnic and class stratification are not dichotomous. But it is possible that the tribal get ethnic transformation and also class transformation simultaneously. It is also possible that they retain their ethnic character without any change and undergo class formation. There is a group of sociologists who argue that the tribals in the process of development and change have taken to caste hierarchy. This is being done by adopting high caste values (preferably some of brahminical values) and practices but the tribals (Bhagat) could never get any status in caste hierarchical system. There are Marxist and non-Marxist sociologists who argue that tribals have not accepted caste model of social stratification. Tribals have jumped it over to caste stratification and have taken to class model of society.

Doshi (1990) argues that tribe, caste and state are closely related. The state as a whole affects and changes the tribal ethnicity and also releases forces of modernization, education, and science and technology. It may strengthen or weaken the structural components of ethnicity and also create class differentiation. As regards ethnicity, Doshi says, 'in Indian context it is difficult to fruitfully employ' this concept. It can be used in two contexts. First, we can use ethnicity as social and cultural characteristic in most of the primordial groups in India. Second, the term 'ethnic' is sometimes used to refer to minorities of various types. Oommen (1986) prefers the use of primordial collectivities in place of ethnic groups. Nair (1985) applied the concept of ethnicity to India's urbanization and uses it as a collectivity of people who: (a) Share some patterns of normative behaviour, and (b) Form a part of a large population, interacting with people from other collectivities within the framework of a social system.

Phadnis (1989) rightly says that the basic attributes of an ethnic group are its distinct cultural identity and ethnic consciousness. She highlighted that the structure of the ethnicity is not static or rigid. It keeps on changing. She says that 'ethnicity is the summation of ethnic consciousness for status and recognition as a distinct social entity. Ethnicity, thus, is not a static, predetermined category but the manifestation of the assertion of the ethnic group in the political arena to defend and/or sustain economic, political and cultural interests.'

All the above discussions of ethnicity brings out some attributes which are relevant for analysing the tribal ethnic structure of India. Race has ceased to be an attribute of Indian tribal ethnicity. Biological cohesiveness based on racial traits is no more visible among the tribals of India. It is because much of inbreeding has taken place among diverse tribal groups and between the tribals and the non-tribals. Therefore, Doshi argues that we have to depend on non-biological attributes peculiar to the tribals. The non-biological traits include: cultural distinctiveness; collective self-consciousness; self-identity; common customs, traditions and institutions; language/dialects; religion; joint farming; subsistence economy; common pride in the land of origin and ethno-political traits. Doshi added the constitutional safeguards and securities (given to the tribals) which have provided a new bond for cohesiveness.

Most of the ethnic traits of the tribals have got weakened during the last six to seven decades of Independence and as a result of breaking of isolation, their cultural distinctiveness has now developed traits of non-tribal culture. Many of the tribals have accepted Christianity and Hinduism (Bhagatism). Pull and push factors have increased the frequency of migration and regular contacts with the non-tribals. Many ethnic traits have undergone substantial changes and some still are continuing. It appears that the ethnic traits or attributes which keep the present day tribal society together are related to cultural distinctiveness, religion, language, dialect, constitutionally granted safeguards and protective discrimination and common participation in tribal movements, particularly those crucial ethnic traits which control their group identity.

It is true that the tribals have imitated the rituals, values, beliefs and lifestyle of Rajputs in the beginning. The Bhils of Rajasthan have borrowed much from the Rajput culture. They claimed to be given a status equivalent to Rajput rulers as they fought for them with Mughals. Rajputs, on the other hand, are not like the Brahmins and the Vaishyas. They are non-vegetarians and take liquor. The tribals who opted and became Bhagat argue that they should be considered in Hindu fold but it never materialized. Bhagat Bhils are teetotallers and left meat, liquor and many bad habits. Hardiman (1984) said that the caste hierarchy is so much rigid that it makes no room for the tribals. He argues that there is some mobilization – up down in the game of snakes and ladders but the board itself never alters. Those who analyse tribal stratification in term of attaining caste status employ ethnic criteria only.

The tribal social stratification is different from caste. In caste stratification, we look for hierarchy among hundreds of castes in terms of purity and pollution of occupation, dietary, dress, house, rituals, and all other things of caste members. This hierarchy is observed or identified not within the caste but among the castes in context with superiority and inferiority. It is true that there is nothing like tribal system as in caste system. Each tribal group, Bhils, Garasias, Saharias, Santhal, or Warli, etc. is endogamous. It is a whole society in itself. A tribal group is not related to the other tribal groups in terms of a system. For all empirical considerations, a tribe is an autonomous, endogamous, whole society not forming any system within the tribal groups found in a region.

While discussing ethnic stratification Doshi (1990) said that 'it could be safely said that the original tribal society with its primordial character got inequality through a change in their ethnicity. Religion constitutes the bedrock of ethnicity. The impact of Hindu religion and also Christianity brought about a lasting change in the tribal stratification'. The tribal (Bhils) society ethnically, got stratified into primordial or Native Bhils, Bhagat Bhils and Christian Bhils. Ethnicity keeps the tribal groups bound together by a number of ties, namely, culture, language, religion, separate identity, common customs and traditions, pride in the land of origin and certain institutions. Out of all these ethnic ties for Indian tribes the constitutional safeties and securities work as the strongest cementing bond. This keeps the tribals segregated from the rest of the population.

Tribals of south Rajasthan retain their ethnic identity by maintaining some primordial traits, namely family, marriage, kinship, village habitation and practices in their day-to-day life regarding food, dress, and visiting of regional fairs and festivals. In changing situation, tribals practice their basic ethnic behaviour with some peripheral changes. The clan structure of tribals also exhibits the traits of ethnicity. And, therefore, the basic aspect of tribal stratification continues to remain ethnic class, ethnicity and state, and these are so interwoven that we cannot understand tribal social change without referring to these aspects.

In short, it can be said that the tribals bear their identity as a social class on the basis of certain ethnic characteristics, particularly among them being cultural distinctiveness, religion, major institutions, partially language and above all the protective discriminations which they all share. This ethnicity is not static. It adopts traits from other ethnicities also. Interaction with other ethnic groups has created new strata among the tribals. The impact of Christianity and Hinduism has stratified the tribal society into ethnic strata such as Christian tribals and Bhagat tribals. It is this which holds the different sub-groups of a tribal group. Different tribal development programmes have improved their class status. With the passage of time, the tribals who benefitted most from the programmes have emerged as rich among the tribals. While others who were small farmers sold out their land and took to agriculture or non-agriculture labour or migrated to towns and cities. In order to keep the flow of benefit or protective discriminations continued to retain their ethnic particularism, the retention of ethnic traits does not deny the formation of classes among them. Their ethnicity has sought its identification with political power.

During the princely and colonial rule, the status of state was only to maintain law and order in its domain so that the exploitation of the masses could be carried on unabated. The state was never a welfare agency. In the present context the status of state has experienced a radical change. In the case of tribals, the state assumes great responsibility. It is obliged by the provisions made in the Constitution to make all efforts for the development of tribals so that they integrate themselves in the mainline culture. Tribal social stratification is different from caste stratification. The attributes of castes determine the rank of the individual caste vis-à-vis the other castes and the caste system as a whole. Basically, the approach toward the sacred, purity and pollution is based on the attributes of a particular caste – highness or lowness, purity and impurity determine its rank among other castes. The attributional and interactional theories of McKim Marriott on the caste stratification do not hold true in the case of tribal stratification. Secular approaches focus politico-economic considerations for stratification. It seems to be consistent with the tribal stratification.

A tribal group is a whole society. It is not a part society like a caste. When tribal stratification is discussed we have to take a departure from the tribal groups forming a system. We do not determine the rank of a tribe in terms of its attributes with other tribes. We identify rank differentiation within a particular tribal group. Similarly, endogamy is a basic attribute in caste stratification, but in tribal stratification, Bhagat and Christian Bhils are not endogamous groups. A Bhagat would accept a match from any section of the tribe provided he or she seeks conversion. The same applies to the Christian Bhils. It is tribal ethnicity that works along with its primordial institutional networks. Clan, kin, totem, taboo, etc. Ethnicity imparts continuity and identity to the tribal group. As a matter of fact even today with the modernization of agriculture and diversification of economy, the tribals are very much influenced by their ethnic traits. Ethnicity runs like a chord at different levels of development and social formation.

Aurora (1972) and Breman (1974) advocated that the tribals are moving from tribe to caste. But Bose (1981), Pathy (1984) and Doshi (1990) argued, on the basis of field data generated from western India (Gujarat, Madhya Pradesh, and Rajasthan) that the direction of change is from tribe to class. But Bose and Pathy among others who argue for class formation among the tribals do not take into consideration, the phenomenon of ethnicity which is emphasized by Doshi only. It is found that whatever status tribal may occupy in society, they continue to retain their ethnic identity among different diverse tribal groups.

Therefore, it can be argued that the continuum scale runs from tribe to class with the homogeneity of ethnicity. It is class based on ethnicity. Certainly, ethnicity contributes social and cultural identity to a tribal group. There are various levels of identity among the tribals of south Rajasthan. The ethnic traits considered for them are *adivasis* and the status of 'scheduled tribe'. These are now considered as their ethnic identity and fundamental identity.

It is also important that the forces of modernization and communication have changed their ethnicity up to a certain level. But the core of ethnicity among all the sections of the tribals of western India, particularly, the Bhils consist of religion, language, scattered pattern of housing, tattooing, drinking liquor, clan and village, falia, exogamy, tribal and plains-hill-forest endogamy and a number of traits associated with social and economic institutions. Although, Natra, bride price, polygamy and the commodity status of tribal women are the peculiar characteristics of the Bhils.

There are some changes. Most of the changes are superficial but the basic structure continues to remain the same. Ethnicity has given emergence to two discrete religious cults, Christianity and Bhagatism. Both have different ways of behaviour. Socially, they deny practicing polygamy, they take bath daily, use water to clean up after defecation and keep house and compounds clean. They do not drink liquor or toddy. Bhagat Bhils do not eat meat or fish. The two groups (Christians and Bhagats) of puritanistic cults appear exclusive to each tribal group. But these both tribal groups carry the core traits of their primordial attributes or ethnic features of the tribe. Similarly, the tradition of bride-price is observed by the followers of both the cults. The Bhagats though deny it but in practice they follow. Scattered pattern of village habitation – arnethnic characteristic of the original stock of the Bhils is also found among all the segments of the tribe living in interior villages.

Some of the tribal reformers tried to attract tribal groups through Bhagat movement. It advocates adopting brahmanical values, deities, festivals, fairs and practices, and in terms of lifestyle, it has motivated them to become teetotaller. It does lead us to the conclusion that they are a part of Hindu society Their incorporation in the Hindu society means falling into caste hierarchy which is based on purity-pollution complex. But they are never accepted by castes and even by tribals themselves. On the other hand, tribals themselves never could leave their core ethnic traits. The participation of the tribals in *rath-yatra* (Rhishabh Deo) never incorporates the tribals into Jainism. Actually, the tribal problem of social change should be viewed and analysed in ethnic framework.

The forces of migration, education, modernization, political participation and democratization are in work in a very complex way. The tribals seek their identity in various development programmes. Tribals are using ethnicity like casteism knowingly or unknowingly. It is because of ethnic traits inherent in the basic structure of tribal institutions. Ethnicity is not a myth; it is a living reality which one can see in the life of the tribals. The breaking of isolation by entry of non-tribal groups to the hills and forests region for trading or government jobs and the migration of tribals to the plains in search of earnings, gave emergence to classes among them. A few join agriculture and many of them joined as non-agriculture labour, i.e. take to government or private sector. Some migrate to industrial or urban cities of the neighbouring states and adopted non-agricultural occupations.

The process of class formation among the tribals has been initiated and strengthened by the government development plans and programmes. The new social formations as a result of capitalist economy are broadly agricultural class, agricultural entrepreneurial class, agricultural labour class, service class, and other wage earning class. A larger number of them earn their livelihood through a diverse economy. The resultant class structure is of the type of class in itself. Clan, kin and ethnic attributes constitute common elements to the Bhil classes based on differential sources of income. The elements of class antagonism have not yet emerged. Though there are segments among them who exploit the tribal Bhils by practicing money lending or adopting clandestine ways, the Bhils have not stood against the Bhils as exploiter and exploited. There is a lack of class crystallization among the tribals but the process of class formation has begun.

## Conclusion

Prior to the Independence, the tribals lived in the hills and forests – fully isolated from the mainline civilization. Their interaction with the state was very much limited and restricted. The inequality among a single tribal group was also insignificant. Basically the tribals in the earlier period were the rulers of the region and often contested the British and feudal domination. The suppression of tribal outbreak is the watershed in the interactions between the tribals who lived in the hills and forests and the rulers. Therefore, the state since its first interaction with the tribals has been the determinant of class formation among the tribals. Soon after Independence, the states in India took to the task of building the country into a nation. Within broader national objective, the fate of the millions of tribals was not different in any way from the fate of the nation as a whole. At this juncture the newly emerging nation's strongest demand is for economic development. It is for economic growth as well as improvements in the level of living, equalization of opportunities by the people in plan and policy decisions. The tribal development programmes have accelerated the process of stratification, acculturation and economic transformation. The tribal sub-plan regions have received priority. As a result of it the elites among tribals have taken larger share of the development cake. Traditionally, the tribal groups have been more or less homogeneous. But whosoever took the fruits of planned development have earned higher social status due to better and improved economic background. Such persons became elites and entered into the creamy layer of the tribals. And, therefore, it initiated the class-based tribal social stratification. But an analysis of emerging tribal social stratification is not possible without referring to tribal ethnicity and the emerging class structure among them. Studies on tribal entrepreneurship (Trivedi, 1990) and tribal migration (Trivedi, 2007) and social mobility (Trivedi, 2007) are also providing the same analysis.

## References

Acharya, S.K. 'Ethnic Processes in North Eastern India', *Economic and Political Weekly* XXIII (21), 1988, pp. 1068–77.

Apte, Mahadev. 'Region, Religion and Language: Parameters of Identity in the Process of Acculturation', in R.E. Holloma, S.A. Arutiunov (eds), *Perspectives on Ethnicity*, Mouton Publishers, Hague, 1978.

Aurora, G.S. *Tribe – Caste – Class Encounters*, Administrative Staff College of India, Hyderabad, 1972.

Banton, Michael. *Race Relations*, Tavistock, London, 1967.

Bariton, Michael. *Racial and Ethnic Competition*, Cambridge University Press, Cambridge, 1983.

Barth, Fredrick (ed.). *Ethnic Groups and Boundaries*, Brown and Company, Boston, 1969.

Baruah, Sanjib. 'Ethnic Conflict as State – Society, Struggle – The Politics and Politics of Assamese Micro-Nationalism', in *Modern Asian Studies*, 28, 1994, pp. 649–71.

Beteille, Andre. *Equality and Universality: Essay in Social and Political Theory*, Oxford University Press, Delhi, 2002.

Beteille, Andre. 'Race, Caste and Ethnic Identity', *International Social Science Journal*, Vol. XXIII, No. 4, 1977, pp. 519–35.

Bhat, Chandra Shekhar. *Ethnicity and Mobility: Emerging Ethnic Identity and Social Mobility among the Waddars of South India*, Concept Publishing Company, New Delhi, 1983.

Bose, N.K. *Culture and Society in India*, Asia Publishing House, Bombay 1967.

Bose, Nirmal Kumar. 'Calcutta: A Premature Metropolis', *Scientific American*, 213(3), 1965, pp. 91–103.

Bose, Pradeep Kumar. 'Stratification Among Tribals in Gujarat', *Economic and Political Weekly*; 7 February, 1981.

Brass, Paul. 'Ethnic Groups and the Slate', in Paul Brass (ed.), *Ethnic Groups and the State*, Croom Helm, London, 1985.

Brass, Paul. *Ethnicity and Nationalism: Theory and Comparison*, Sage Publication, New Delhi, 1991.

Breman, Jan. 'Mobilization of Landless Laborers, Halpatis of South Gujarat', *Economic and Political Weekly*, IX, 1974.

Bromley, Willian (ed.). *Soviet Ethnology and Anthropology Today*, Mouton Publishers, Hague, 1974.

Bromley, Yulian. 'Soviet Ethnography: Main Trends', *Social Science Today*, Moscow, 1977.

Chauhan, Brij Raj. *Towns in the Tribal Setting*, National, Delhi, 1970, p. 27.

Cohen, Abner (ed.). *Urban Ethnicity*, Tavistock Publications, London, 1974.

Cohn, B.S. and Singer, M. (eds). *Structure and Change in Indian Society*, Aldine Publishing Company, Chicago, 1968.

Danda, Ajit K. 'Ethnicity and Social Transformation in North-East India', *Man in India*, 72(2), 1992, pp. 131–140.

Das Gupta, Jyotirindra. 'Ethnicity, Language Demands and National Development in India', in Nathan, Glazer and Daniel P. Moynihan (ed.), *Ethnicity: Theory and Experience*, Harvard University Press, Cambridge, 1975.

Datta, Amal. 'Land and Ethnicity in Sikkim', *Man in India*, 72(2), 1992, pp. 165–178.

Deliege, Robert. *The Bhils of Western India*, National, Delhi, 1985.

Doshi, S.L. *Tribal Ethnicity, Class and Integration*, Rawat Publications, Jaipur, 1990.

Epstein, A.L. *Politics in an Urban African Community*, Manchester University Press, Manchester, 1958.

Eriksen, Thomas H. *Us and Them in Modern Societies: Ethnicity and Nationalism in Trinidad, Mauritius and Beyond*, Scandinavian University Press, Oslo, 1992.

Eriksen, Thomas H. *Ethnicity and Nationalism: Anthropological Perspective*, Pluto Press, London, 1993.

Francis, E.K. 'The Nature of Ethnic Group', *American Journal of Sociology*, 52, 1945.

Ghurye, G.S. *The Aborigines: 'So Called' – And Their Future*, Gokhale Institute of Politics and Economics, Poona, 1943.

Glazer, Nathan and Moynihan, Daniel A. (eds). *Ethnicity: Theory and Experience*, Harvard University Press, Cambridge, 1975.

Glazer, Nathan and Moynihan, Daniel Patrick. *Beyond the Melting Pot: The Negroes, Puerto Ricans, Jews, Italians, and Irish – A Study of Ethnic Groups of New York (1963)*, MIT and Harvard University Press, Cambridge, 1970.

Gluckman, M. 'Anthropological Problems Arising from African Industrial Revolution', in A. Southal (ed.), *Social Change in Modern Africa*, Oxford University Press, London, 1961.

Gordon, M.M. *Assimilation in American Life*, Oxford University Press, New York, 1964.

Hardgrave, Robert L. Jr. 'Urbanization and the Structure of Caste' in M.S.A. Rao, C. Bhat and L.N. Kadekar (eds), *A Reader in Urban Sociology*, Orient Longman, New Delhi, 1991.

Hardiman, David. 'Adivasi Assertion in South Gujarat: The Devi Movement of 1922–23', in *Subaltern Studies*, III, Oxford University Press, New Delhi, 1984.

Hobsbawm, E.J. and Guha, Ranjit (ed.). 'Ethnicity and Nationalism in Europe Today', *Anthropology Today*, 8(1), 1992, pp. 3–8.

Hopkins, E.W. The Social and Military Position of the Ruling Caste in Ancient India, as represented by the Sanskrit Epic; with an Appendix on the Status of Women, Varanasi, 1972 (1889).

Jam, Ranu. 'Jam Oswal of Calcutta as an Ethnic Group – A Socio-historical Perspective', *Man in India*, vol. 67, no. 4, December, 1987, pp. 383–403.

Jha, Vivekanand. 'From Tribe to Untouchable: The Case of Nisadas', in R.S. Sharma (ed.), *Indian Society: Historical Probing*, Peoples Publishing House, New Delhi, 1974, p. 67.

Kothari, Rajani. 'Ethnicity' in David Kumar and Santasilan Kadirgamar (eds), *Ethnicity: Identity, Conflict and Crisis*, Arena Press, Hong Kong, 1989.

Kumaran, K.P. 'Ethnic Minority Associations and their Socio-Cultural Functions', *Man in India*, 72(2), 1992, pp. 141–52.

Levinson, David. *Ethnic Relations: A Cross Cultural Encyclopedia*, ABC – CLIO, Santa Barbara, California, 1994.

Malcolm, J. *A Memoir of Central India*, Thacker, Spink and Co., Calcutta, 1880, p. 148.

Mason (eds). *Theories of Race and Race Relations*, Cambridge University Press, Cambridge, 1986, pp. 170–86.

Mitchell, J.C. *The Kabla Dance*, Manchester University Press, Manchester, 1956.

Mythilli, K.L. 'Little Madras in Bombay City', in M.SA. Rao (ed.), *Urban Sociology in India*, Orient Longman, Delhi, 1992.

Nair, K.S. *Ethnicity and Urbanization*, Shanta Publications, Delhi, 1985.

Oommen, T.K. 'Insiders and Outsiders in India: Primordial Collectivism and Cultural Pluralism in Nation Building', *International Sociology* Vol. 1, March, 1986.

Padgaonkar, D. 'In Conversation with M.N. Srinvas', *Sunday Times of India*, 12 December 1993.

Pandian, J. *Caste, Nationality and Ethnicity: An Interpretation of Tamil Cultural History and Social Order*, Popular Prakashan, Bombay, 1987.

Pathy, Jagannath. *Tribal Peasantry Dynamics of Development*, Inter-India Publication, New Delhi, 1984.

Phadnis, Urmila. *Ethnicity and National-Building in South Asia: A Case Study of Sri Lanka*, Sage Publications, Delhi, 1987.

Punekar, V. *Assimilation*, Popular Prakashan, Bombay, 1974.

Rao, M.S.A. (ed.). *Urban Sociology in India*, Orient Longman, New Delhi, 1974.

Rao, M.S.A. 'Some Aspects of Sociology of Migration', in *Sociological Bulletin*, Vol. 30, No. 1, March, 1991.

Sabharwal, Gopa. *Ethnicity and Class: Social Divisions in an Indian City*, Oxford University Press, New Delhi, 2006.

Schermerhom, R.A. *Ethnic Plurality in India*, University of Arizona Press, Arizona, 1978.

Sharma, R.S. *Material Culture and Social Formation in Ancient India*, MacMillan India Ltd., Delhi, 1983.

Singh, Andrea Menefee. *Neighborhood and Social Networks in Urban India*, Marwah, New Delhi, 1976.

Singh, K.S. 'A Study in State-Formation among Tribal Communities', in R.S. Sharma (ed.), *Indian Society: Historical Probing*, People's Publishing House, New Delhi, 1984, p. 318.

Singh, K.S. (ed.). *Ethnicity, Caste and People: Proceedings of the Indo-Soviet Seminars*, (Calcutta and Leningrad in 1990) Manohar Publication, Delhi, 1992.

Singh, Yogendra. *Indian Sociology*, Vistaar Publication, New Delhi, 1986, p. 3.

Srinivas, M.N. *Caste in Modern India and Other Essays*, Asia Publishing House, Bombay, 1962.

Subba, Tanka B. 'Inter-Ethnic Relationship in North-East India and the Negative Solidarity', *Man in India*, 72(2), 1992, pp. 153–64.

Trivedi, M.S. *Entrepreneurship among Tribals*, Printwell Publications, Jaipur, 1990.

Trivedi, M.S. *Homogeneity to Heterogeneity: A Study of Impact of Migration on the Bhil Society*, Himanshu Publications, New Delhi, 2007.

Trivedi, Mridula. *Towards Social Mobility: A Study of the Bhils of South Rajasthan*, Himanshu Publications, New Delhi, 2007.

Trivedi, Madhu Sudan. 'Migration, Development and Crisis to Traditional Tribal Identity,' in *Tribals in India: The Changing Scenario*, S.N. Tripathi (ed.), Discovery Publishing House, New Delhi, 1998, p. 173.

van den Berghe, P.L. *Race and Racism: A Comparative Perspective*, John Wiley and Sons, New York, 1967.

Wanner, W. Lloyd and Srole, Leo. *The Social System of American Ethnic Groups*, Vol. III, Yankee City Series, Yale University Press, New Haven, 1965 (first published in 1945).

Weiner, Myron. *The Sons of the Soil: Migration and Ethnic Conflict in India*, Oxford University Press, Delhi, 1978.

# 4

# Tribal Situation in Gujarat

**Chandrakant Upadhyaya**

The tribal area of Gujarat state is spread across three distinct ecological zones. The hills and plateaus, characterized by rocky upland with small, scattered deposits of minerals and tropical mixed as well as moist forests, make the first ecological zone. Second zone comprises the valleys dominated by a fertile cultivable land intersected by rivers and streams. The third ecological zone is marked with luxuriant growth of wild trees, bamboos and other fibrous plants. Most of the tribal communities of Gujarat live in the southern part of Gujarat covered by forest.

The entire strip of eastern part of the state that runs right from the north to the south and cutting across the geographical boundary of three Indian states, viz., Rajasthan, Madhya Pradesh and Maharashtra, is mountainous and covered with forests of varying dimensions. This strip comprises the tribal belt of the state in which the traditional habitat of a number of tribal communities have been formed since centuries. In the north, the tribal region nestles in the Aravalli and Satapura mountain ranges while in the southern east are the Sahayadri mountain ranges. In the valleys constituting the second ecological zone and on the escarpments and slopes of these hilly ranges, the tribal settlements are situated in a scattered manner. While the width of the land between the eastern and western boundary is very large in north and centre, it is quite reduced in the south. As a result, this strip of land in south Gujarat, which is lying between the Sahayadri ranges and the Arabian Sea, is narrow. It becomes narrower still in the extreme south.

## Tribal Population

There are 26 tribal communities living in the state of Gujarat where more than half of them are very small in number. The detail demographic profile of the tribal population of the state would be clear from Table 1.[1]

**Table 1**

*Major Tribes of Gujarat (2011)*

| *Sl. No.* | *Name of the Schedule Tribe* | *Total Population* | *Percentage* |
|---|---|---|---|
| 1. | Bhil | 42, 15,603 | 47.27% |
| 2. | Halpati | 6, 43,120 | 7.21% |
| 3. | Dhodia | 6, 35,695 | 7.12% |
| 4. | Gamit | 3, 78,445 | 4.24% |
| 5. | Naika, Naikada | 4, 59,908 | 5.15% |
| 6. | Choudhary | 3, 02,958 | 3.39% |
| 7. | Rathwa | 6, 42,348 | 7.20% |
| 8. | Dhanka | 2, 80,949 | 3.15% |
| 9. | Konkna | 3, 61,587 | 4.05% |
| 10. | Warli | 3, 28,194 | 3.68% |
| 11. | Patelia | 1, 14,414 | 1.28% |
| 12. | Kanbi | 60,646 | 0.68% |

*Source:* Census of India, 2011.

The above mentioned tribes are considered as the major tribes in the state on the basis of their linguistic, cultural and demographic characteristics. The important minor tribes are as shown in 'Drashtikshep'.[2]

The minor tribes are also known as Primitive Tribal Groups or Particularly Vulnerable Tribes. These communities lag behind other tribes in terms of the socio-economic indicators as framed by the government. They also live in remote area compared to other tribal groups. The details of the these tribal communities are as indicated in Table 2 and Table 3:

**Table 2**

*Particularly Vulnerable Tribes of Gujarat (2011)*

| *Sl. No.* | *Name of the Schedule Tribe* | *Total Population* | *Percentage* |
|---|---|---|---|
| 1. | Kolgha | 67,119 | 0.75% |
| 2. | Kotwalia | 24,249 | 0.27% |
| 3. | Siddi | 8,661 | 0.09% |
| 4. | Kathodi | 13,632 | 0.15% |
| 5. | Padhar | 30,932 | 0.34% |

**Table 3**

*Other Tribal Groups (2011)*

| *Sl. No.* | *Name of the Schedule Tribe* | *Total Population* | *Percentage* |
|---|---|---|---|
| 1. | Rabari (Ness) | 59,995 | 0.67% |
| 2. | Paradhi (Phanse, Advin, Chincher) | 3,450 | 0.03% |
| 3. | Bavcha, Bamcha | 2,889 | 0.03% |
| 4. | Charan (Ness) | 2,890 | 0.03% |
| 5. | Bharwad (Ness) | 1,672 | 0.01% |
| 6. | Gond, Rajgond | 2,965 | 0.03% |
| 7. | Pomla | 687 | 0.007% |
| 8. | Barda | 748 | 0.008% |

So far as development of tribes in Gujarat is concerned, some tribes have progressed more compared to others. Thus, till now, only the major tribes have been considered for purpose of development. Further, within the major tribal groups, there is a disparity in the level of socio-economic development. Among some of the tribes, such as Dhodia, Choudhary, Patelia and Dungri Garasia (a sub-group of Bhil tribe as indicated in the list of Scheduled Tribes, otherwise having a separate entity), the process of social and economic changes appears to be of such magnitude that they may lead to rapid change in their culture. In fact, there appears to be a clear case of tribal groups in the process of 'detribalization'. This word is being used here in the sociological sense which implies the dropping or the rejection of tribal modes of behaviour and adoption of standards of behaviour other than tribes or sub-groups of major tribes such as Bhil of Dangs. Kathodi, Kolgha, Kotwalia and Naikda of Panchmahal continue to have a primitive existence. Other tribes of the state are, by and large, in between these two socio-cultural levels of development. The large ethnic and cultural variety, prevailing among tribals of this state naturally provides a fertile field of anthropological and ethnographical studies. It also provides the greatest challenge to researchers to make available the results of their research for the improvement of the quality of life of the tribal people.

Tribal population of the state as per the latest data is 89 lakh (15% of the total population) and found mostly in the eastern belt of the Gujarat state. Gujarat occupies the fifth position in the country, after Madhya Pradesh, Maharashtra, Orissa and Rajasthan. Out of 33 districts of Gujarat, 14 districts – Banaskantha, Sabarkantha, Aravalli, Mahisagar, Panchmahal, Dahod, Chhota Udepur, Bharuch, Narmada, Surat, Tapi, Navsari, Valsad and Dangs have sizeable tribal population. Out of the above said districts, district of Dangs, Tapi, Narmada, Dahod and Valsad have 94.6, 84.2, 81.6, 74.3 and 52.9 per cent of tribal population respectively out of the total population in these districts.

Besides the discussed 14 tribal concentrated districts explained above, there are a few small tribal pockets found in Junagadh, Kuchchh, Surendranagar, Jamnagar and Ahmedabad districts of the state. The minor tribes discussed earlier like Padhar, Rabari, Barda, etc. are found in this area. The population of these small tribal groups is not of much significance but it is of much importance culturally as the different tribal groups living in these pockets display a very colourful and rich heritage. Of course, now those communities, which have been designated as primitive ones are being given emphasis for development. Apart from these, there is another category of tribal population, known as 'dispersed tribals', living in such villages which have predominantly non-tribal population. The post-Fifth Plan strategy (other than one for scheduled area) tried to attack the tribal problem from three angles classifying the tribals into three categories: (a) tribals in the area of tribal concentration; (b) primitive tribes; and (c) dispersed tribals in other areas.

For ascertaining the exact distribution of the majority of the tribal groups, it will be worthwhile to divide entire eastern belt into three zones: northern, central and southern. These are, of course, arbitrary divisions. Northern zone comprises

Banaskantha, Sabarkantha and Aravalli districts and the major tribes found are Bhil and its sub-groups, viz., Rajput Garasia, Dungari Garasia and Bhil Garasia.[3] In this zone, a primitive tribe known as Kathodi lives.

Mahisagar, Panchmahal, Dahod and Chhota Udepur districts are found in the Central zone where tribes like Bhils, Patelias, Dhankas, Naikdas and Rathwas are found. In the vast tribal tract of the southern Gujarat, the major tribes found are Vasava (a group of Bhil), Tadavi, Halpati, Gamit, Konkna, Dhodias, Warli, Bhil, Naika and Choudhary. Also a few primitive tribes like Kathodi, Kolgha and Kotwalia are found in southern Gujarat. Bharuch, Narmada, Surat, Tapi, Navsari, Valsad and Dangs districts are found in this zone.

Apart from these tribal talukas which fall under the jurisdictions of different Integrated Tribal Development Projects[4] in the state some more areas which are identified as tribal pockets also has sizeable tribal population.[5]

## The North Zone

Table 4 gives data on Taluka-wise tribal population of the 14 districts discussed above. Looking at the taluka-wise concentration of different tribal groups, following picture emerges:

> North zone of the tribal belt of Gujarat comprises Danta, Amirgadh, Khedbrahma, Vijaynagar, and Poshina, Bhiloda and Meghraj taluka where most parts are covered under forest. In Danta and Vijaynagar, respectively 59.2 per cent and 68.4 per cent of land is covered by forest. Out of the available cultivable land very little has irrigation facility and agriculture depends on monsoon. Hence tribal people of this region work very hard to earn a livelihood. Among total land available in these regions, almost all the land has no facilities for irrigation. Only a very small amount of land in this region can be accounted as under irrigation. Land alienation is also reported from this zone. This adds woe to the existing problems of poverty of the tribal people.

Garasia, Dungari Garasia, Bhil Garasia and Bhil tribes are found in this region. Garasia is a separate tribal group in Rajasthan and they are also found in Gujarat known as Dungari Garasia or Bhil Garasia – a sub-group of Bhil, which is the largest tribal group in this belt. All these tribes have many cultural traits

**Table 4**

*District and Taluka-wise Tribal Population of Gujarat (2011)*

| Sl. No. | Name of the District | % of tribal population in the District (2011) | Name of the Taluka | % of Population in the Taluka (2011) | Main Tribes |
|---|---|---|---|---|---|
| 1. | Banaskantha | 9.10 | Danta | 56.36 | Bhil Garasia, Rajput Garasiya |
| | | | Amirgadh | 58.53 | |
| 2. | Sabarkantha | 22.32 | Khedbrahma | 75.38 | Sokla Garasia, Dungari Garasia, Bhil Garasiya |
| | | | Vijaynagar | 78.45 | Sokla Garasia, Dungari Garasia |
| | | | Poshina | – | Sokla Garasia, Dungari Garasia |
| 3. | Aravalli | – | Bhiloda | 57.57 | Dungri Garasia, Bhil Garasiya |
| | | | Meghrej | 37.03 | Dungri Garasia, Bhil Garasiya |
| 4. | Mahisagar | – | Santrampur | 80.32 | Bhil, Patelia, Naikada |
| | | | Kadana | 78.20 | Bhil, Patelia |
| 5. | Panchmahal | 30.18 | Ghogamba | 41.51 | Bhil, Naika, Rathwa |
| 6. | Dahod | 74.31 | Dahod | 77.34 | Bhil, Patelia |
| | | | Garbada | 94.83 | Bhil, Patelia |
| | | | Jhalod | 90.13 | Bhil, Patelia |
| | | | Fatehpura | 93.45 | Bhil |
| | | | Limkheda | 63.07 | Bhil, Patelia, Naikada |
| | | | Dhanpur | 71.07 | Bhil, Rathwa |

*Cont'd...*

...Cont'd

| | | | | | |
|---|---|---|---|---|---|
| | | | Devgadh Bariya | 20.03 | Bhil, Rathwa |
| | | | Sajeli | – | Bhil |
| 7. | Chhota Udepur | – | Chota Udepur | 87.62 | Rathwa, Dhanka, Naika |
| | | | Nasvadi | 87.72 | Tadvi, Rathwa, Naika |
| | | | Kwant | 93.51 | Rathwa, Naika |
| | | | Pavi Jetpur | 83.33 | Rathwa, Naika |
| 8. | Bharuch | 31.47 | Zaghadiya | 78.25 | Vasava Bhil |
| | | | Valiya | 55.42 | Vasava Bhil, Gamit, Dhanka |
| 9. | Narmada | 81.55 | Tilakwada | 73.29 | – |
| | | | Nandod | 96.41 | Vasava Bhil |
| | | | Dediyapada | 91.19 | Vasava Bhil |
| | | | Sagbara | 77.07 | Vasava Bhil, Gamit, Dhanka |
| 10. | Surat | 14.09 | Mandavi | 45.70 | Halpati, Chaudhary, Vasava |
| | | | Mangarol | 45.70 | Halpati, Chaudhary, Vasava |
| | | | Bardoli | 45.25 | Halpati, Chaudhary |
| | | | Mahuwa | 81.21 | Halpati, Chaudhary |
| 11. | Tapi | 84.17 | Umberpada | 96.73 | Vasava, Halpati |
| | | | Songadh | 84.91 | Gamit, Vasava Bhil, Chaudhary |
| | | | Uchhal | 98.05 | Vasava Bhil, Gamit |
| | | | Nizar | 80.82 | Vasava Bhil, Gamit, Dhanka |

Cont'd...

...*Cont'd*

| | | | | |
|---|---|---|---|---|
| | | Vyara | 84.84 | Chaudhary, Dhodiya, Halpati, Gamit, Kotwalia |
| | | Valod | 71.63 | Chaudhary, Dhodiya, Halpati, Gamit |
| 12. Navsari | 48.10 | Chikhli | 71.05 | Halpati, Kolgha |
| | | Bansda | 90.59 | Konkna, Warli, Dhodia, Naika, Kolgha |
| | | Konkna | – | Dhodia, Halpati, Naika, Khergam |
| 13. Valsad | 52.92 | Pardi | 32.75 | Dhodia, Halpati, Naika |
| | | Umbergaon | 46.49 | Warli, Halpati, Dhodia |
| | | Dharampur | 91.92 | Konkna, Warli, Dhodia, Naika, Halpati |
| | | Kaprada | 96.20 | Warli, Konkna, Dhodia, Naika, Halpati |
| 14. Dang | 94.64 | Ahwa | 94.64 | Konkna, Kunbis, Bhil, Warli, Gamit, Kathodi, Kotwalia |
| | | Subir | – | Kunbis, Bhil, Warli, Gamit, Kathodi, Konkna |
| | | Vaghai | – | Gamit, Konkna, Kunbis, Bhil, Warli, Gamit, Kotwalia |

in common, especially clan names, traditional deities and other socio-religious beliefs, folklore, scattered hutments, etc. Not much difference can be found by an outsider. They are incorporated under the generic term 'Bhil'. This is exactly what has happened in the case of Garasia.

Although the forest land is in greater proportion, it is not very rich in timber wood. Formerly, the forests used to play important role in tribals' economic life, but because of the ruthless exploitation of the forests in this region, they are not providing much support to tribal's economy. This has definitely resulted in making the economic life of these people poorer. This has also led to occurrences of frequent drought condition in this region.

Majority of the workers in this region are in agricultural vocation. But, the agricultural practices of the tribals of this belt, barring a few pockets in Vijaynagar, Bhiloda and Khedbrahma, have always been in crude form. Being ignorant of improved practices of agriculture, improved implements, improved seeds and use of fertilizers, etc., till recently they were doing agriculture on traditional pattern in which those new innovations had no place. However, due to government's development programme, a small section of the elites among these people have been able to adopt new practices but the majority of the population still have the traditional agriculture.

They follow their own traditional saran method to irrigate the land for raising wheat crops. But that was an erratic way, entirely dependent on good rainfall. Due to paucity of potential rivers, tanks and underground water, there has never been much potential in putting the land under irrigation.

The main crops grown in this region are maize, *bajra*, *jowar*, wheat, oilseeds, cotton and groundnut. The major crops out of the mentioned region are always maize and *kodra* – a coarse millet grain. Cotton also helps the tribals to earn some cash.

Thus, altogether a depressing picture emerges regarding the state of agrarian economy of the tribals of this region. As regards the agricultural labour work, till recently, the poor tribals were engaged in such work for which they got very low wage. Besides, they were provided with *bidis* (country cigarette). They were required to work for 9–10 hours for a meagre wage. Opportunities for getting engaged as labourers in construction work, etc. were few and far between, and not within easy reach. Hence, the second line of defence for their subsistence was forest from where they were able to bring minor forest produce and sell off. They also gather edible roots and fruits for consumption and try to get wage labour work.

So far as agricultural development in tribal area is concerned, much progress is achieved in terms of productivity and yield. This is due to Vanbandhu Kalyan Yojana and other agricultural development programmes.

In case of cooperative movement in tribal areas, large numbers of co-operatives were opened due to which tribal dependency on money lenders has been drastically reduced. They have used this in agriculture due to which there is a positive impact on agricultural productivity. However there is a need for change in the rules of the cooperatives in tribal areas.

In the field of education, there has been considerable expansion in number of schools in this region over the last couple of years. Literacy rate has improved among tribes compared to the past.

### The Central Zone

The central belt comprises the tribal talukas of Mahisagar, Panchmahal, Dahod and Chhota Udepur districts. As in north, this region too is hilly and wooded, though the land under forest is comparatively of small area; e.g. 17.1 per cent of the total land in Jhalod taluka of Dahod district and 40.7 per cent in Chhota Udepur taluka of Chhota Udepur district of the agricultural land available in this region. The same story is here too. Only a small area of the total agricultural land has been put under irrigation. The entire belt provides a unique example of a backward area located within relatively prosperous districts. The main tribal population in this region consists of Bhils, Patelias, Dhankas, Naikdas and Rathwas. Patelias and Dhankas are more progressive than Bhils, Rathwas and Naikdas are in the sphere of agriculture and education. Although a greater amount of land is available for cultivation, compared to the northern sector, the density of population in this region was relatively higher. For instance, in Chhota Udepur taluka, there were 274 persons per 50 mile as against the state average of 290. More than 90 per cent of the population live in rural areas. The economy of the region was heavily dependent upon agriculture and agriculture labour with more than 78.97 per cent of the working population engaged in primary sector. The principal crop is maize while wheat and gram are also grown on a small scale by the tribals. Due to lack of sufficient rainfall, drought had become a regular phenomenon in this area. Land being of poor quality, crop yield is invariably low. As the forests have disappeared to a great extent, chances of getting even temporary employment as forest labourers have also been reduced to a great extent. These factors have been instrumental in driving a large number of tribals after the rainy season to faraway places in search of gainful employment. It is a common sight on National Highway 8 and Ahmedabad-Bombay railroad to find the tribals of Panchmahal in vast number engaged as labourers doing major and minor repair work. Other occupational opportunities in their own area are meagre.

However, in Chhota Udepur taluka, a fluorspar project has been started where one of the world's largest fluorspar deposits has been found. Mining operations have provided lower rung unskilled employment opportunities to the local tribals. As has been observed in a research project on impact of industrialization, the tribals were mostly unskilled wage earners in the project, while most of the technical personnel have been recruited from non-tribal area, which has disturbed the harmony of tribal life. Same thing has been repeated in this project due to lack of skilled industrial labourers from amongst the tribals. In near future, more ITIs catering to the requirement of the skilled manpower for the industries coming up in the area can be planned in advance.

The tribal development programmes initiated by the government have brought positive changes and tribals are looking forward for a better future. In education, a lot of progress has been made as compared to previous years.

## The South Zone

The south zone comprises Narmada-Tapti tribal tract spread in seven districts, namely Bharuch, Narmada, Surat, Tapi, Navsari, Valsad and Dangs. The eastern part of the first three districts and Dangs is demarcated from Maharashtra by the tapering off the Satpura and Sahayadri ranges. This entire region is the forest and hills belt of south Gujarat. This eastern region of south Gujarat is composed of undulating terrain through which many rivers pass and flow down towards plains in the west. In the valleys and depressions, good black soil is often found while on the slopes and uplands it is generally reddish in colour. Not more than 20 to 25 per cent of the total land is under cultivation. The rest of the area is either under forest or not fit for cultivation. Earlier times, the economy of the tribals of this region revolved round the forest. The forest, among all things, first, provided them suitable land for slash-and-burn cultivation which was the main source of subsistence. But, gradually, the tribals have become settled agriculturists although rudiments of shifting cultivation is still evident in their burning of dry leaves and twigs in the cultivable field before sowing. The yearwise work cycle of the people of this region is such that from June (the monsoon usually breaks in about the middle of June) to January they remain busy in agriculture and for about three month during this period they are fully employed while for the rest of the period, they are underemployed and so take recourse to collection of minor forest produce.

From February to May, they do not have any agriculture operations and as such either collect forest produce or work in the logging of woods and other allied activities in the forest area or work as labourer on daily wages. Since there is no regular organization for providing employment for this labour force, the wage rates fall down considerably during this period, in view of large surplus manpower available.

Nearly two-thirds of the total cultivable land is used for food crops. In some areas, the groundnut has been only recently introduced. In recent years, the area under food crops seems to have increased. In the plains of Surat and Valsad districts, sugarcane has become a popular cash crop.

Now there is more concentration on growing food crops. Among cereals, *nagli,* rice and *jowar* are the main crops. Besides these, several varieties of inferior types of cereals, such as *varai, banti* and *samo kodra* are also grown. These crops are universally grown by nearly all the cultivators of this belt for the consumption of the family. The *rabi* crops are also cultivated by the tribal. A large number of well and watershed are constructed with the help of government programme to cater to the need of irrigation in the area. In recent years, the farmers are growing cashew and mangoes in plenty. This has resulted in an increase in their income.

Development programmes have been directed to change the ride form of agriculture and to popularize settled type of cultivation and ultimately to improve methods of cultivation. Agricultural extension and animal husbandry programmes have been given priority. But these programmes have not been able to reach out. As a result, by and large, the rural scene in this tribal region has remained unchanged. Except the gradual disappearance of forest, not much change is visible during the last 10 years or so. One can certainly see signs of developmental activities in the form of new buildings, such as veterinary hospitals, primary health dispensaries, schools, cooperative godowns, etc., but the economic life of the tribals appears to be unaltered. As such, one gets the impression that the large part of amount, meant for development programmes, has been spent on construction of buildings and purchase of equipment but efforts on matters which would have been of direct benefit to the tribals have not been made to the same extent as to construction activities.

The government has provided educational facilities in each village. Primary schools do exist in each village. As a result the literacy rate in this region has increased to 69.01 per cent according to 2011 Census.

## Livelihood Pattern

In tribal belts of Gujarat, as in other parts of India, tribals speak dialects of their own. In spite of the provisions in Article 350 of the Indian Constitution and resolution passed by the Central Education Board way back in 1949, the right of getting at least lower primary education, in their own mother-tongue, is being denied to lakhs of tribal children in Gujarat, as in many other parts of India, by showing utter negligence in preparation of text books in tribal dialects as well as in providing tribal dialect-knowing teachers. With the advancement of education in tribal Gujarat, today, there is no dearth of teachers knowing tribal dialects from amongst the tribals themselves.

In the sphere of cooperative movement it seems that this has not touched even the fringe of the economic life of the people of this region. Forest co-operative societies have mushroomed but the real benefits have gone to the tribals of the plain areas. The tribals of this hilly region have been sadly neglected to reap benefits from these forest co-operative societies. It may be pertinent to mention that in forest and other cooperative societies, enrollment of the tribal people has not been encouraging. These co-operative societies have been instrumental in creating a small minority of elite group in the tribal societies who have, in a way and indirectly, become trained to exploit their own brethren. Recently milk co-operative societies have been established in this area. Tribal have been benefitted much from milk co-operative.

**Table 5**

*Occupation-Wise Tribal Workers in Gujarat*

| *Industrial Classification* | *Percentage of Tribal Workers* | | | | | |
|---|---|---|---|---|---|---|
| | *1961* | *1971* | *1981* | *1991* | *2001* | *2011* |
| As cultivator | 59.14 | 48.34 | 45.94 | 45.70 | 41.88 | 34.23 |
| As agriculture labourers | 31.09 | 42.33 | 40.10 | 39.16 | 36.04 | 44.74 |
| Household industry | 1.57 | 2.33 | 0.83 | 1.77 | 2.00 | 0.70 |
| Manufacturing process, servicing, repairs others* | 8.20 | 7.00 | 13.13 | 13.37 | 20.08 | 20.33 |
| Total | 100.0 | 100.0 | 100.0 | 100.0 | 100.0 | 100.0 |

*Others include transport and communication, trade and commerce, construction jobs, mining, etc.

For majority of tribal people in the state, settled dry cultivation has been the primary mode of food production. A look into the data clearly suggests that land is the major source for employment and agriculture is the most dominant occupation. Tribal people in the state are genuinely peasantry and are earthbound in the strict sense of the term. In the tribal economy, land is important, being the principal source of livelihood.

As is evident from the figures in Table 5, there has been an alarming deterioration in the number of cultivators amongst the tribal working population within five decades, viz., 1961–71, 1971–81, 1981–91, 1991–2001 and 2001–2011. The percentage of cultivators fell from 59.14 per cent (1961 Census) to 34.23 per cent (2011 Census). However, it slightly went up to 45.94 per cent in 1981 Census. The percentage of agricultural labourers went up from 31.09 per cent (1961 Census) to 42.33 per cent (1971 Census), and again went up to 44.74 per cent in 2011 Census. Although these changes have occurred in the domain of agricultural occupations, there has been no difference in the percentage of workers depending upon the primary mode of production during 1961 and 1971 Censuses. But, in the 2011 Census, the percentage of workers in secondary and tertiary sectors has gone up from 7 per cent (1971 Census) to 20.33 per cent (2011 Census). This means that due to the various programmes initiated under the tribal sub-plan, a large number of tribals have been able to move to secondary and tertiary sectors from the primary sector. This is a commendable trend due to the limitations inherent in agricultural development in tribal areas.

However, the overall picture that emerge is that of a low income population in which a vast majority are dependent on primary sector of occupations. Due to the low participation in the secondary and tertiary sectors and limited scope of extension of the primary sector, the economics of the majority of the tribal in this state belongs to what is known as traditional and backward sector. By and large, there has not been much change in the occupational pattern of most of the tribal communities. Exceptions, however, may be made in case of a few tribal groups such as Dhodias and Choudharys of south Gujarat and Patelias of Dahod district. But vast majority of them still remain 'underdeveloped' and live a precarious economic existence. In all, 28.05 per cent of the total tribal families have been identified as living below poverty line. In fact, the real poverty line remained substantially high especially when deflated to the rising price level. In the words of Dantwala, 'the success achieved in the realization of this goal (eradication of poverty and unemployment) has been patently disappointing'.[6] Similarly, Vyas asserts that 'in spite of decades of planning, there is no indication of any remarkable achievement in this regard'.[7]

In such a situation their dependency on external aid for development of primary sector, i.e. agriculture and allied activities as well as of secondary and tertiary industries assumed much importance. Thus, the official agencies which are involved in the implementation of the programmes of economic betterment of the tribals will have to perform a dual role. They are also required to perform equally the important role of realizing the great development potential of the primary sector, and making it available for greater production. Since, in the traditional economic set-up of the tribal societies in Gujarat, there is virtually no scope for outside development agencies, whether belonging to the government sector or non-government sector, they will have to play the role of catalytic agent to bring greater returns.

It is also a matter of vital importance to diversify the occupational pattern among the tribals so that more and more tribals get weaned away from the sector in order to move into secondary and tertiary sectors. But when tribals take to secondary and tertiary occupations, they remain, in most cases, restricted to teaching/nursing and unorganized daily wage labour work. Thus, there is an urgent need to make efforts to diversify their occupational base.

But, the low level of literacy amongst the different tribal groups, barring a few ones, proves to be a major impediment in the diversification of the occupational pattern. Amongst the tribal groups in Gujarat, Dhodia has the highest rate of literacy, i.e. 83.67 per cent (2011 Census). This is also such a tribal group in the state amongst whom one finds a rapidly growing class of new entrepreneurs. Quite an encouraging number of persons among the Dhodia and Choudhary tribes (literacy rate being 72.93% according to 2011 Census) are able to operate in the secondary and tertiary sectors of occupations. But, for the great mass of tribal society in Gujarat, the bane of illiteracy hampers in the efforts to promote diversification in their occupational pattern.

**Table 6**

*Literacy Rate Among Major Tribal Groups*

| *Sr. No.* | *Name of the Tribe* | *Literacy Rate 1961–2011 (in %)* | | | | | |
|---|---|---|---|---|---|---|---|
| | | *1961* | *1971* | *1981* | *1991* | *2001* | *2011* |
| 1. | Bhil | 9.80 | 11.73 | 18.18 | 26.69 | 35.59 | 59.80 |
| 2. | Halpati | 11.61 | 13.74 | 17.92 | 26.99 | 40.79 | 65.46 |
| 3. | Dhodia | 23.94 | 31.19 | 44.96 | 57.13 | 67.05 | 83.67 |
| 4. | Gamit | 11.93 | 14.86 | 24.39 | 33.47 | 45.63 | 67.07 |
| 5. | Naika-Naikda | 10.79 | 9.55 | 13.85 | 19.74 | 29.28 | 50.05 |
| 6. | Choudhary | 13.43 | 22.4 | 32.24 | 41.71 | 54.89 | 72.93 |
| 7. | Rathwa | 4.81 | 5.65 | 12.19 | 20.83 | 30.05 | 52.87 |
| 8. | Dhanka | 15.83 | 17.05 | 26.20 | 32.98 | 44.71 | 65.35 |
| 9. | Kokna | 8.92 | 12.56 | 19.94 | 30.83 | 42.98 | 66.48 |
| 10. | Warli | 4.43 | 5.03 | 9.81 | 15.95 | 25.35 | 52.74 |
| | Gujarat State (Total) | 30.45 | 35.79 | 43.70 | 51.15 | 69.01 | 78.03 |
| | Schedule Tribes (Total) | 11.69 | 14.12 | 21.14 | 29.67 | 47.74 | 62.48 |

*Source:* Census of India: 1961–2011

One of the distinguishing features of the tribal sub-plan is that the programme has to be pumped with specific needs of the area which will aim to improve the quality of life of the tribal people within 10 years. Keeping these objectives in mind in reviewing the development efforts made in the first and the second tribal sub-plan, it appears that a clear perspective about the long-term strategy for development of tribals of specific region has not yet emerged. For instance, it had been clearly spelt out that the economy of tribals in several regions revolves around the forests. In view of such a significance of forests in tribal's economic life, the subject of management as well as policy regarding forests in tribal areas assumes a pivotal concern to merit serious discussion.

Although the forest policy does make a mention about the local needs, the investment policy has been more attuned to the exotic needs of the economy of the wider society. The investments now going into the forestry have always been accruing towards commercial considerations, pushing aspects of improving the economy of the tribals in the background. Although there is consensus at the material level on the issue of planning forest-based programmes which subserve the tribal economy, concrete efforts in this direction have not yet been attempted.

### *Development Administration and NGOs*

In areas like Dangs, Dharampur, Vadodara, Songadh, Sagbara, Dediapada, Chhota Udepur, Ratanmal (in Godhra district), planning programmes of tribal development or forest development in isolation has no meaning, the two must reinforce each other. In these areas, forest-based economy should be planned in which agriculture and allied activities could be assigned secondary position. As indicated earlier, the potential of agricultural development in these areas has obvious limitations because of the poor soil, undulating land and almost complete absence of irrigation facilities. Due to these reasons, both tribal development and forest development should be included on a priority basis in all forestry plans, whether conventional, intensive or commercial.

There has been almost a complete absence of programmes to generate countervailing forces of sufficient dimensions so as to help the tribal community to become equal partner in the process of growth. And here one is reminded of the plights of Bhils of

Dangs, Warlis of the Dharampur and Umbergaon talukas, Naikas of the Pardi taluka, Naikdas of Godhra district, etc. Whenever, one went in these areas, it was very much obvious that people of these tribal communities have not been included in appreciable number in the process of implementation of the scheme. Who benefits the most from the tribal development programmes? It is likely that prized rewards are being cornered by a limited segment of only a few tribes. The more advantaged tribal groups get a major share of benefits from tribal development programmes. Even more depressing is the fact that some other groups benefitted at the expense of the tribal people. Roads are often said to be beneficial for economic development but their main effect seems to be stimulation of commodity production; and they make it easier for rich farmers to cart away their surplus of grain to markets.

One can easily get supportive evidence for this contention when he/she cares to examine the phenomenal rise of commercial town and centres in tribal districts, like Vyara, Songadh, Valod (in Tapi district) Bardoli (in Surat district), Pardi, Umbergaon (in Valsad district), Valiya, Netrang (in Bharuch district) and Jhalod, Dahod, Devgadh Bariya (in Dahod district).

Thus, in one way or other, the development programmes are being geared to encourage class stratification in the tribal societies of these areas, a situation which is clearly far away from the laid down objectives of the tribal sub-plan. It is far from the objective of planning for development to make available all resources as well as opportunities for development to some resourceful communities. If these tribal groups, as mentioned above, continue to be left behind and a few communities continue to allow reaping the entire benefits, serious repercussions would follow.

The fact that the phenomenon of seasonal migration, which has started recently in some tribal areas when a vigorous effort in the form of tribal sub-plan is being made, is a serious blot on the development machinery. The goal of economic development of the tribals is to bring economic opportunities to the tribals in their own habitat. But if the assumption regarding rapid increase in the scale of seasonal migration of the tribals is correct, it speaks of far-reaching consequences in our efforts towards economic development of these tribals.

Under these circumstances, a strenuous effort is needed to mobilize the poor tribal communities as well as to chalk out programmes especially for them. The implementers, in order to make their task easier, concentrated only on already developed tribal communities. This brings the question of how to motivate the implementers of the development programmes to mobilize and motivate the poor tribal communities like Bhil, Warli, Naikda and so on. One way is to make it obligatory on them. Besides, the officials should be made responsible in a statutory manner to cover certain fixed proportion of families from such tribal communities whose economic situation is very bleak.

The programmes of immediate benefits to the tribals are generally small with modest financial investments. Preference to bigger programmes, even though some of them may not be of direct relevance to the tribals, persists in most of the sectors. Greater emphasis, thus, would have to be given to beneficiary oriented programmes. A high proportion of the investment by each sector must go into projects that directly benefit the tribals. The economic contents of the plan must be strong.

Let us not be under the illusion that a good plan would necessarily produce good results. There are several intervening variables between planning and implementation. For instance, many schools were set up in tribal areas but there was no way of ensuring regular presence of the teacher within the school premises on working days. Truancy of teacher in remote tribal areas is well known. Similarly, even though the Constitution of India, under Article 350A, affirms that every state must provide adequate facilities for instruction to pupils in their mother tongues, decades have passed and state governments have ignored this prescription for tribal people. Since initial instruction to the tribals is given in an alien language, they understand and assimilate very little. Children cannot understand the teacher, let alone answer questions.

In all the major tribal communities of Gujarat, especially among the Dhodia, Choudhary, Gamit, Patelia, Dungri Garasia and Kokna, which are undergoing the process of political development, we behold the familiar lineaments of the modernizing society, professional political men and all which is creating new relationship between people whose fathers and grandfathers were isolated from all but their nearest neighbours.

This group of political men, who are conceptualized as elites, provides impetus for political development and in turn place themselves strategically to move upwards within the system. The nature of this group of political elites and the socio-political history of the particular community very much shape the political development of that tribal society. In the changing 'encapsulated' political system of the tribal societies in Gujarat, the tribal elites play specialized political roles as mediating agency through which much of the modernity, especially the socio-political orientation, is reaching the masses, and consequently towards widening the political horizons of the masses. But, with the tribals being less developed, the community has to compete with comparatively advanced groups of people under a common political system. They find themselves at a disadvantage. This motivates tribal leadership to increase the tempo of political socialization of the members of their community towards realization of their identity as a political unit. Due to the nature of pluralistic society of the state, the degree of hostility between competing ethnic groups gets sharper and the social tensions go deep down. Ethnic group influences appear to be the greatest among members of tribal societies that feel threatened by a larger group. As such, tribal societies living in different regions of Gujarat have also developed significant political sub-culture. Tribal communities, like Dhodia and Choudhary, form an important segment of the Gujarat society and hence the bearing of their distinctive political sub-culture upon the structure and operation of the state political system is of far-reaching importance. One can cite examples from the rehabilitation process of oustees of Narmada project, suppression of Valia tribals, management of forest co-operatives, etc.

Thus, without the requisite political will, excellently drawn plans can be left to adorn office shelves. Bureaucratic inertia often leads to the ritualistic exercises. It has become very difficult to induce the bureaucracy to carry out goal-oriented and time-bound programmes with dedication. There are some notable officers who work with commitment but a sizeable section of them tends to adopt the line of least resistance. It is unfortunate but true that mediocrity and routine often get away with the cherished rewards and public servants who cut the red-tape and innovate, to attain the desired objections, get penalized. This stifles initiative and experimentation. The implementation of tribal sub-plan strategy requires tedious and hard work, both at the stages of planning and implementation.

Absence of high motivation is responsible for feeble results. If the objectives have to be attained within a stipulated period, a re-energized bureaucratic machinery will have to be geared to action.

Lastly, the task of tribal development acquires yet another dimension because of the recognition of the desirability of preserving and enriching the equality of tribal life. This question should not be dismissed lightly. It is emerging as the focus of much of the discussion and debate on tribal development. A serious threat is hovering over the tribal people who are trying to engulf their whole culture and substitute it with an alien culture. The tribal man faces the prospects of seeing his distinctive style of life wiped off from the ethnic map of India.

Development to be real must be total, that is to say, it must transcend purely economic dimensions in order to include social considerations and the whole dimension of cultural life, embracing creativity, quality of life and the rights of the tribal people as human beings.

The danger is coming, not from outside, but from our foppish and hob-nob handling of tribal affairs. The tribal man, who once had veritable free spirit, has lost it and has acquired the mental cast of a Hindu of the depressed class. He has now begun, on the one hand, to nurse grievances and, on the other hand, to depend more and more on alien agencies. He has fallen prey to the inferiority complex, something which he had never done before. It will be a colossal loss to India.

It will be worthwhile here to speak that the role of voluntary organizations in stimulating and guiding social change among the different tribal societies of Gujarat has been a vital one. Mahatma Gandhi himself got interested in reconstructing the tribal societies of south Gujarat and this inspired several social workers who plunged themselves to carry out the mass scale attempt to mobilize the immobile tribal groups. Prominent among them were A.V. Thakkar who later on became as 'Thakkar Bapa' and Jugat Ram Dave. The organizations created by them (Bhil Seva Mandal by Thakkar Bapa and Rani Paraj Seva Sangh by Jugat Ram Dave), in course of time, developed into pioneer voluntary organizations engaged in works of tribal development, by the time India became independent, a firm root of voluntary efforts had been established in the state and a climate for the need of social change through voluntary efforts was created. Today, we find that those tribal groups are much more developed among whom these organizations had started the work of mobilizing and organizing them. On account of their pioneering efforts, today, there are 452 ashram schools and 74 post basic high schools in the tribal areas of the state, all managed by voluntary organizations. In recent times, besides Bhil Seva Mandal and Rani Paraj Seva Sangh, other notable voluntary organizations actively working in tribal areas of Gujarat are Arch Vahini, SEWA (Jhagadia), Bhartiya Agro-Industries Federation S. (BAIF), Sad Guru Seva Sangh, Adivasi Seva Samiti, AKRSP, etc.

The Government of Gujarat launched the Vanbandhu Kalyan Yojana in the year 2007 with an Eleventh Plan allocation of ₹ 15,000 crore for speedy development of tribal areas of the State. The vision is to double the income of all tribal families, with a special focus on the migrant families and the Particularly Vulnerable Tribal Groups.

The VKY has done commendable work in the field of tribal development in the state of Gujarat.

Lastly, there is an imperceptible and yet unmistakable link between the quality of research and the tribal development. In view of this, social scientists must make their researches qualitatively above reproach. It is necessary to have a clear perception about what the contribution of social sciences should be to the total process of tribal development. In order to prevail in the call to serve the tribal people, social science researches will have to be organized appropriately, with a firm intellectual and emotional commitment, to understand the problems of tribal societies and propose means of action for them. We must have commitment, individually and collectively to better the world for the poor, deprived, underprivileged, downtrodden and exploited tribal people, in fact for all these people.

## Notes

1. 2001 Census and 2011 Census reports of Government of India.

2. 2011 Drashtikshep, Tribal Research and Training Institute, Ahmedabad.
3. Dungri Garasia, Bhil Garasia and Rajput Garasia have been included among Bhils in the list of Scheduled Tribes.
4. There are 14 Integrated Tribal Development Projects operating in Gujarat state. The name of the ITDP are Dang, Bansda, Mandvi, Songadh, Rajpipla, Chota Udepur, Dohad, Khedbrahma, Palanpur, Lunawada, Modasa and Bharuch
5. In certain talukas (other than those covered under tribal sub-plan), there are some villages which have more than 50 per cent of their population comprising Scheduled Tribes. Such villages are grouped together and identified as tribal pockets for the purpose of tribal sub-plan programmes.
6. Dantwala, M.L., Rural Employment: Facts and Issues, in *Economic and Political Weekly*, Vol. XIV, No. 25, 23 June 1979.
7. Vyas, V.S., Introduction to a Research Programmes in Rural Development for Rural People; Dharampur Project, Indian Institute of Management, Ahmedabad, 1975 (Mimeo).

# 5

# Tribal Situation in Madhya Pradesh

**Ganesh Patel**

According to 2011 Census, the total population of the state of Madhya Pradesh was 7,26,26,809. The tribal population among this was almost 21 per cent. The tribal people of the state habitate in far off places. There are 46 tribal communities residing in the state. They have their own distinct culture and dialects. Mostly Bhilly, Korkoo, Gondi, Begani, etc. are prevalent dialects. The literacy rate among women, as compared to men, is very low. In each tribal community, they have their own physical appearance and also distinct ways of marriage. As compared to any other state, the tribal population in Madhya Pradesh is the highest.

The tribal people in this state are economically very poor. Their main occupations are agriculture and agriculture labour work. Since the land holding is very less, the tribals migrate to other outer places in search of labour work. The literacy rate among girls is very low. The government has opened schools and ashrams for their education; but there is an increasing trend of school drop-outs among tribal girls. In fact, they are ignorant about importance of education. The level of Health and Nutrition in their community is very low. One can find malnutrition among children in 0–6 age group. Similarly, the child mortality rate is also higher. The government, under ICDS programme, have opened a number of anganwadis, but the level of malnutrition has not come down. Likewise, in this region, there are more number of child labourers. The child labourers also migrate to other states in search of labour work. Similarly, the girls also migrate outside the region in search of work. They are exploited there. Since, the tribal community is illiterate, they have more faith on ghosts and witches. The crime rate is also going higher.

**Table 1**

*Population of Tribals in MP*

| *Sr. No.* | *Name of the District* | *Percentage of Tribal population* |
|---|---|---|
| 1. | Alirajpur | 89 |
| 2. | Zabuwa | 87 |
| 3., | Badwani | 69 |
| 4. | Dindori | 64 |
| 5. | Mandla | 57 |
| 6. | Dhar | 55 |
| 7. | Anooppur | 47 |
| 8. | Shahdol | 44 |
| 9. | Baitul | 42 |
| 10. | Khargon | 39 |
| 11. | Khandwa | 35 |
| 12. | Singroli | 32 |
| 13. | Chhindwada | 36 |
| 14. | Harda | 28 |
| 15. | Burhanpur | 30 |
| 16. | Raisen | 17 |
| 17. | Dewas | 17 |
| 18. | Sivani | 37 |
| 19. | Balaghat | 22 |

In the State of Madhya Pradesh, overall population of tribal people is 21 per cent. As mentioned in Table 1, there are 19 districts, which have larger number of tribal people. The largest number, i.e. more than 80 per cent tribal population, can be found in the districts of Alirajpur and Zabuwa. The districts of Badwani, Dindori, Mandala and Dhar have more than 50 per cent of tribal populations. The districts of Anooppur, Shahdol, Baitul, Khargon, Khandwa, Singroli, Chhindwada, Sivni and Burhanpur have more than 30 per cent tribal population.

**Table 2**

*Literacy among Tribals (2011)*

| | *Year 2001* | *Year 2011* |
|---|---|---|
| India | 47.1 | 58.2 |
| Madhya Pradesh | 41.2 | 50.6 |

As shown in Table 2, in the year 2001, the literacy rate in India was 47.1 per cent, which rose to 58.7 per cent in the year 2011. Likewise, in Madhya Pradesh, in 2001, the literacy rate was 41.2 per cent; which rose to 50.6 per cent in the year 2011.

**Table 3**

*Tribal Literacy Rate District-wise (Census 2011)*

| *Literacy rate more than 50%* | *Literacy rate more than 40%* | *Literacy rate more than 30%* |
|---|---|---|
| Balaghat, Bhopal, Jabalpur, Shajapur, Narsinhpur, Sivni, Ujjain, Dindori, Mandala, Hoshangabad, Anooppur, Raisen, Bhind, Chhindwada, Raigadh, Muraina, Indore, Sagar, Mandsore, Umariya, Katni, Shahdol, Dahoh, Sidhi, Baitul, Datiya, Reewa, Harda (Total 30 districts) | Dewas, Gwalior, Singroli, Khandwa, Panna, Vidisha, Dhar, Ratlam, Khargon, Guna, Nimach, Chhatarpur, Ashoknagar, Shivpuri, Tikamgadh, Sihore (Total 16 districts) | Badwani, Burhanpur, Zabuwa, Alirajpur, (Total 4 district) |

In the state, the literacy rate among tribals is 50 per cent. As shown in Table 3, in 30 districts of the state, according to 2011 Census, the literacy rate is more than 50 per cent; in 16 districts it is more than 40 per cent and in four district, it is more than 30 per cent.

It can be seen from Table 4 that the literacy level below primary education is 47.1 per cent among people in Bhil and Kol communities. Likewise, in Bhil community, 21.2 per cent people have gone up to primary level; 8.2 per cent up to middle class level, 6.3 per cent up to higher secondary school level and even 1.6 per cent up to graduation level. In Gond tribe, 45 per cent of people have not reached up to primary level; 27.4 per cent have passed primary level; 10.9 per cent have reached up to middle school level; 7.0 per cent have reached up to higher secondary school level; and 1.2 per cent have reached up to graduation level also. In Kol tribe, 47 per cent have not reached up to even primary level, 26.9 per cent have reached primary level, 11.4 per cent have reached middle school level; 6.6 per cent have reached higher secondary level and 0.6 per cent have reached graduation level.

**Table 4**

*Literacy Rate Among Main Tribes*

| *Sr. No.* | *Name of the Tribe* | *Literacy Rate* | *Less than Primary Level* | *Primary Level* | *Middle School Level* | *Higher Secondary School Level* | *Graduation Level* |
|---|---|---|---|---|---|---|---|
| 1. | Bhil | 15.5 | 47.1 | 21.2 | 8.2 | 6.3 | 1.6 |
| 2. | Gond | 8.4 | 45.0 | 27.4 | 10.9 | 7.0 | 1.2 |
| 3. | Kol | 7.2 | 47.1 | 26.9 | 11.4 | 6.6 | 0.6 |
| 4. | Korku | 10.1 | 56.0 | 22.9 | 6.8 | 3.6 | 0.5 |
| 5. | Sahariya | 15.4 | 62.2 | 16.1 | 4.0 | 1.8 | 0.5 |
| 6. | Baiga | 11.4 | 50.4 | 26.0 | 8.3 | 3.4 | 0.5 |

In Korkoo tribe, 56 per cent have not reached up to even primary education level; 22.96 have passed primary level; 6.8 per cent have reached up to middle school level; 3.6 per cent have reached up to higher secondary level and only 0.5 per cent have reached up to Graduation level.

In Sahariya tribe, 62.2 per cent have not crossed primary level; 16 per cent have gone up to primary level; only 4 per cent could reach middle school level, less than 2 per cent (1.8%) have reached higher secondary level and just half (0.5) per cent have reached up to graduation level.

In Baiga tribe, 50 per cent have reached only up to less than primary level; 26 per cent could pass the primary level, 8.3 per cent reached middle school level; just 3.4 per cent reached higher secondary level; and 0.5 per cent could reach up to graduation level also.

Table 5 clearly indicates the trends towards literacy among female tribals. The maximum literacy level in female is in Gond community, which is little more than one-third, i.e. 36.4 per cent. Among Korkoos, Kols, Bhils and Baiga, the female literacy rate ranges between 20 to 24 per cent (Korkoo 24, Kol 22.9%, Bhil 23% and Baiga 20.1%). Among Sahariya, the female literacy rate is only 15.9 per cent.

**Table 5**

*Female Literacy Among Main Tribal Communities*

| Gond | Korkoo | Kol | Bhil | Baiga | Sahariya |
|---|---|---|---|---|---|
| 36.4 | 24.0 | 22.9 | 23.0 | 20.1 | 15.9 |

Thus, general literacy rate among tribals is less; but it is much less among tribal females. In seems, females have no aptitude for learning. People do not get their daughters educated. Girls are mainly associated with household work; and therefore, they are not encouraged to attend the schools. Even where they are enrolled, most give up in between and drop out from the schools.

**Table 6**

*Habitations of Main Tribes in MP*

| Tribe | Districts where concentrated |
|---|---|
| Gond | Chhindwada, Shahdol, Mandala, Dindori, Sivni Balaghat, Narsinhpur. |
| Bhils | Dhar, Zabuwa, Alirajpur, Ratlam, Badwani, Khargon |
| Korkoo | Khandwa, Harda |
| Sahariya | Sahopur, Gwalior, Shivpuri, Guna, Vidisha, Ashoknagar |
| Baiga | Mandla, Dindori, Umariya, Shahdol, Balaghat, Sidi |
| Kol | Shahdol, Satna, Sidhi |

As shown in Table 6, Gond tribe people mainly habitate in seven of the districts of MP, whereas Bhil tribe is mainly concentrated in six districts, Korkoos are found in only two districts but Sahariyas are found in six districts. Kol tribe people mainly habitate in three districts of the state.

**Table 7**

*Tribe Population*

| Tribes having larger no. of people | Tribes having very few no. of people |
|---|---|
| Gond, Bhil, Korkoo, Sahariya, Baiga and Kol | Manzi, Kherwar, Mowari, Panika, Ondh, Birhor, Parja and Nagesiya |

As shown in Table 7, there are six tribes, viz. Gond, Bhil, Korkoo, Sahariya, Baiga and Kol which have larger population in the state; but the tribes like Manzi, Kherwar, Mowari, Panika,

Ondh, Birhor, Parja and Nagesia have very less number of people. Their population is much less.

**Table 8**

*Dances of Main Tribes of MP*

| *Sr. No.* | *Name of the Tribe* | *Specific Dances* |
|---|---|---|
| 1. | Gond | Shaila, Karma, Birha, Bhadoni |
| 2. | Bhil | Bhagoriya, Lahari, Dansolo, Chabadi, Ghodi |
| 3. | Baiga | Dadariya, Begakarma |
| 4. | Sahariya | Tejabi, Gatha, Fag |
| 5. | Korkoo | Gadhari, Gogaryan, Mandal, Chuladi |

As shown in Table 8, different main tribes have their distinctive dances. In fact, a particular dance is an identification mark of a tribe. Among Gonds, four dances, viz. Shaila, Karmo, Birha and Bhadani, are most prevalent. Among Bhil tribe, the dances of Bhagoriya, Lahri, Dansolo, Chabadi and Ghodi are most prevalent. The Bhagoriya dance is performed in the month of Fagan, i.e. during Holi/Dhuleti festivals. The Baiga tribe performs Dadariya and Begakarma dances. The Sahariya tribe is known for its Tejabi, Gatha and Fag dances. Among Korkoo tribe, dances like Gandhari, Gogaryan, Mandal and Chuladi are prevalent.

**Table 9**

*Main Tribal Dialects*

| *Sr. No.* | *Name of the Tribe* | *Their dialects* |
|---|---|---|
| 1. | Bhil, Bhilala | Bhili, Bareli, Pataliya |
| 2. | Korkoo | Korkoo |
| 3. | Gond | Gondi |
| 4. | Mavasi | Mavosi |
| 5. | Baiga | Baigani |
| 6. | Sahariya | Bundeli |

In Madhya Pradesh, various tribal dialects are gradually decaying. As shown in Table 9, Among Bhil or Bhilala tribe, their Bhili dialect is still in use. The Korkoo tribals talk in Korkoo dialects, Mavoasi tribe people communicate in their own Mavosi dialect; and Baiga tribals use Baigani dialects. Similarly, Sahariya tribals speak Bundeli dialect.

While summing up the paper we may say that in regards to the square area, Madhya Pradesh occupies second place among the Indian states. About 40 per cent of total Indian population is in Madhya Pradesh. The Baigas, Bhariya and Sahariya are the most backward tribes. As such, there are as many as 46 tribes. The main occupation of tribals is agriculture and agricultural labour work. They are also dependent on forests. There is maximum malnutrition in 0–5 age-group children. Almost 60 per cent of these children are below normal weight. Almost 50 per cent of children suffer from malnutrition. Atrocities on women and children is rampant. There is lack of health and hygiene facilities in tribal areas. Tribal people migrate to other places in search of labour work. In 19 districts of the state, most of tribal people habitate. Among tribals, the literacy rate is 50.6 per cent. In 30 districts of the state, the literacy rate is above 50 per cent and in 16 districts, the literacy rate is above 40 per cent. Among Bhil tribe, 1.6 per cent have reached up to graduation level. In Gond tribe, it is 1.2 per cent. In rest of the tribes, the percentage of graduation is below 1 per cent.

# 6

# Tribal Situations in Maharashtra

**Sarbeswara Sahoo**

The state of Maharashtra lies between the latitudes 15°36′20 to 22°1′40′′ and longitudes 72°40′30′′ to 80°56′30′′ covering an area of 3,07,713 sq km. The state is bounded in the north and north east by Gujarat, Madhya Pradesh, and Chhattisgarh states. In the south and south east by Karnataka and Telengana and in the west by Union Territory of Dadra and Nagar Haveli and Arabian Sea.[1] It is one of the richest states of India contributing 23.2 per cent of GDP to Indian economy.

## Tribal Area and Population of Maharashtra

The state of Maharashtra has the second largest tribal population in the country next only to that of Madhya Pradesh. The major tribal communities are the Bhils, Gonds, Mahadev Kolis, Warlis, Koknas and Thakars, while the Katkaris, Kolam and Madia Gonds are classified as primitive tribes. Of the 47 Scheduled Tribes (ST) communities, 19 ST communities have a population of less than 1,000. The Scheduled Area notified by the Government of India consists of 5,809 villages and 16 towns in 12 districts covering an area of 46,531 sq km, which is about 15.1 per cent of the area of the state. These districts are Thane, Pune, Nashik, Dhule, Nandurbar, Jalgaon, Ahmednagar, Nanded, Amravati, Yeotmal, Gadchiroli and Chandrapur. The tribal districts of Maharashtra are indicated in yellow colour in the map shown in Figure 1 are border to the tribal districts of Gujarat, Madhya Pradesh, Chhattisgarh and Karnataka. Tribals are found in geographically backward parts of the state i.e. north-western part and north-eastern parts of the state are comparatively less developed, where on an average 25 per cent tribal population lives.

In Maharashtra, geographically the concentrations of tribal are found in the following regions:

(1) *Sahyadri Region:* The Sahyadri region comprises Thane, Raigad, Nashik and Pune districts, where Warlis, Kokanas, Thakurs, Mahadeo Kolis, Malhar Kolis, Dhor Kolis, Katkaris, etc. tribal groups are found.
(2) *Satpudas Region:* The Satpudas region incorporates Nandurbar, Dhule, Jalgaon, Aurangabad and Amravati districts and Bhils, Kokanas, Dublas, Dhankas; Korkus are the main tribal groups seen here.
(3) *Gondwana Region:* The Gondwana region includes districts like Chandrapur, Gadchiroli, Bhandara, Yavatmal and

**Figure 1**

*Tribal Commisionerate Offices in the ITDP area of Maharashtra*

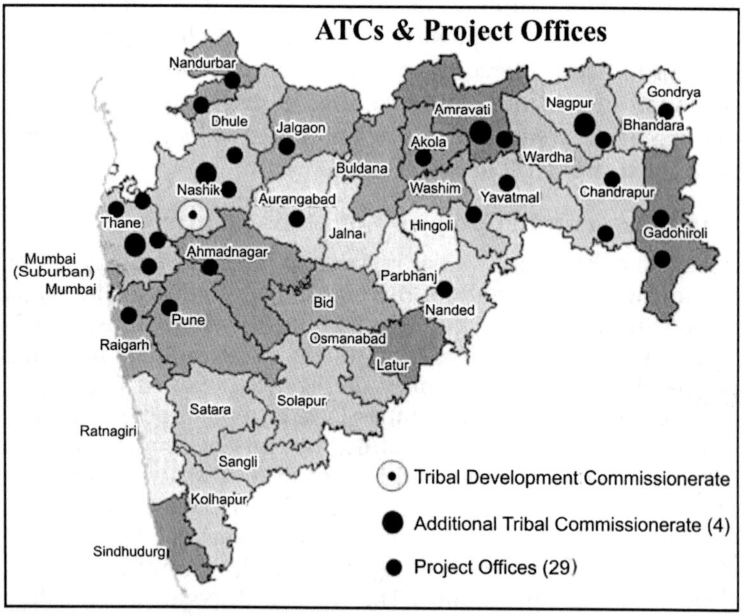


*Source:* Tribal Commissioner Office, Government of Maharashtra.

Nagpur and Gonds, Madia Gonds, Korkus, Kolams, Paradhans, Andhs, etc. are the main tribal groups found in this region. Tribal sub-plan concept was introduced by the Government of India for overall development of tribal dominated pockets. Integrated Tribal Development Agencies were set up in these areas. Figure 1 shows the TSP areas and ITDP pockets of the Maharashtra state.

**Table 1**

*Major Tribal Communities in Maharashtra: Showing Geographic Location*

| *Name of the Tribe* | *District wise Location* |
|---|---|
| Bhil | Nandurbar, Dhule, Nashik |
| Gond | Gharchiroli, Chandrapur, Wardha, Nagpur, Bhandara, Gondia, Yavatmal |
| Mahadev | Ahmednagar, Thane |
| Koli | Nasik Buldana |
| Warli | Thane Nasik Mumbai |
| Kokna | Thane Nasik |
| Thakar | Raigad, Thanke, Nasik |

*Source:* Tribal Commissioner Office, Government of Maharashtra

Thus, the tribal areas are located in the north, north-east and north-western part of the state. There are 47 tribal communities and three particularly vulnerable tribes found in the state of Maharashtra. The major tribes along with the areas where they are found are explained in Table 1.

Demographic details of Tribal Population of Maharashtra is explained in Table 2.

**Table 2**

*Tribal Population of the Maharashtra State*

| *Census Year* | *State's Total Population (lakh)* | *Tribal Population (lakh)* | *Percentage* |
|---|---|---|---|
| 1971 | 504.12 | 38.41 | 7.62 |
| 1981 | 627.84 | 57.72 | 9.19 |
| 1991 | 789.37 | 73.18 | 9.27 |
| 2001 | 968.79 | 85.77 | 8.85 |
| 2011 | 112.37 | 90.06 | 10.1 |

*Source:* Census of India.

Tribal population of the state has increased from 7.62 per cent in the year 1971 to 10.1 per cent in the year 2011. In terms of tribal population, Maharashtra is second, next to Madhya Pradesh. The rise in the number of tribals shows that the life expectancy of the Scheduled Tribes has increased over the years due to overall development. State-wise share of tribal population to total population in the country is explained in Figure 2.

However, the decadal change of tribal population of Maharashtra is 22.5 per cent lower than the national average of 23.7 per cent.

**Table 3**

*Sex Ratio (ST)*

| *Sex Ratio: ST* | *2001* | *2011* |
|---|---|---|
| Maharashtra | 973 | 977 |
| India | 978 | 990 |

**Figure 2**

*Share of Tribal Population to Total in India (2011)*

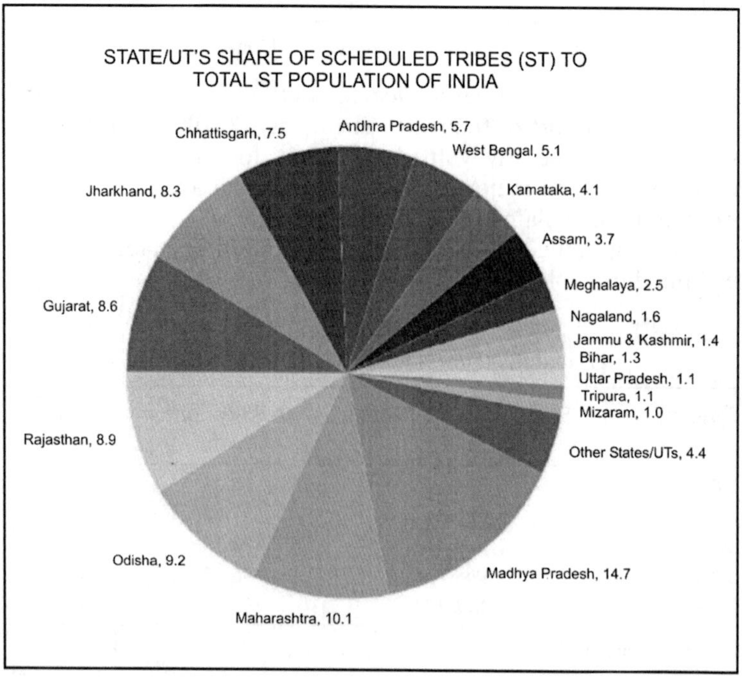

Generally, sex ratio is favourable in case of tribals. However, the data in Table 3 shows that the number of female per thousand of male for tribal population in case of Maharashtra is less than the country. It was 977 against 990 for the whole country for tribal people.

**Table 4**

*Tribal Communities in Maharashtra with Population (2011 Census)*

| *ST Name* | *ST Population* | *Male Population* | *Female Population* |
|---|---|---|---|
| All Schedule Tribes | 1,05,10,213 | 53,15,025 | 51,95,188 |
| Andh | 4,74,110 | 2,43,300 | 2,30,810 |
| Baiga | 333 | 195 | 138 |
| Barda | 1,247 | 628 | 619 |
| Bavacha, Bamcha | 345 | 186 | 159 |
| Bhaina | 270 | 148 | 122 |
| Bharia Bhumia, Bhuinhar Bhumia, Pando | 1,348 | 750 | 598 |
| Bhattra | 66 | 31 | 35 |
| Bhil, Bhil Garasia, Dholi Bhil, Dungri Bhil, Dungri Garasia, Mewasi Bhil, Rawal Bhil, Tadvi Bhil, Bhagalia, Bhilala, Pawra, Vasava, Vasave | 25,88,659 | 13,06,793 | 12,81,866 |
| Bhunjia | 2,136 | 1,155 | 981 |
| Binjhwar | 8,567 | 4,256 | 4,311 |
| Birhul, Birhor | 145 | 90 | 55 |
| Dhanka, Tadvi, Tetaria, Valvi | 35,104 | 17,969 | 17,135 |
| Dhanwar | 4,094 | 2,125 | 1,969 |
| Dhodia | 17,520 | 8,652 | 8,868 |
| Dubla, Talavia, Halpati | 18,697 | 9,204 | 9,493 |
| Gamit, Gamta, Gavit, Mavchi, Padvi | 67,796 | 33,911 | 33,885 |
| Gond, Rajgond, Arakh, Arrakh, Agaria, Asur, Badi Maria, Bada Maria, Bhatola, Bhimma, Bhuta, Koilabhuta, Koilabhuti, Bhar, Bisonhorn Maria, Chota Maria, Dandami Maria, Dhuru, Dhurwa, Dhoba, Dhulia, Dorla, Gaiki, Gatta, Gatti, Gaita, Gond Gowari, Hill Maria, Kandra, Kalanga, Khatola, Koitar, Koya, Khirwar, Khirwara, Kucha Maria, Kuchaki Maria, Madia, Maria, Mana, Mannewar, Moghya, Mogia, Monghya, Mudia, Muria, Nagarchi, Naikpod, Nagwanshi, Ojha, Raj, Sonjhari Jhareka, Thatia, Thotya, Wade Maria, Vade Maria | 16,18,090 | 8,18,955 | 7,99,135 |

*Cont'd...*

*...Cont'd*

| | | | |
|---|---|---|---|
| Halba, Halbi | 2,61,011 | 1,32,245 | 1,28,766 |
| Kamar | 1,391 | 793 | 598 |
| Kathodi, Katkari, Dhor Kathodi, Dhor Kathkari, Son Kathodi, Son Katkari | 2,85,334 | 1,42,619 | 1,42,715 |
| Kawar, Kanwar, Kaur, Cherwa, Rathia, Tanwar, Chattri | 26,354 | 13,697 | 12,657 |
| Khairwar | 1,843 | 1,107 | 736 |
| Kharia | 745 | 370 | 375 |
| Kokna, Kokni, Kukna | 6,87,431 | 3,46,001 | 3,41,430 |
| Kol | 6,874 | 3,548 | 3,326 |
| Kolam, Mannervarlu | 1,94,671 | 98,319 | 96,352 |
| Koli Dhor, Tokre Koli, Kolcha, Kolgha | 2,20,074 | 1,12,666 | 1,07,408 |
| Koli Mahadev, Dongar Koli | 14,59,565 | 7,42,439 | 7,17,126 |
| Koli Malhar | 2,82,868 | 1,41,698 | 1,41,170 |
| Kondh, Khond, Kandh | 515 | 272 | 243 |
| Korku, Bopchi, Mouasi, Nihal, Nahul, Bondhi, Bondeya | 2,64,492 | 1,34,931 | 1,29,561 |
| Koya, Bhine Koya, Rajkoya | 388 | 209 | 179 |
| Nagesia, Nagasia | 133 | 75 | 58 |
| Naikda, Nayaka, Cholivala Nayaka, Kapadia Nayaka, Mota Nayaka, Nana Nayaka | 22,307 | 11,717 | 10,590 |
| Oraon, Dhangad | 43,060 | 22943 | 20,117 |
| Pardhan, Pathari, Saroti | 1,45,131 | 73,575 | 71,556 |
| Pardhi, Advichincher, Phans Pardhi, Phanse Pardhi, Langoli Pardhi, Bahelia, Bahellia, Chita Pardhi, Shikari, Takankar, Takia | 2,23,527 | 1,13,380 | 1,10,147 |
| Parja | 315 | 184 | 131 |
| Patelia | 2,574 | 1,372 | 1,202 |
| Pomla | 44 | 26 | 18 |
| Rathawa | 488 | 262 | 226 |
| Sawar, Sawara | 348 | 206 | 142 |
| Thakur, Thakar, Ka Thakur, Ka Thakar, Ma Thakur, Ma Thakar | 5,67,968 | 2,87,764 | 2,80,204 |
| Varli | 7,96,245 | 3,94,144 | 4,02,101 |
| Vitolia, Kotwalia, Barodia | 448 | 228 | 220 |

*Source:* Census of India, 2011

As mentioned earlier, there are 47 tribal communities in the state. The details of the tribals along with their population as per the 2011 Census is provided in Table 4.

The number of Bhil tribes are the highest and Pomla being the lowest. As discussed, there are three particularly vulnerable tribal groups in the state of Maharashtra. They are Katkeri, Kollom and Madia Gond. The population of particularly vulnerable tribal groups are as shown in Table 5:

**Table 5**

*District-Wise Population of Particularly Vulnerable Tribal Groups in Maharashtra*

| *Sr. No.* | *Primitive Tribe* | *District* | *Population as per* | | | | |
|---|---|---|---|---|---|---|---|
| | | | *1971 Census* | *1981 Census* | *1991 Census* | *2001 Census* | *2011 Census* |
| 1. | Katkari/ Kathodi | 1. Thane | 56,330 | 57,456 | 73,700 | 91,429 | |
| | | 2. Raigad | 67,563 | 75,680 | 93,484 | 1,03,244 | |
| | | 3. Ratnagiri | 9,453 | 21,265 | 3,452 | 6,034 | |
| | | 4. Pune | 7,101 | 8,885 | 12,054 | 11,935 | |
| | | 5. Nashik | 3,804 | 4,444 | 5,437 | 7,194 | |
| | | 6. Other Districts | 2,534 | 6,872 | 14,070 | 15,186 | |
| | | Total | 1,46,785 | 1,74,602 | 2,02,203 | 2,35,022 | 2,85,334 |
| 2. | Kolam | 1. Yavatmal | 49,775 | 65,707 | 76,802 | 9,39,329 | |
| | | 2. Nanded | 3,626 | 3,953 | 49,556 | 51,653 | |
| | | 3. Chandrapur | 2,656 | 4,903 | 3,962 | 6,376 | |
| | | 4. Other Districts | 4 | 11,510 | 17,523 | 21,688 | |
| | | Total | 56,061 | 1,18,073 | 1,47,843 | 1,73,646 | 1,94,671 |
| 3. | Madia Gond | 1. Gadchiroli | 3,31,798 | 11,62,735 | 14,42,986 | 15,54,894 | |
| | | 2. Other Districts | – | – | – | – | |
| | | Total | 3,31,798 | 11,62,735 | 14,42,986 | 15,54,894 | N.A. |
| | Maharashtra State | | 5,34,644 | 14,55,410 | 17,93,022 | 19,63,562 | |

*Source:* Tribal Development Commissioner, Government of Maharashtra

Thus Katakari among the PVTG are having the largest share. As per 2011 Census, the total population was 2,85,334. Not only that, condition of the Katkari is one of the worse and need attention. The subsequent paragraphs describe the situation of Katkari in Maharashtra.

## Situation of Vulnerable Tribes: A Case of Katkari

As usual the conditions of Particularly Vulnerable Tribes are worse compared to the Schedules Tribes. They live in abject poverty marred by illiteracy ignorance and exploitation. The conditions are same in the state of Maharashtra, an industrially developed state. Out of the three PVTG, the condition of Katkari that lives under the nose of the commercial capital of India is worst and much under discussion.

The Katkari of today is a fragmented and very scattered community, highly dependent on others for their livelihoods and for a place to live. Most Katkari are landless workers with only periodic and tenuous connections to their original nomadic, forest-based livelihoods. Many have become bonded labourers working on the brick kilns and charcoal units serving the urban and industrial interests of Greater Mumbai. They are also called the vanishing tribes of India. More than a third of the Katkari hamlets are in Raigad and Thane districts. They depend on the local landlord for livelihood. As most of the land owners are selling their land to the builders, the Katkari are witnessing migration. Despite their service, the Katkari community is firmly excluded from membership in village society. Particular expressions of untouchability, including physical exclusion, the assumption of criminality and a visceral reaction to Katkari food habits have created an extreme distance of the Katkari from the caste-based agrarian order.[2] Other PVTG found are slightly in a better position compared to the Katkari. Therefore, it is important for the government to see that the vulnerable conditions of the Katkari needs to be improved.

## Literacy Rate of Scheduled Tribes in Maharashtra

Raising literacy among the tribals is a very basic initiative for their development. In the state of Maharashtra the tribal literacy rate in the year 2011 was 65.7 per cent (Table 6), which is much less than the average literacy of 82.9 per cent for the non-tribal population. Literacy gap is still as high as 18–26 per cent that needs to be reduced. There are five districts, for instance, Dhule, Raigarh, Thane, Nashik and Gadchiroli, which are identified with very low tribal literacy rate. These districts are such, where the tribal concentration is very high, confined to north-western part, and one district in the north-eastern part of the state to be a graduate in tribal society is a very big achievement considering their level of living and their residential location in very remote and inaccessible areas. The state government as well as Central government has provided certain opportunities by providing scholarship, fellowship, and ashramshala to raise their educational level and a huge amount has been spent on various programmes right from Third Plan and more especially in the Fifth Plan. The mass illiteracy among the tribals forms the very basis of their vicious circle of poverty.

**Table 6**

*Literacy Rate of Schedule Tribes and Non-Tribals of the State of Maharashtra, Literacy Percentage for Total and Tribal Peoples of Maharashtra State, during the Period 1961 to 2011*

| *Census Year* | *Literacy Percentage* | | | | | |
|---|---|---|---|---|---|---|
| | *Total* | | | *Scheduled Tribe* | | |
| | *Male* | *Female* | *Total* | *Male* | Female | Total |
| | *Male+Female* | | | *Male+Female* | | |
| 1961 | 40.04% | 16.76% | 29.82% | 12.55% | 1.75% | 7,21% |
| 1971 | 51.04% | 26.43% | 39.13% | 19.06% | 4.21% | 11.74% |
| 1981 | 58.65% | 34.63% | 47.02% | 32.38% | 11.94% | 22.29% |
| 1991 | 76.56% | 53.30% | 64.87% | 49.08% | 24.08% | 36.77% |
| 2001 | 86.00% | 67.00% | 76.90% | 67.00% | 43.10% | 55.20% |
| 2011 | – | – | 82.90% | – | – | 65.70% |

*Source:* Census of India.

**Table 7**

*Government Ashram Schools in Maharashtra (2011)*

| *Additional Tribal Commissionerate Office* | *Total No. of Ashram Schools* | *Boys* | *Girls* | *Total* |
|---|---|---|---|---|
| A.T.C., Nashik | 222 | 43,983 | 38,634 | 82,617 |
| A.T.C., Thane | 123 | 25,544 | 17,038 | 42,582 |
| A.T.C., Amravati | 100 | 16,671 | 13,114 | 29,785 |
| A.T.C., Nagpur | 102 | 16,534 | 15,698 | 32,232 |
| Total | 547 | 1,02,732 | 84,484 | 1,87,216 |

*Source:* Tribal Development Commissionerate, Maharashtra.

In order to improve educational situation, Government of India and State tribal development department emphasized the role of ashram schools, stipend and scholarships. Table 7 provides the details of ashram schools for Scheduled Tribes of Maharashtra. The total number of ashram schools operating in Maharashtra are 547 where 1,87,216 students are enrolled.

However, there have been media reports on poor conditions of about the ashram schools in the state of Maharashtra. Not only that, the Standing Committee on Social Justice and Empowerment, Government of India, also reported the poor conditions of ashram schools. The Committee[3] pointed out that 793 children died in ashram schools in Maharashtra between 2001–02 and 2012–13 as a result of scorpion/snake bites and minor illnesses.[4]

## Livelihood Situations of Scheduled Tribes in Maharashtra

Most of the tribals of Maharashtra lives in rural areas depends on Agriculture, Forest and Wage works. Landlessness among the Scheduled Tribes in the state is as high as 43 per cent. Agricultural productivity is also quite low, 1,017 kg per hectare, and hence has kept the large number of Scheduled Tribes below poverty line. Tribal areas are land scarce in the state and hence forest especially Common Property Forest and other resources become a major source of livelihood.

## Forest and Tribals in Maharashtra

Most of the tribal population in the state resides near and around forest areas, particularly in Thane, Nashik, Dhule, Nandurbar, Jalgaon, Pune, Nanded, Amravati, Gadchiroli and Chandrapur Districts. The total forest area in the state is 63,867 sq km, this is about 21 per cent of the total geographical area of the state. Out of this 31,277 sq km of forest area, i.e. 49 per cent, is in the tribal sub plan area of the state. Forestry works, therefore, play an important role in the socio-economic development of the tribals. They depend on forest for harvesting of major and minor forest produce, afforestation and plantation, wildlife and nature conservation, forest protection, etc. Employment for tribals is generated from forest related activities done by the Forest Department, Forest Labourers' Co-Operative Societies, Maharashtra State Co-Operative Tribal Development Corporation, Forest Development Corporation, etc. From time to time, skills of the tribals are improved through training programmes undertaken by the department.

In past, the tribals due to their illiteracy and ignorance were exploited by unscrupulous forest contractors. The state government with the intention to free tribals from exploitation enacted the following Acts:

1. The Maharashtra Sale of Trees by Occupants belonging to Scheduled Tribes (Regulation) Act, 1969
2. The Maharashtra Tribals Economic Condition (Improvement) Act, 1976
3. The Nationalization of Tendu and Apta leaves under the former Act of 1969.

The Forest Department under the Maharashtra Sale of Trees Act, 1969 allow the tribals to sell a selected list of trees from selected areas.

Under the Act of 1976, lending by private agencies and marketing of certain agricultural and minor forest produce in the tribal sub plan area by any other agencies except those notified by the state government from time to time are prohibited. The Maharashtra State Co-operative Tribal Development Corporation is the major administrative organization entrusted with the task of implementing the Act of 1976.[5]

## Poverty and Migration

The overall landlessness of tribals in Maharashtra is 43 per cent. Amongst tribes, landlessness is highest among the Primitive Tribal Group of Katkaris (83%) and Kolams (63%). However, the other Primitive Tribal Group of Madia Gonds is mainly landed, with only 17 per cent of them being landless. Poverty situation of the tribals of Maharashtra is same as that of the tribals of the Indian subcontinent.

From Table 8 it can be observed that poverty of rural and urban areas of the Maharashtra is quite high compared to other state of India. As a result of poverty there is intra-state and inter-state of migration of the Schedule Tribes. Poverty stricken districts are observed to be affected by left wing extremism. Many of the Scheduled Tribes of the border districts, like Nadurbar and Khandesh region, migrate to sugar cane industries of Maharashtra and Gujarat and live in worst conditions. Due to poverty and hunger, malnutrition is found among Scheduled Tribes. This also has associated health problems due to which mortality rate among tribes is very high. Table 9 shows the infant mortality rate among the Scheduled Tribes.

**Table 8**

*State-wise Percentage of Population Below Poverty Line (Social Groups-Wise) 2004–05*

| Sr. No. | States | Rural | | | | Urban | | | |
|---|---|---|---|---|---|---|---|---|---|
| | | ST | SC | OBC | Others | ST | SC | OBC | Others |
| 1 | Andhra Pradesh | 30.5 | 15.4 | 9.5 | 4.1 | 50.0 | 39.9 | 28.9 | 20.6 |
| 2 | Assam | 14.1 | 27.7 | 18.8 | 25.4 | 4.8 | 8.6 | 8.6 | 4.2 |
| 3 | Bihar | 53.3 | 64 | 37.8 | 26.6 | 57.2 | 67.2 | 41.4 | 18.3 |
| 4 | Chhattisgarh | 54.7 | 32.7 | 33.9 | 29.2 | 41.0 | 52.0 | 52.7 | 21.4 |
| 5 | Delhi | 0.0 | 0.0 | 0.0 | 10.6 | 9.4 | 35.8 | 18.3 | 6.4 |
| 6 | Gujarat | 34.7 | 21.8 | 19.1 | 4.8 | 21.4 | 16.0 | 22.9 | 7.0 |
| 7 | Haryana | 0.0 | 26.8 | 13.9 | 4.2 | 4.6 | 33.4 | 22.5 | 5.9 |
| 8 | Himachal Pradesh | 14.9 | 19.6 | 9.1 | 6.4 | 2.4 | 5.6 | 10.1 | 2.0 |
| 9 | Jammu & Kashmir | 8.8 | 5.2 | 10.0 | 3.3 | 0.0 | 13.7 | 4.8 | 7.8 |
| 10 | Jharkhand | 54.2 | 57.9 | 40.2 | 37.1 | 45.1 | 47.2 | 19.1 | 9.2 |
| 11 | Karnataka | 23.5 | 31.8 | 20.9 | 13.8 | 58.3 | 50.6 | 39.1 | 20.3 |
| 12 | Kerala | 44.3 | 21.6 | 13.7 | 6.6 | 19.2 | 32.5 | 24.3 | 7.8 |
| 13 | Madhya Pradesh | 58.6 | 42.8 | 29.6 | 13.4 | 44.7 | 67.3 | 55.5 | 20.8 |
| 14 | Maharashtra | 56.6 | 44.8 | 23.9 | 18.9 | 40.4 | 43.2 | 35.6 | 26.8 |
| 15 | Orissa | 75.6 | 50.2 | 36.9 | 23.4 | 61.8 | 72.6 | 50.2 | 28.9 |
| 16 | Punjab | 30.7 | 14.6 | 10.6 | 2.2 | 2.1 | 16.1 | 8.4 | 2.9 |
| 17 | Rajasthan | 32.6 | 28.7 | 13.1 | 8.2 | 24.1 | 52.1 | 35.6 | 20.7 |
| 18 | Tamil Nadu | 32.1 | 31.2 | 19.8 | 19.1 | 32.5 | 40.2 | 20.9 | 6.5 |
| 19 | Uttar Pradesh | 32.4 | 44.8 | 32.9 | 19.7 | 37.4 | 44.9 | 36.6 | 19.2 |
| 20 | Uttarakhand | 43.2 | 54.2 | 44.8 | 33.5 | 64.4 | 65.7 | 46.5 | 25.5 |
| 21 | West Bengal | 42.4 | 29.5 | 18.3 | 27.5 | 25.7 | 28.5 | 10.4 | 13.0 |
| | All India | 47.3 | 36.8 | 26.7 | 16.1 | 33.3 | 39.9 | 31.4 | 16.0 |

*Source:* Planning Commission, New Delhi.

**Table 9**

*Infant Mortality*

| | Neonatal Mortality Rate | | Infant Mortality Rate | | Under-five Mortality Rate | |
|---|---|---|---|---|---|---|
| | Scheduled Tribes | Other | Other | Scheduled Tribes | Scheduled Tribes | Other |
| Maharashtra | 32.5 | 34.3 | 51.4 | 40.5 | 69.8 | 47.4 |
| India | 39.9 | 34.5 | 62.1 | 48.9 | 95.7 | 59.2 |

*Source:* National Family Health Survey, 2005–06.

## Health and Nutrition Status of Scheduled Tribes in Maharashtra

As discussed earlier, tribal people live in remote places and remain isolated, living in remote forest and hilly areas. Majority of them have poor health status, peculiar health needs and a wide prevalence of red blood cell genetic disorders that complicates their health problems further. Moreover, the inadequate health infrastructure in tribal areas to deal with such complicated health problems is a matter of grave concern (Kate, 2000).[6] Health problems of the tribal population in the state can be summarized as follows:

- Deficiency of essential components in diet leading to malnutrition, protein calorie malnutrition and micronutrient deficiencies (vitamin A, iron and iodine) are common. Goitre of various grades is also endemic in some of the tribal areas.
- Water borne and communicable diseases: Gastrointestinal disorders, particularly dysentery and parasitic infections are very common, leading to marked morbidity and malnutrition. Malaria and tuberculosis still remain a problem in many tribal areas, while the spectrums of viral and venereal diseases have not been studied in depth.
- High prevalence of genetic disorders mostly involving red blood cells: Genetically transmitted disorders like sickle cell anaemia, glucose 6 phosphate dehydrogenase deficiency and different forms of thalassaemia are also common. All these defects lead to the early destruction of red blood cells and add to the overall anaemia (Kate, 2000).
- Excess consumption of alcohol: The brewing of alcohol from Mohua flower and fruits has been practiced traditionally. However, the switch over to commercially available liquor is likely to be a major threat.
    - Superstitions particularly related to health problems.
    - Extreme poverty.

Thus, the tribals of Maharashtra as that of elsewhere in this country face many health problems leading to death. However, sickle cell anaemia is one of the most painful diseases leading to the death of Scheduled Tribes but has been discussed very little (Table 10). Recently the Ministry of Tribal Affairs, Government of India, devised a strategy to tackle the issues of sickle cell anaemia. Following paragraphs provide the details of sickle cell anaemia among the Scheduled Tribes in the state of Maharashtra.

**Table 10**

*Summary of the Distribution of Sickle Cell Trait Among Different Tribal Groups of Maharashtra (2000)*

| Sr. No. | Tribal Group | District | Sickle Cell Carriers (%) |
|---|---|---|---|
| 1 | Otkar | Gadchiroli | 35 |
| 2 | Pardhan | Nanded, Yeotmal | 33.7 |
| 3 | Pawara | Dhule, Jalgaon | 25.18 |
| 4 | Madia, Gond | Gadchiroli, Yeotmal | 20.8 |
| 5 | Bhil | Nandurbar | 20.6 |
| 6 | Halbi | Gadchiroli | 13.93 |
| 7 | Malhar Koli | Thane | 13.88 |
| 8 | Rajgond | Gadchiroli | 10.88 |
| 9 | Korku | Amravati | 9.49 |
| 10 | Tandvi | Jalgaon | 8.33 |
| 11 | Kolam | Yeotmal | 8.33 |
| 12 | Warli | Thane | 8.04 |
| 13 | Katkari | Pune, Raigad, Ratnagiri | 5.90 |
| 14 | Kokana | Dhule, Nasik | 3.50 |
| 15 | Andha | Nanded | 1.97 |
| 16 | Mahadeo Koli | Pune, Nasik | 0.81 |
| 17 | Thakur | Pune, Thane, Raigad, Ahmednagar | 0.00 |

*Source:* Kate, S.L., 2000.

One may find that the tribals in Maharashtra or elsewhere are the most vulnerable groups among whom the nutritional deficiency occurs more frequently and to a more severe degree, which requires special attention to look into their problem. In Maharashtra, mostly in the tribal areas, serious problem of malnutrition exists due to which many tribal children die. This is primarily due to poverty and low access to nutritious food as unemployment is a common phenomena.

According to a study (Tagade, 2012), malnutrition is found to be very high among tribals due to food insecurity. The share of chronic undernutrition (stunting) in this region constitute more than 54 per cent, while acute undernutrition (wasting) is more than 44 per cent, indicating that 50 per cent of the children are undernourished in some way or the other. The underlying cause for a substantially higher level of chronic undernutrition compared to acute state of under nutrition in the study region is attributed to insufficient food intake followed by the inadequate health care facilities (Tagade, 2012). The study also found that the malnourishment is higher among tribal compared to non-tribals in the study region.

## Displacement and Rehabilitation Issues of Scheduled Tribes in Maharashtra

Due to construction of Sardar Sarovar Dam on Narmada river people, mostly the tribals of three states, i.e. Gujarat, Madhya Pradesh and Maharashtra, were affected. In all, it is estimated that 33,000 families in central Madhya Pradesh and 3,100 and 4,600 families, respectively, in the western states of Maharashtra and Gujarat were affected.

Of these, 245 villages are in Madhya Pradesh, 33 in Maharashtra and 19 in Gujarat. In terms of percentage 80 per cent, 12 per cent and 8 per cent of the families are from Madhya Pradesh, Maharashtra and Gujarat respectively.[7] The detail status of displacement of tribes is explained in Table 11.

**Table 11**

*Displacement by Narmada River: In Maharashtra*[8]

| | |
|---|---|
| Submergence affected<br>Compensatory afforestation/ | 3,300+ PAFs in 33 villages (balance as on today approximately 2,000)<br>There is no estimate for the number of families affected by these environmental protective measures. It is being carried out in at least 49 tribal villages in Akrani Tehsil and tens of villages in Akkalkua Tehsil of Nandurbar district over Tribal lands. (approximately 3,000–5,000 tribal families) |
| Secondary displacement due to loss of lands to resettlement sites rights of the original tribal who have been | This is a serious issue here. The PAFs are being relocated in tribal lands where the |
| This death R&R | living there have not been recognized. has led to serious conflict and even the of two original inhabitants at one of the sites. |

Due to construction of Sardar Sarovar Project, nine villages from Akkalkuwa and 24 villages from Akrani taluka, a total of 33 villages of Nandurbar District of Maharashtra are being affected. Total land coming under submergence is 933 ha. of which 1,519 ha. is cultivable, private land is 6,288 ha. and forest land is 1,592 ha. Government land comprising rivers and *nallas*. Total no of affected families are 4,227 out of which 1,472 are landowners, 748 are landless and 955 are major sons/daughters. Modi (2004), in her paper, reported a lot of negative impact of the displacement like exclusion of project affected people due to faulty definition, poor quality of land allotted, conflict as same patch of land distributed to more than one family, etc. There are still many project affected families who are yet be rehabilitated in the state of Maharashtra. The balance number of PAFs in Maharashtra would be around 1,700 to 2,000 and at least 5,000 hectares of irrigable agricultural land will be required.

## Left Wing Extremism

There are six districts of Maharashtra affected by Left wing extremist activities. These districts are Gadchiroli, Gondia, Nanded, Yavatmal, Chandrapur, and Bhandara. Due to this movement, a lot of causality has happened. The LWE area of Maharashtra is shown in Figure 3.

A recent report by the Ministry of Home Affairs says that, there are 436 deaths in all, i.e. civilians, security personnel and

**Figure 3**

*Leftwing Districts of Maharashtra*

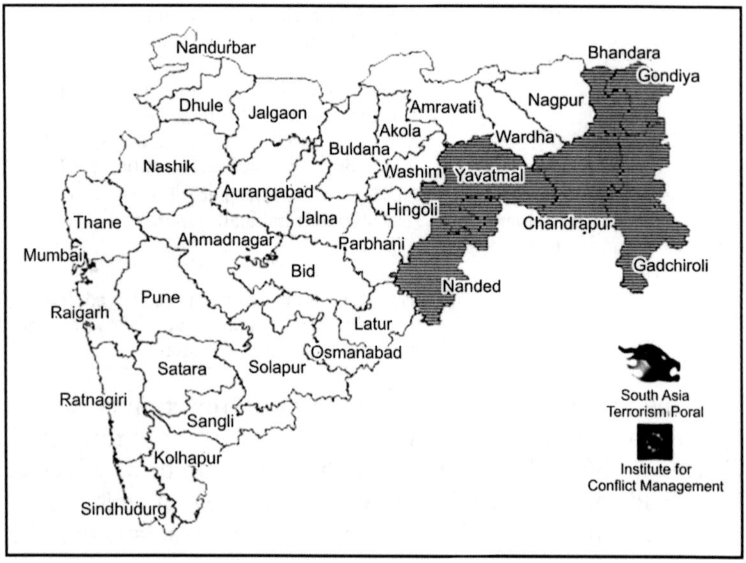

the ultras due to this. Year-wise casualty due to Left wing activities in the state is given in Table 12.

This is quite alarming in the state and hence needs to be tackle sensibly. Gadchiroli has become the Red bastion in Maharashtra, whereas Chandrapur, Gondiya, Yavatmal, Bhandara and Nanded districts are declared 'Naxal prone areas'. All these districts are situated adjoining to the Naxal-infested regions of Andhra Pradesh, Chhattisgarh, and Madhya Pradesh. Gadchiroli is one of the least developed districts in Maharashtra where the poorest of the poor live amidst extreme violence and abject poverty. Apart from this favourable geographical setting, the economic backwardness and undulating terrain of these districts are fertile grounds for Left extremism.[9]

**Table 12**

*Casualty Related to LWE Activities in Maharashtra*

| *Year* | *Civilians* | *SFs* | *Terrorists* | *Total* |
|---|---|---|---|---|
| 2005 | 2 | 17 | 8 | 27 |
| 2006 | 13 | 3 | 33 | 49 |
| 2007 | 9 | 2 | 8 | 19 |
| 2008 | 2 | 5 | 7 | 14 |
| 2009 | 12 | 52 | 23 | 87 |
| 2010 | 22 | 15 | 3 | 40 |
| 2011 | 34 | 10 | 25 | 69 |
| 2012 | 21 | 14 | 5 | 40 |
| 2013 | 10 | 7 | 28 | 45 |
| 2014 | 9 | 11 | 10 | 30 |
| 2015 | 10 | 4 | 2 | 16 |
| Total* | 144 | 140 | 152 | 436 |

*Data till 8 November, 2015.

*Source:* http://www.satp.org/satporgtp/countries/india/maoist/data_sheets anl_cas_mha.asp

## Tribal Welfare and Development Programmes

In order to improve socio-economic and health life of tribal across the country, the Ministry of Tribal Affairs supports the state government. The most important effort being the tribal sub-plan programmes. The Government of Maharashtra also implements several programme with reference to livelihood, health and educational improvement programmes. The outlay earmarked for TSP under the twelfth five year plan is 24,475 crore, which is 8.9

per cent of the State's total outlay. Some of the important schemes of the government are:

- Navsanjivani Yojana (NSY) is being implemented to reduce MMR and IMR in tribal areas of 15 districts of the State covering 8,419 villages. Under NSY various schemes are being implemented to reduce MMR and IMR like Matrutva Anudan Yojana (MAY), Dai meetings, pre monsoon activities, provision of food and loss of wages, etc.[10]
- Matrutva Anudan Yojana: (MAY) is being implemented under NSY to provide health services like ANC registration, regular health check-up and required medicines to pregnant women in tribal areas.
- *Shabari Aadiwasi Vitta Va Vikas Mahamandal Maryadit* (SAVVM) is established by the Government of Maharashtra for economic welfare of the tribal community. At present, authorized share capital of this corporation is 200 crore and paid up capital is 71.36 crore, of which 51 per cent share is of the Government of Maharashtra and 49 per cent is of the Government of India. The corporation implements various schemes of National Scheduled Tribes Finance and Development Corporation (NSTFDC). Some of other schemes for welfare of Schedule Tribes in Maharashtra in brief are:
    - Special Action Plan for inaccessible tribal area
    - Adivasi Utthan Scheme: Comprehensive Rural Health Project
    - Thakkar Bappa Scheme
    - Nav Sanjivan Yojana
    - Mahila Sabalikaran Yojana: Women Self Help Group
    - Kanyadan Scheme
    - Assistance to Ashram Schools
    - Ekalavya English Medium Schools
    - Motor Driving Training for the Scheduled Tribes

There are many other programmes implemented by the Tribal Development Department, Government of Maharashtra from time to time for welfare and development of Scheduled Tribes in the state.

## Conclusion

Despite all efforts to bring tribals into the mainstream society by the Central and the state government, it has made little impact.

Despite being a developed state, the conditions of Scheduled Tribes especially that of the PVTG is not different from Scheduled Tribes of the poorer states. Tribals lag far behind the non-tribals in all the parameters of Human Development. The government has to emphasize on removal of poverty of Scheduled Tribes and set a deadline for that. Removal of poverty only will enable the tribals to improve other parameters of Human Development like health, education, and gender, etc.

## Notes

1. http://164.100.47.134/lsscommittee/Social%20Justice%20&%20Empowerment/15_Social_Justice_And_Empowerment_44.pdf
2. http://mainstreamweekly.net/article4598.html
3. http://nandurbar.nic.in/html_docs/sardarsarover/rehabilation.htm
4. http://shodhganga.inflibnet.ac.in/bitstream/10603/25487/15/15_chapter_07.pdf- by K.C. Ramotra – 2014
5. http://www.adiyuva.in/2010/07/tribal-areas-and-population-in.html
6. http://www.firstfoundation.in/Soc/List_ST.htm
7. http://www.idsa.in/system/files/BG_MaoistMovement.pdf
8. http://www.satp.org/satporgtp/countries/india/maoist/data_sheets/anl_cas_mha.asp
9. https://en.wikipedia.org/wiki/Maharashtra
10. Kujur Rajat http://www.ipcs.org/article/naxalite-violence/naxal-warning-in-maharashtra-1925.html.

## Selected Readings

Modi, Renu. 'Coping with Displacement', *Economic and Political Weekly,* 13 March, 2004.

Pawar, S.K. 'Socio-economic Status of Tribal Population in Maharashtra: A Geographical Analysis', Unpublished Ph.D. Thesis, Department of Geography, Shivaji University, Kolhapur, 2012.

Tagade, N. Food Insecurity in Tribal Regions of Maharashtra: Explaining Differentials between the Tribal and Non-Tribal Communities, Working Paper, Institute for Social and Economic Change, Bangalore, 2012.

# 7

# Tribes, Land and Forests

## Emerging Legal Implications with Reference to PESA and FRA

**Satyakam Joshi**

The objective of this paper is to highlight a series of policy developments that influenced forest governance during pre- and post-colonial India. There is no denying that colonial forest administration was revenue-centric and exploitative, and thus recognized no rights and concessions for forest dwellers, especially tribals. To address the common domain, this paper also briefly traces the history of forest laws and policies in India (colonial and post-colonial) and their impacts on tribal people, with particular focus on the two recent landmark legislations, the Panchayat Extension to Scheduled Area Act (1996) and the Forest Rights Act (2006), promulgated to recognize rights over forests and forest lands.

Forest is an integral part for tribals. They were used to cultivating land collectively for their subsistence. Many engaged in shifting cultivation and did not cultivate a given area for a long period. There is historical evidence of non-tribal landed gentry continuously pushing tribals into the interior regions of forest and hills. Many tribal owners, thus, became unrecorded tenants and/or labourers in the less fertile highlands or bonded or semi-bonded labourers in the fertile lowlands or forest areas. The British were primarily interested in timber and other incomes from forests and, therefore, framed laws to evict the local inhabitants. Land settlements were introduced and the state granted alienable title to land to individual males on the payment of cash. The relationship with land was now mediated by the state and the community ceased to exist in the eyes of the courts. Until 1887, the main aim of the rulers was conquest with a strong military thrust into the forest depths and hill tops. 'Good governance' also led to the administration opening up tribal areas to contractors, civil and military officers, traders, alcohol vendors, timber contractors and merchants. In 1927, the government passed the Indian Forest Act, under which it could constitute any forest or waste land which was the property of government into a reserved area, by issuing a notification. However, since the settlement of rights had not been carried out, large areas remained unsurveyed. Unaware of administrative complexities, most tribal cultivators remained without official land titles. Forest areas were defined as reserved, protected and unclassified. Under the first, no one was allowed to use any forest product without permission from the Forest Department. In Gujarat, 7 per cent of the land area is forested. Of this, 71.26 per cent falls within the reserved forest area. *Adivasis* as well as non-tribals, who were traditional cultivators without formal titles, began to be treated as encroachers.

The Wildlife Protection Act, 1972, provided for creation of protected areas and wildlife habitats whereby *adivasis* lost access to lands and livelihoods based on forests. Again, the settlements of rights were not carried out completely. Hence, all *adivasis* became 'encroachers' when they cultivated lands they had tilled for generations. The Forest Conservation Act acknowledged 'the traditional right of the tribal people on forest land', but no effort was made to protect these rights. The Forest Department continued to treat *adivasis* as encroachers and destroyed their crops. Moreover, the department began plantations on tribal land as a strategy to evict them.

## Pre-Independence Forest History in India

The state and local communities have competed fiercely over Indian forests. Colonial forest policy changed the relationship between forest dwelling communities and forests, changing the way forests were perceived and owned. The colonial state established property rights over forests in the 1860s, prior to which usufruct was unrestricted. Today, forests continue to be state property and control over them rests with the Forest Department (FD). Ramachandra Guha (1983) has argued that before 1947, our forests served the strategic interests of British imperialism. After Independence, they served the needs of the mercantile and industrial bourgeoisie. Colonial forest policies in India had begun to take concrete shape around the middle of the 19th century, when in keeping with the bourgeois outlook towards forests, the British turned towards maximizing the revenue. Down to the middle of the 19th century, traditional dues and cesses, which accrued to the colonial rulers, were the main source of forest revenues to the British.

In 1850, a commission mandated by the colonial administration prepared a report that concluded that Indian forests were being destroyed because of mismanagement by the local people (Agrawal, 1985). Consequently, a full-fledged forest department was created in 1864. From then onwards, the assertion of state monopoly and the exclusion of forest communities marked the organizing principles of forest administration. Towards this end, the first Forest Act was passed in 1865. As commercial considerations and revenue generation became overriding, this was found inadequate and replaced by a much more repressive Act in 1878. In fact, all provisions of the 1865 Act were found to be defective, except Section 8, which according to Baden-Powell, chief architect of the 1878 Act, 'gives the one satisfactory power in the Act, and must be maintained in the new law; arrest without warrant is absolutely essential' (Guha, 1983: 1941). The 1878 Act was a comprehensive document. Compared to the previous legislation the new Act was entirely different in form and content. While the 1865 Act had only 19 Sections, the 1878 Act had 83 Sections, divided into 14 Chapters and a Preamble. For the 1878 Act, establishment of absolute state property rights and so a firm settlement between the state and its subjects over their respective rights in the forests represented the chief concern. As Brandis puts it, 'Act VII of 1865 is incomplete in many respects – the most important omission being the absence of all provisions regarding the definition, regulation, commutation and extinction of customary rights ... (by the state) ...' (Guha, 1983: 1944).

Thus, the establishment of state property and the separation of customary rights became primary objectives of the 1878 Act. Towards this end, the classification of forests into reserved forests, protected forests and village forests – and the procedure for forest settlement in these, were the twin features. The demarcation, an inherent feature of the definition of forests, is based purely on administrative grounds. However, commerce was the guiding principle. In reserved forests (Chapter II), lands were the absolute property of the government. In protected forests (Chapter IV), although lands were the property of the government, the use-rights of the villagers remained. In village forests (Chapter III), the government held only the rights of management. Village forests consisted of residual wastelands with negligible Forest Department control. The reserved/protected classification was guided by the goal of profit from timber. In village forests, profit was absent. To begin with only areas needed for national requirements and for export to England were designated as reserved. However, it was not possible to assess these needs immediately. With time, the area under reserved forests increased. Protected forests were designated with the goal of converting them into reserved forests. Such conversion took place as the demand for forest resources increased. There were 14,000 square miles of state forests in 1878. This increased to 56,000 square miles of reserved forests and 20,000 square miles, of protected forests in 1890 and to 81,400 and 8,300 square miles respectively in 1900 (Gadgil and Guha, 1992: 134). The several amendments to the 1878 Act and the ambiguous language used necessitated a single piece of legislation that would do away with ambivalence. This led to the promulgation of the 1927 Act. In fact, the differences between the Acts of 1927 and 1878 (read along with the various amendments) are minor.

The 1927 Act continues to be the basis of Indian forest legislation. The Indian Forest Act of 1927 is timber oriented. Its title says, 'An Act to consolidate the law relating to forests, the transit of forest produce and the duty leviable on timber and other forest produce'. There is no mention of conservation. According to the Act, no person can claim a right to private property in forested land merely because he is domiciled there, or his forefathers lived there for centuries. Nor do such people have any rights over forest produce. The purpose behind the Forest Act is clearly to lay down the procedure by which the government can acquire property and generate revenue from it. Two fundamental issues can be identified. The first pertains to the method by which government acquires land, the nature of its control over it, and the way it may negotiate its proprietary rights with existing rights holders and claimants. The second pertains to the control of timber and other forest produce in transit, the duty leviable on them and the collection of drift and stranded timber.

## Forest Policy After Independence

The Government of India announced its Forest Policy in 1952. Prior to this, one of the prime concerns of the Forest Department had been to increase revenue generation from forests. The Forest Policy added the objective of increasing forest cover. It envisaged a tree cover of 33 per cent of the total geographical area, regardless of the composition of the forests, and regardless of the opinions of, and impact upon forest-dependent communities. Consequently, eucalyptus was planted in various places throughout the country (Vira, 1995). On the other hand, forests were recognized as useful for the needs of the mercantile and industrial bourgeoisie – increased forest cover meant increased availability of forest products, especially timber. Government short-sightedness after Independence was also evident in the failure to amend the Act of 1878. The 1894 policy had spoken of the rights of rural communities over forest produce. Gradually this came to mean 'rights and privileges', which were given legal status in the Indian Forest Act of 1927. The sovereign government of India could have undone the damage, instead of which its 1952 policy adopted the phrase 'rights and concessions'. Forests were not perceived as a whole, and the focus was on timber, which is but a component of a complex whole. The colonial government had turned land without individual titles into state property, and forest dwellers into 'encroachers'. After Independence, the process intensified. As a result, tree cover declined from 70 million ha in 1950 to 35 million ha in 1990.

In 1961, at the start of Third Five Year Plan, it had been recognized that there was a large and growing gap between the demand and supply of forest produce. The plan estimated that by 1975, the shortfall of fuel wood would be 100 million tonnes. Despite this, nearly 75 per cent of the Third Plan outlay on afforestation was targeted towards production forestry. During the 1960s, a massive programme was initiated to clear existing forests, which were to be replaced by monoculture plantation of fast growing commercially useful species, predominantly eucalyptus and tropical pine. This process continued till the end of the Fifth Plan, with an emphasis on self-sufficiency in commercial products, especially pulp, newsprint, wood panel products and matches. Through this period, forests generated high revenues for the state. The Forest Department's surplus increased from ₹ 133.9 million annually, averaged over 1951–52 to ₹ 1,547.2 million in 1980–81.

Afforestation was an important component of state-initiated forestry programmes, and comprised 50.06 per cent of total public sector outlay in forests between 1951 and 1980. The Fourth Five Year Plan stressed the need to achieve self-sufficiency in forest products, especially those required by forest-based industries and proposed greater efforts at creating large scale plantations of quick-growing species and species of economic and industrial importance. By the start of the Fifth Five Year Plan in 1974–75, of the total outlay on afforestation, 80.40 per cent had been spent on production forestry, which accounted for 65.14 per cent of the physical area covered. The need to accelerate these efforts was emphasized by the National Commission on Agriculture in 1976, which suggested the use of forest lands for production forestry to meet industrial needs. The report suggested the establishment of State Forest Development Corporations in order to attract institutional funding for industrial forestry. To lighten the burden on production forestry, the report recommended a programme of social forestry in non-forest areas, private farms and community lands to meet the subsistence needs of rural populations.

This programme had two components: farm forestry, targeted at private landholders; and community forestry, linked to various categories of public and community land, excluding forest land. The Forest Development Corporation was established in different provinces to promote production forestry. All these corporations depended upon industrial finance as well as re-investment of profits. The space opened up by felling was used for the monoculture of quick growing species. Natural forests were on their way to being replaced by man-made plantations. But the policy was doomed from the start, because conservation or exploitation of forests requires the scientific understanding of delicately balanced forest ecology. The results have, indeed, been catastrophical. Thus, there has been continuous process of decreasing forest which forced government to enact the law in 1980 which had direct impact on forest dwelling communities i.e. *adivasis* of India.

## The Forest Conservation Act 1980 and its Impact on Forest Dwellers

The Forest Conservation Act of 1980 (FCA) was a crisis-driven response. It was introduced by Prime Minister Indira Gandhi in the 1970s, when remote sensing data showed a remarkable decline in forest cover (about one million hectares a year over the decade). The Act was promulgated to stop the use of forestlands for roads, dams and buildings. The Central Government now had sole authority for granting such permissions. The result was that state governments neglected small but important activities and requirements of villagers to build schools, electric poles or bridges. As a result, Uttarakhand, the very area which gave birth to the Chipko Movement saw a Jangal Kato (forest felling) Andolan in the 1980s against the Act. The FCA was a two-page document that strengthened the 1927 Act, empowering the Minister to make decisions about forest lands. It is a law on land use and its implementation depends upon the whims of the minister. Further, it only forbids 'reserve forests' from being denotified by the states. The Act's mandate even extends to lands for which only notifications under Section 4 of the Indian Forest Act (IFA) have so far been issued Section 4(1)(c) of the IFA of 1927. This declares the state's intention to reserve an area as a forest, and requires appointment of the forest settlement officer (FSO) to settle claims of pre-existing occupants and users. This safety clause has often been dispensed with. An area is formally notified as a forest only after the formalities associated with Section 20 and 29 are completed. Areas recorded as 'forests' in any government record also comes under the Act's purview. As neither the IFA nor the FCA defined a 'forest', on 12–12–1996 the Supreme Court ruled (Godavarman case) that the Act's provisions would apply to any area conforming to the dictionary definition, irrespective of ownership. This also includes all lands entered in any government record as 'forest', whether or not that land has any tree cover and whether or not preliminary notifications were issued. It also applies to all community-managed forests on revenue lands – forests which have been maintained and nurtured precisely because villagers did not follow the Forest Department's 'scientific forestry' prescriptions, which would have involved clear felling and mono-cultural plantations for sustained yield of timber.

Given the disarray in government land records, and the diverse categories of land in different contexts for which the term 'forest' has used in them, a very wide range of common lands critical for local livelihoods could now be brought under the 'scientific' management of the forest department's 'working plans'. There is no requirement to verify the current status of these lands, whether any forest on them ever existed in the past or still exist, the rights people enjoy in them or the function these lands play in people's livelihoods. The court does not seem to have noticed that many of these lands are riddled with disputes, including pending claims for land rights by their indigenous inhabitants.

Due to non-recognition of their rights, tribal people (as per FCA, 1980) who were rooted in forests for ages came to be looked upon as encroachers. The threat of eviction looms large in their psyche. This historical injustice and insecurity is the reason why tribal communities feel emotionally and physically alienated from government. Tribals, NGOs and radical activists have protested against the Act. They have argued that the FCA's aim was to deny customary rights over natural resources, and to exploit resources under state forestry, which resulted in the degradation of forests. There were series of protests all over the country against this Act by tribals and NGOs activists, and the government was compelled to address their demands. The National Forest Policy, 1988, stresses that forests are first charge to tribal communities. Their livelihood needs are paramount and superior to commercial needs. While recognizing the symbiotic relationship between tribal people and forests, the policy also safeguards the customary rights and interests of tribal people and dwellers on forest lands. This policy provided for the association of tribal people with the protection, regeneration and development of forests with a view to providing gainful employment to people living in and around forests, with special attention to:

1. Replacement of contractors by tribal cooperatives.
2. Protection, regeneration and optimum collection of minor forest produce along with institutional arrangements for marketing.
3. Development of forest villages on par with revenue villages, family-oriented schemes for improving the status of tribal beneficiaries.
4. Undertaking integrated area-development programmes to support the tribal economy.

The requirements of forest-dependent communities now acquired a priority. In order to fulfil the commitments enshrined in the 1988 policy, the Central Ministry of Environment and Forest (MoEF) issued six circulars on 18.9.1990 for the settlement of disputed claims. As per these circulars, pre-1980 encroachments on forest lands were eligible for regularization provided the state governments had evolved eligibility criteria in accordance with local needs and conditions and had decided to regularize such encroachments. These circulars provided for:

1. Appointment of joint teams of Revenue, Forest and Tribal Welfare Departments.
2. Involvement of Gram Sabhas.
3. Banning agriculture practices on certain slopes; claims established through proper inquiry.
4. Demarcation of land to be restored to the claimant-no ceiling on size of holding.
5. Proposal for de-notification of forest lands along with the proposal for compensatory afforestation.
6. Elimination of intermediaries and replacement of contractors by tribal cooperatives, etc.
7. Protection of tribals and non-engagement of outside labour in forestry activities.
8. Conversion of forest villages in remote and inaccessible forest areas into revenue villages with a view to providing uninterrupted manpower for forestry operations.
9. An acceptance that it would not be appropriate to deny inhabitants of forest villages legitimate rights over lands allotted to them decades ago for settlement and have been continuously their occupation since then.
10. Restricting admissible evidences mainly to first Offence Report and thus in practical terms denying recognition.

However, the MoEF could not implement its decision wholly or partly due to enactment of the FCA 1980. The 1988 amendment to the FCA 1980 places all forestland under the jurisdiction of the Forest Department. Thus, while on the one hand, the Indian government has adopted a policy sympathetic to the needs of the forest dwellers, on the other it has enacted laws that restrict access of these people to the forest. Putting this situation in perspective the environmentalist Singh noted, 'In the case of the government of India, the left hand does not know what the right hand is doing. As regards forest development, the right hand is undoing what the left hand is trying to do.'

## Evolution and Implications Pro-Tribal Forest Legislations in India

Since the primary intention of colonial laws was to take over lands and deny the rights of communities, the 'settlement' process initiated during the late 19th and early 20th centuries was hardly effective. Surveys were often incomplete or not done (82.9% of Madhya Pradesh's forest blocks have not been surveyed to date, while in Orissa more than 40% of state forests are 'deemed' reserved forests where no settlement of rights took place). Where the claims process did occur, the rights of socially weaker communities – particularly tribals – were rarely recorded. The problem became worse particularly after Independence, when the lands declared 'forests' by the Princely states, the *zamindars*, and the private owners were transferred to the Forest Department through blanket notifications. In short, what the government records called 'forests' often included large areas of land that were not and never were forest at all. Moreover, those areas that were in fact forest included the traditional homelands of communities. As such consolidation of government forests did not settle existing claims on land; all people, mostly tribals, who lived in these forests, were subsequently declared 'encroachers,' as they did not have recognized rights and claims to their ancestral homelands.

## Panchayats Extension to Schedule Areas Act, 1996

During the 1990s, the eminent domain of the government was challenged by activists and human rights movements. Rights of the tribals over local resources were considered sacrosanct and non-negotiable and a move was initiated to secure constitutional recognition for these rights. The sustained campaign led first to the 73rd Amendment of the Constitution to give recognition to decentralized governance in rural areas and then the Constitution of the Bhuria Committee to look at tribal rights over resources through extension of the provisions of this Amendment to the Schedule V areas. Based on the recommendations of the committee, the Parliament passed a separate legislation in 1996 as an annexure to the 73rd Amendment specifying special provisions for *panchayats*[5] in Schedule V areas. Known as the Panchayats Extension to Schedule Areas[6] (PESA), 1996, it decentralized existing approaches to forest governance by bringing the Gram Sabha centre stage and recognized the traditional rights of tribals over community resources meaning land, water, and forests. PESA was important not just because it provided for a wide range of rights and privileges, but also because it provided a principle as well as a basis for future law making concerning the tribals. According to the Central government law, the states promulgated their own laws supposedly giving rights to tribals over local resources. It is almost two decades since PESA came into effect, but the obstacles in enforcing its provisions have remained largely unaddressed. Its avowed objective of power to the people has yet to take shape. The states are struggling to devise definitive procedures to define rights over forests and minor forest produce. Meanwhile, some states like Maharashtra, Gujarat, and Orissa, in an effort to perpetuate State control over forest resources, tried to dilute the provisions of PESA although they had no legal jurisdiction to do so.

There are four points that need particular emphasis here. First, there are critical omissions of some of the fundamental principles without which the spirit of PESA can never be realized. Secondly, the state legislations, perhaps by design, twist certain words from the Central PESA that has resulted in powers being taken away from the Gram Sabha – the collectivity of all village adults where the need for empowerment is most critical for making local self-governance a reality in the country especially in relation to managing common pool resources. Thirdly, even where it affirmed some provisions of the law in principle, their applicability was made subject to framing of rules/orders or 'as may be prescribed'. As stated earlier, such enabling rules are not yet in place in most cases. Finally, few rules and prescriptions began to surface in early 2000 primarily through revocable official circulars but which again have been totally inoperative because of the ambiguity and lack of clarity of these provisions. Thus, it is not surprising that even these are waiting to be taken to the ground. The operative provisions being not in place, a promising radical law has been reduced largely to a paper law.

## People's Movements Against Repressive Forest Laws and Enactment of FRA-2006

The policy relating to forest underwent a sea change in 1988. The role of the village communities in the preservation and management of the forests came to be recognized. This historical turnaround gave birth to the policy of Joint Forest Management (JFM). The JFM implies the handing over certain rights to village communities to appropriate natural resources for their own use. However, the lack of a clear definition of the rights holders and the kinds of rights and sanctions that can be applied has impeded the process of establishing social institutions. The policy failed to understand social and economic features at local level and user's responses to changes. One reason for the failure of the JFM is its top-down approach, and lack of people's participation in planning. On the other hand, there has been an effort to regularize forest lands that tribals had long been cultivating. But every one of these efforts stayed within the existing structure. Some regularization orders even required proof that the claimant had earlier been booked for 'encroachment'. As per MoEF figure in response to starred question no. 284 in Lok Sabha, 16.8.2004, the total area under pre-1980 eligible encroachment regularized so far is 3.66 lakh hectare against the 13.43 hectare of forest land is under encroachment in the country.

The consequences of this failure became apparent on 3 May 2002, when the Inspector General of Forests (IGF) wrote to the Chief Secretaries of all state governments informing them that in response to the problem of encroachment raised in the *Godaverman Thirumulpad vs. Union of India* case (Interlocutory Application No. 703, Writ Petition No. 202/95), the Supreme Court had (23 November 2001) restrained the Central Government from regularizing encroachments without its permission. The letter directed state authorities to prepare a time-bound programme for summary eviction of all encroachments not eligible for regularization as per the Ministry's 1990 guidelines by 30 September. In the month following this letter, forced evictions of *adivasis* occurred across the country at a scale unprecedented in recent history. As many as 40,000 families were evicted in Assam and the countrywide total was estimated at 3 lakh families. *Adivasis* were evicted from about 1.52 lakh hectares of forest area. These mass evictions triggered the first real steps forward. In Maharashtra, after a demonstration by more than one lakh tribals in Mumbai on 10 October 2002, the government announced new regulations that recognized tribal rights over forest lands. But this was not replicated elsewhere in the country. People's movements and organizations now began organizing to resist evictions. Some organizations filed interventions before the Supreme Court, while others filed applications before the Central Empowered Committee. But most importantly, concerted resistance via protest demonstrations, Jail Bharo Andolans, and written counter replies to the forest department's eviction notices amplified people's views on this issue. 'There are no *adivasis* without forests and no forest without *adivasis*, we are one. We will not give up our rights. Try and evict us!'

The gross violation of democratic rights of *adivasis* and other forest communities by the forest department continues to be a matter of grave concern. It is in this context that the Campaign for Survival and Dignity (CSD) organized a Public Hearing in Delhi on 19–20 July 2003. The CSD, a federation of tribal and forest community organizations from 10 states, merged to resist evictions. Subsequently, the NDA government issued two circulars (stayed by the Supreme Court). The UPA government's Common Minimum Programme called for a halt to evictions. Forest issues had acquired national status responding to the Supreme Court stay, in July 2004, the MoEF filed an affidavit in which it admitted that forest communities had suffered a 'historical injustice' and that the 'rural poor, especially tribals, had been deprived of their livelihood rights'. The Ministry did nothing to follow up on this admission, but in January, following pressure from the CSD, other indigenous groups demand and UPA government commitment to implement its common minimum programmes, the Prime Minister directed the Ministry of Tribal Affairs to draft a law on forest rights. The choice of the Ministry was another popular victory – the government accepted that forest authorities would not and could not draft a just law.

## Forest Rights Act, 2006

The Scheduled Tribes and Other Traditional Forest Dwellers (Recognition of Forest Rights) Act 2006, popularly known as the Forest Rights Act (FRA), is a watershed in the hard-fought and prolonged struggle of *adivasis* and other forest dwellers of India. The new law attempts to right that historic injustice and gives forest communities a primary role in forest management. The statement of object and reason (SOR) of the FRA, attributed the delay in recognizing forest rights to colonial rule which had ignored this reality for economic gain. The SOR admitted that after Independence, in its enthusiasm to protect natural resources, the state had persisted with colonial practices. The simplicity of tribal people and their general ignorance of modern regulatory frameworks precluded them from asserting their genuine claims. The SOR suggested that insecurity of tenure and fear of eviction had engendered a sense of alienation amongst tribal communities. The SOR explained the rationale of the FRA in terms of vesting forest rights and occupation of forest land with forest-dwelling communities who were integral to the survival and sustainability of the forest ecosystem, but whose rights could not be recorded. The FRA's salient features are as follows:

1. The Act recognizes and vests rights and occupation in forest land in forest-dwelling Scheduled Tribes and other traditional forest-dwellers who have resided in such forests for generations but whose rights were not recorded.
2. The Act provides for recognition of forest rights of other traditional forest-dwellers provided they have for at least three generations prior to 13.12.2005 primarily resided in and have depended on the forest or forestlands for bonafide livelihood needs. A generation would mean a period of 25 years.
3. The cut-off date for the recognition and vesting of forest rights under the Act will be 13.12.2005.
4. The Act provides for the ceiling of occupation of forestland for purposes of recognition of forest rights to the area under occupation and in no case exceeding an area of four hectares.
5. The Act provides for conferring rights in national parks and sanctuaries habitat.
6. The Act provides for the right to hold and live in forest land under individual or common occupation for habitation or for self-cultivation for livelihood by a member or members of

forest-dwelling Scheduled Tribes and other traditional forest-dwellers.

7. The Act recognizes the right of ownership access to collect, use and dispose of minor forest produce which was traditionally collected within or outside village boundaries. The Act defines minor forest produce to include all non-timber forest produce of plant origin, including bamboo, brush wood, stumps, cane, *tussar*, cocoons, honey, wax, *lac*, *tendu* or *kendu* leaves, medicinal plants and herbs roots and tubers.
8. The Act recognizes the right to in situ rehabilitation including alternative land in cases where Scheduled Tribes and other traditional forest-dwellers have been illegally evicted or displaced from forest land of any description without granting their legal entitlement to rehabilitation prior to 13.12.2005.
9. The Act provides for forest rights relating to government providing for diversion of forest land for schools, hospitals, anganwadis, drinking water, water pipelines, roads, electric and telecommunications lines.
10. The rights conferred under the Act are heritable but not alienable or transferable and to be registered jointly in the name of both spouses in the case of married persons and a single head in the case of households headed by a single person. In the absence of a direct heir the heritable right shall pass on to the next of kin.
11. The Act provides that no member of a forest-dwelling Scheduled Tribes or other traditional forest-dwellers shall be evicted or removed from forest land under his occupation until the recognition and verification procedure is completed.
12. Gram Sabhas have been designated as competent authorities for initiating the process of determining the nature and extent of individual or community forest rights or both that may be given to forest-dwellers.

## Implementation Status of FRA in Gujarat

After the Act being enacted various steps being taken by the tribal development department in order to implement the Act. This includes, arranging Gram Sabha and forming of Forest Right Committee (FRC) at village level, printing in huge number of application forms for land claiming and managed to distributed at all villages, prepared a booklet on explaining the Act in simple language and distributed at village level. Thus, there was a serious attempt by government to address the key issues for implementing the Act. Further to it, department had conducted training camp on how to fill the forms and what are the evidences that require to attached with the forms. In May 2008 the Department of Tribal Development had organized a workshop with NGOs and activists of Adivasi Maha Sabha at Ahmedabad, who are working in tribal areas for implementing the Act. Various problems related with implementing the Act were discussed in the workshop. As a result many problems were sorted out on the spot. After the workshop the department started a help line for claimants and still it is working effectively. Initial work by the FRC was very effective and they could manage to submit the claimant's forms on time with proper documents of proof to the Gram Sabha. After preparing claimant's application for land with proper evidences were submitted to Gram Sabha, Gram Sabha after proper verification submitted it to block level committee (BLC). It should be noted here that Adivasi Maha Sabha activists have trained the FRC members about how to fill up the forms as well as what type of documents need to be attached with the application. Between June 2008 and January 2009, there have been more than 26 training programmes organized by the Adivasi Maha Sabha covering all 45 tribal talukas of the state. In each training programme, around 200 to 300 FRC members attended the training. Due to this FRCs managed to submit claims in advanced. In the Dediapada taluka of Narmada district, FRC of 25 villages had submitted satellite imaginary photos of the forest lands on which people are cultivating. This is unique and government officials were astonished with these evidences. In short FRCs had played a pivotal role in submitting claims.

As per the latest figure on implementation of FRA in Gujarat, total claims recommended by Gram Sabha to SDLC are 1,86,495 (1,80,414 individual and 6,081 community. Number of claims recommended by SDLC to DLC are 73,057 (69,201 individual and 3,865 community). Number of claims approved by the DLC for title are 73,057 (69,201 individual and 3,856 community). Number of titles distributed are 72,625 (68,769 individual and 3,856 community). Extent of forest land for which the title deeds issued is 10,97,843 (in acres) (98,436 individual and 9,99,407 community). It should be noted here that a member of Gujarat Tribal Advisory Council had raised concern over high rate of rejected claims and the matter was discussed in the meeting held on 1 July 2011 and it was decided to review all rejected claims at various levels. Following the decision of GTAC, the government of Gujarat created a special review cell on 1 August 2011 and circulated procedure to review all the rejected claims. As a result, a number of claims disposed of has been reduced considerably.

With the advent of the British rule the tribals not only started losing their lands but forests also became state property. The creation of 'reserved' and 'protected' forests during the colonial period considerably affected the tribal rights in such forest areas which had provided an important source for their livelihood. This policy was further extended during post-Independence period particularly due to the enactment of fresh legislation like the Forest Conservation Act, 1980 and legislation on wildlife. The latter legislations displaced the tribals from national parks and sanctuaries and the tribals who have been cultivating the land in the forest area for generations have been labelled as encroachers. Only in 1988, the forest policy recognized the rights of tribals over forest land. But recognition never became a reality. Only FRA 2006 provided some hope for doing justice to tribals. The FRA 2006 is a good piece of law but still the motive of the state is not in favour of the tribals. The *adivasis* of Gujarat demanded the abrogation of the principle of eminent domain and restricting the meaning of 'public purpose' after six decades of Independence. But colonial minded bureaucracy and lack of political will on the part of elected representatives is not allowing tribals to get their due share. But still there is hope and law must and will remain part of the struggle for *adivasi* rights.

## Emerging Legal Implications

*Adivasi* rights (in a legal sense) offer a site through which to explore how these contradictory social forces shape the making and working of the law. In the immediate post-Independence period, the law served as an important instrument of the state in recognizing *adivasi* rights. While Nehru's five principles provided a vision of respecting the 'uniqueness' of *adivasi* communities and their customary claims to land, law has been a critical means to act upon this vision. Article 342 of the Constitution, by providing the President the power to notify communities as Scheduled Tribes, implicitly recognizes the fact that Scheduled Tribe communities are the ones who have suffered some of the worst types of deprivation. Under Article 46 of the Directive Principles of State Policy, the state is obliged to ensure the educational and economic interests of the weaker sections, especially those of the Scheduled Castes and Scheduled Tribes. In addition, Article 14 speaks about the right to equality and Article 15 prohibits discrimination due to religion, caste, sex, etc. Article 13 prevents the state from making laws that deny people their fundamental rights. Scheduled tribes are also guaranteed various forms of reservation by Articles 320, 332 and 334 of the Constitution (Bijoy, 1999: 1332; Mohanty, 2001: 3857).

The most significant Article in the Constitution vis-à-vis *adivasi* rights is Article 244. The logic of Article 244, in the spirit of Nehru's five principles, is that for the traditions and culture of Scheduled Tribe communities to be respected scheduled areas should function autonomously. The fifth schedule allows the president to declare areas as scheduled and the governor the power by public notification to not apply Acts of Parliament or modify them in accordance with the needs of Scheduled Tribe communities. Crucially the fifth schedule permits the governor (on the recommendation of the tribal advisory council) to prohibit the transfer of land by or amongst Scheduled Tribes as well as regulate the allotment of land to non-scheduled tribes and the working of money lenders (Bijoy, 2000).

In addition to these constitutional provisions, a number of other acts have been passed in order to uphold *adivasi* rights ranging from land tenancy acts and revenue codes (Bijoy, 1999: 1331) to most recently the 1996 Panchayat (Extension to Scheduled Areas) Act (PESA), that gives *adivasi* communities substantive powers with regard to natural resource management and self-governance. According to PESA, Gram Sabhas are empowered to preserve their cultural identity, community resources, modes of dispute resolution, and equally important the right to approve government plans, programmes and projects within their jurisdiction (Mukul, 1997: 929). Moreover, the Gram Sabhas or the panchayats at the appropriate level have to be consulted before the acquisition of land for development in scheduled areas. The FRA, which aims at providing adivasis rights to forest land already occupied by them and access to forest produce for livelihood purposes, is the latest in a line of legal initiatives to address *adivasi* rights.

But while laws to uphold *adivasi* rights have been enacted, the state's concern for development (pushed by other social forces) has been responsible for denying *adivasis* these very rights.

Pro-*adivasi* judgments must be understood keeping in mind the wider hierarchy of rights that the courts seem to uphold. First, for the most part, *adivasi* rights are upheld when they are deemed to be not in conflict with the 'greater common good' or 'sustainable development'. Second, when *adivasi* rights (in the form of land or forest rights or more broadly livelihood rights) are juxtaposed with development concerns, these rights are often limited or redefined. For example, in the context of large-scale development projects, the courts have tended to privilege development both at the expense of social rights and the environment. Third, there are a number of 'environmental' cases where the protection of 'pristine nature' results in limits placed on rights of use to natural resources such as forests and fisheries. The Doon Valley and Silent Valley cases are notable examples (Upadhyay, 2000: 3790). In such cases, the environment takes precedence over development too. This can be explained by the fact that the environment, imagined in terms of pristine wildlife sanctuaries, unpolluted urban middle class localities, for example, are very much part of the middle class imagination that influences the judiciary either directly or indirectly.

While few would deny the importance of the greater common good or sustainable development, it is the manner in which these concerns become important (or do not become important) that is worrisome. Sustainable development is rarely invoked when large-scale infrastructure projects wreak havoc in the environment, but become important when *adivasis* collect non-timber forest produce. Similarly, while there is no denying that preservation of 'natural' habitats and wildlife is a must, why is it again that this happens in the context of *adivasi* claims to land and not when industry or game poachers stake their claims? Sustainable development requires first of all a much more critical and comprehensive analysis of what it is that makes development unsustainable.

## References


Agrawal, Anil (ed.). *The Sate of India's Environment: A Second Citizen's Report*, Centre for Science and Environment, New Delhi.

Bijoy, C.R. 'Adivasis Betrayed: Adivasi Land Rights In Kerala', *Economic and Political Weekly*, 34 (22), 29 May, 1999, pp. 1329–93.

——. 'Adivasi Rights and Struggles of Autonomy: A Review of the Indian Experience', in K. Krishnan (ed.) *Adivasi Groups in 2000*, mimeo, 2000.

Endangered Symbiosis. Evictions and India's Forest Communities, Report of the Jan Sunwai, (Public Hearing) July, 2003. Campaign for Survival and Dignity, Dahanu, Maharashtra.

Farnandes, Walter (ed.). *Drafting a People's Forest Bill: A Forest Dweller-Social Activist Alternative*, Indian Social Institute, New Delhi, 1996.

Forest (Conservation) Act, 1980 with Amendments Made in 1988. htpp://www.envfor.nic.in/legis/forest/forest2.html.

Forest Rights, Advocacy Internet, Vol. 6, Issue No. 6, November–December, 2006.

Gadgil, M. and Guha, R. *This Fissured Land: An Ecological History of India*, Oxford University Press, New Delhi, 1992.

——. *Ecology and Equity: The Use and Abuse of Nature in Contemporary India*, Penguin Books, New York, 1985.

Guha, Ramachandra. 'Forestry in British and Post-British India: An Historical Analysis', *Economic and Political Weekly*, 29 October and 5 November, 1983, pp. 1882 and 1940.

——. *The Unquiet Woods: Ecological Changes and Peasant Resistance in the Himalaya*, Oxford University Press, New Delhi, 1989.

——, 'An Early Environment Debate: The Making of the 1878 Act', *Indian Economic and Social History Review*, 27, 1, 1990.

Hope and Fear: Notification of Forest Rights Law Stirs Up Tribal Belt, *Frontline*, 29 February 2008.

Kothari, Smitu. 'Challenging Centralize Governance: The Struggle for Self Rule' in Singh, Satyajit and Sharma, Pradeep (eds.) *Decentralization Institution and Politics in Rural India*, Oxford University Press, New Delhi, 2007.

Joshi, Satyakam. 'A Study of Forest Labour Cooperative Societies of South Gujarat' (Unpublished Ph.D. Thesis), South Gujarat University, Surat, 1993.

——. *Development, Deprivation and Discontent: A Case of Dangs Tribals*, in Development and Deprivation in Gujarat edited by Ghanshyam Shah and others, Sage Publication, New Delhi, 2002.

——. 'Forest and Tribals: Issues and Challenges', *Dhol*, Dipawali Special Issue, 2003.

——. 'Tribals, Forest Policy and Forest Rights Act 2006', *Arthat*, Vol. 24, No. 3–4 October–December, 2005.

——. 'Local Governance and Social Change in Gujarat' in Baviskar B.S. and George, Mathew (eds), *Inclusion and Exclusion in Local Governance: Field Studies from Rural India*, Sage Publication, New Delhi, 2009.

Menon, P.S.K. and Sinha, Bakshi. *Panchayati Raj in Schedule Areas*, Concept Publishing Company, Delhi, 2003.

Mohanty, B.B. 'Land Distribution among Scheduled Castes and Tribes', *Economic and Political Weekly*, 36(40), 6 October 2001, pp. 3857–68.

Mukul. 'Tribal Areas: Transition to Self–Governance', *Economic and Political Weekly*, 32(8), 3 May 1997, pp. 928–29.

Munshi, Indra. 'Scheduled Tribes Bill', *Economic and Political Weekly*, Vol. XL No. 41, 8–14 October 2005.

Nambiar, M. 'Making the Gram Sabha Work', *Economic and Political Weekly*, 26(33), 2001.

Parekh, Trupti. 'Tribals in the Midst of Forest', *Khoj*, May–June, Vol. II, No. 1, 2005.

Prasad, Archana. Fine In Spirit, Not In Letter, Scheduled Tribes Bill needs crucial fine-tuning, *Times of India*, October 20, Ahmedabad Edition, 2005.

Rangrajan, Mahesh. 'Fire in the Forest', *Economic and Political Weekly*, Vol. XL No. 47, 9–25 November 2005.

Samata. 'A Study on Process of Acquisition of Land for development of Mining Industry in Schedule-V Areas with a Focus on Violation of PESA in Light of the Mining and the Industrialisation Process in the Scheduled-V Areas, 2003', Draft Report, Hyderabad.

Sarin, Madhu. 'Who Is Gaining? Who Is Losing? Gender and Equity Concerns in Joint Forest Management', Working Paper by the Gender and Equity Sub-group, National Support Group for JFM, Society for Wasteland Development, New Delhi, 1996.

Shah, Ghanshyam and Joshi, Satyakam. et al. *Panchayati Raj in Gujarat*, Surat: Centre for Social Studies, (mimeo), 1997.

Shah, Mihir. 'First You Push Them In, Then You Throw Them Out', *Economic and Political Weekly*, Vol. XL No. 47, 19 November 2005.

Singh, Chattrapati. *Common Property and Common Poverty: India's Forest Dweller and the Law*, Oxford University Press, New Delhi, 1986.

Singh, Bhupinder. 'Democratic Decentralisation in Tribal Area', Rajiv Gandhi Institute for Contemporary Studies, Paper No. 20, Rajiv Gandhi Foundation, New Delhi, 1995.

Singh, Gurdip. *Environment Law*, Lawman (India) Private Limited, New Delhi, pp. 185, 1995.

Singh, Karter and Vishwa Ballabh (ed.). *Cooperative Management of Natural Resources*, Sage Publication, New Delhi, 1996.

The Scheduled Tribes and Other Traditional Forest Dwellers (Recognition of Forest Rights) Bill, 2006.

Tribals and Forest. Let's Understand Them: Adivasi Mahasabha Gujarat, December, 2003.

Upadhyay Sanjay. 'Tribal Self-Rule Law and Common Property Resources in Scheduled Areas of India – A new Paradigm Shift or Another Ineffective Step?' Paper Presented at the Tenth Biennial Conference of International Association for the Study of Common Property (IASCP) 'The Commons in an Age of Global Transition Challenges, Risks and Opportunities' Hosted by the Instituto de InvestigacionersSociales, Universidad Nacional Autonoma De Maxico Oaxaca, Mexico, 9–13 August 2004.

Upadhyay, Videh. 'Forest People and Courts; Utilising Legal Spaces', *Economic and Political Weekly*, 35 (43 and 44), 16 June 2000, pp. 3789–92.

Upadhyay, Videh. 'Changing Judicial Power: Courts on Infrastructure Projects and Environment', *Economic and Political Weekly*, 36(24) 28 October 2001, pp. 2131–34.

Vira, Bhaskar. Institutional Changes in India's Forest Sector, 1976–1994 – Relations on State Policy, Oxford Centre for the Environment, Ethic and Society (OCEES) Research Papers, Oxford, UK, November, 1995.

Xaxa, Virginius. 'Tribes in India', in Veena Das (ed.), *The Oxford India Companion to Society and Social Anthropology*, Oxford University Press, Delhi, 2003.

# 8

# Land and Tribals of Gujarat

**Vidyut Joshi**

Writing on land reforms in India, P.C. Joshi of the Institute of Economic Growth, Delhi rightly observes: 'There was in India hardly any important problem the economic aspect of which could be understood in isolation from say, the social, the cultural, the psychological, the technological, the political or the geographical aspect.' Keeping this general point of view in mind, an attempt is made here to identify variations and patterns of tribal land systems in post-Independence period have more of socio-economic and cultural significance than merely legal, judicial or rational. We have also thought it appropriate to shift the focus from the analysis of the land systems as such to an analysis of overall change in this specific field in tribal areas in the context of development and change in this specific field in tribal areas in the context of development and change in the knowledge, production technology and social relationships among the tribals and non-tribals.

In brief, we have tried to study the crucial role of land in moulding values, attitudes and behaviour of the tribals and non-tribals in context of realignment of forces in relation to broad social stratification and power structure both among the backward and the progressive tribal communities.

The history of tribal land in general is quite complex. By the end of the 19th century, steps were taken for survey and settlement of land revenue, under Section 73 of Land Revenue Code, in the tribal areas directly governed by the British. Wherever scarcity conditions prevailed due to natural calamities, the tribals found it extremely difficult to maintain themselves in absence of any source of livelihood. The scarcity-hit people were not able to pay land revenue in such hard days and even when the assessment was revised to a lower level, they opposed it tooth and nail.

With a view to safeguard the land of such persons in backward areas, the British Government, in 1901, passed an amendment bill in the Bombay Land Revenue Code, introducing a new Section 73A imposing a ban on transfer of land without the permission of the Collector in such backward villages where survey and settlement was not introduced. The government had powers to do this by issuing a notification.

Before proceeding to explain further on the above section, it will be expendient to mention here that there already existed Section 68, under which an occupant of agricultural land was entitled to the use and occupation of his land for the period to which his tenure was limited. If the tenure is unlimited or a survey settlement has been extended to the land, he is so entitled in perpetuity, conditionally, on payment of amounts on account of land revenue for the same and on fulfilment of any other terms or conditions lawfully annexed to his tenure. The lands to which survey and settlement was extended were, thus, considered liable to payment of revenue. And, as no terms and conditions were annexed to the tenure, these lands enjoyed the status of old tenure and were alienable and partible. There was a provision, inserted in the year 1901 in Section 68, that when unoccupied and (government waste) land happened to be granted to any person, the District Collector could impose the conditions restricting the alienation and partition of land subject to rules made by the government. Lands granted by the Collector on these conditions were termed as new tenure lands.

Section 73 of the Land Revenue Code was substituted for the first time and it provided that all occupancies subject to conditions, lawfully annexed to the tenure, shall be heritable and transferable. The 'new' or 'restricted' tenure came into being by insertion of provision to Section 68 and enactment of a new Section 73A.

In Gujarat, the legal provision existing at present for prohibiting alienation of tribal land and for restoring tribal lands unauthorizedly occupied and contained in Section 73! and 79A, respectively, which were inserted in the erstwhile Bombay State in the year 1901. These two sections read as under:

(1) Power to Restrict Right to Transfer:

> Section 73A(1). Notwithstanding anything in the foregoing section, in any tract or village to which the State Government may, by notification published before the introduction therein of an original survey settlement under Section 103, declare the provisions of this section applicable, occupancies shall not after the date of such notification be transferable without the previous sanction of the Collector.
>
> Section 73A(2). The State Government may, by notification in the Official Gazettee, from time to time, exempt any part of such tract or village or any person or class of persons from the operation of this section.

(2) Summary Eviction of Person: Unauthorizedly Occupying Land:

> Section 79A. Any person unauthorizedly occupying, or wrongfully in possession of any land (1) to the use or occupation of which by reason of any of the provisions of this Act he is not entitled, or (b) which is not transferable without previous sanction under Section 73A or by virtue of any condition lawfully annexed to the tenure under the provisions of Section 62, 67 or 68 may be summarily evicted by the Collector.

Out of 32 tribal talukas covered under tribal-sub-plan (TSP) area in Gujarat, lands in about 16 talukas are treated as surveyed and settled and so tribal lands of labour half the TSP area were without any restriction on alienation, and the tribals freely alienate their lands under pressure of circumstances or due to underhand dealings of the interested parties. There was no legal provision whatsoever to prohibit alienation of tribal land in these 16 talukas.

So far as unsurveyed and unsettled areas are concerned, publication of government notification is a condition precedent to application of Section 73A. These areas are those which were governed mostly by the former princely states and merged/integrated with other territories of Indian Union in the year 1948. There was practically no restriction on alienation of tribal land during the period of more than 12 years from 1948 to 1961, until the Gujarat Government issued notification applying Section 73A in ex-princely states' areas, covering 16 talukas.

During this period of 12 years, there was no such restriction, and alienation of tribal lands freely took place, and there was no legal remedy to revert consideration of cases of such alienation for want of notification. Thus, it becomes most significant to note that until the year 1961, there was practically no restriction on alienation of tribal land in all the 32 tribal talukas covered under the TSP.

After 1961, 16 tribal talukas (covered by ex-princely states) were brought under the purview of Section 73 by issue of a Government notification. But, the trend of alienation of the tribal lands which had already set in, continued unchecked, because the administrative machinery to detect alienation was strengthened only in 1977 by creation of LND-5 units (headed by Deputy Collector) under the TSP.

Next to land alienation, there are five major problems of tribal land system, viz., tenancy legislation, ceiling on land, fragmentation and consolidation of landholdings, forest land, indebtedness and moneylending.

## Tenancy Act

The following two amendments were made by the Gujarat state in the Bombay Tenancy and Agricultural Land Act, 1948. It is hereinafter referred to as Gujarat Tenancy Act V of 1973 which came into force with effect from 9 March 1973.

(a) In no case shall a tenancy be terminated for personal cultivation and non-agricultural use by the landlord, if the tenant is a member of the Scheduled Caste or Scheduled Tribe Section 31B(4).

(b) Surrender of tenancy rights in favour of landlord has been barred. All surrenders can be made only in favour of the State government and such land will vest with the State government free from all encumbrances for disposal according to the provisions of the Act in accordance with the priority list.

Before the above amendments came into force, the landlords had right to terminate the tenancy of tribal tenants on the ground of personal cultivation or non-agricultural use of land up to a specified period. Similarly, landlords were also able to get the land voluntarily surrendered by a tribal tenant up to a specified period. During this period, tactful and intelligent landlords of tribal tenants availed of the legal provisions in getting back the land from the tribal tenants on the ground of personal cultivation or by voluntary surrender. The tribal tenants who made voluntary surrender have done so on account of poverty and illiteracy, indebtedness and influence of landlords. Some of these surrenders might be fictitious and fake.

The departmental information shows that the figures of lands lost by tribal tenants for personal cultivation by landlords and lands surrendered in favour of landlords in respect of only 14 tribal talukas and one tribal pocket. In all 3,317 tribals voluntarily surrendered 3,203 hectares of land and 1,450 tribals lost legal right over 2,095 hectares of land for personal cultivation by landlords. Thus, a total of 4,767 tribal tenants lost 5,298 hectares of land one the above two counts and were, therefore deprived of becoming deemed purchasers.

The above two amendments which could have protected them were made at a very late stage. It is likely that the figures of tribal tenants and the lands lost by them as revealed from the limited department data on the above two counts, if studied in detail in all 32 talukas and 15 pockets, would go much higher.

From the above it can be inferred that the tribal tenants' lack of knowledge about their legal right in land and their inferior social and financial status as compared to their non-tribal landlords are among the main handicaps which virtually nullify their rights under the vital provision of the law.

## Ceiling Law

The study of the ceiling law and its implementation brings out the following points for serious consideration by the Gujarat government:

1. The Gujarat Agricultural Ceiling Act, 1960, has made a provision that a person belonging to a Scheduled Tribe shall have precedence over other persons for the allotment of land declared surplus. The occupancy price to be charged from the

allottees is equal to the amount of compensation to be paid to the landholder whose land has been declared surplus. The amount of compensation of cultivated land ranges from 80 to 200 times the assessment of the land. Looking at the extremely poor financial condition of the tribals, it is very difficult for them to pay such heavy price. It is, therefore, suggested that the concessional occupancy price at the rate of six times the assessment should be charged to the tribal allottee and the remaining amount of difference between the full and the concessional occupancy price should be met from the subsidy to the concerned tribal from the TSP. The concessional occupancy price at six times the assessment may be given as interest-free loan to be recovered in 12 annual equal instalments from the TSP.

2. To evade the precise provisions of the ceiling law, the following devices are reported to have adopted by tactful and intelligent landlords so that their land in excess of the ceiling limit may not be declared surplus: (a) Partitioning land among family members by unregistered ante-dated documents, and (b) creating rights of tenants in the names of persons who are acquainted or related to them and thus enabling them to become deemed purchasers under the tenancy law. Cases are also reported where such landlords have taken money in advance and they have given tenancy rights to others who become occupants as deemed purchasers under the tenancy law and, thus, they also got the purchase price in addition to advance money. Thus, they were able to manage to get full value of their land by adopting such tactful methods, on account of unforeseen loopholes by the makers of the law.

## Prevention of Fragmentation and Consolidation of Holdings Act

### *Fragmentation*

Different parcels of lands held by a tribal landholder in a village are generally situated at different places. For instance, some are on rocky and hilly areas while a few are in somewhat plain areas. The fertility of each parcel of land is naturally different. And so, each and every heir of a deceased landholder prefers to have his share by sub-dividing each parcel of land with differences in the fertility of the soil. This results in smaller and uneconomic fragments and at times these fragments are of the size below the standard area prescribed by the above Act. However, in the records, names of all the heirs of a deceased are shown against each parcel of land under joint possession, though the position on the ground is different, as indicated above. In the record of rights, therefore, there appears no fragments, while fragments existed as cultivated by the heirs of tribal ancestor on the spot.

The only reasonable solution that can be suggested is to persuade different heirs to manage the cultivation of such lands jointly and to share the expenditure involved and divide the produce of the lands among themselves. This is the only way in which the position at the ground level and in the records can be retained undisturbed.

## *Consolidation*

Out of 54 villages selected for field survey (39 of tribal talukas and 15 of tribal pockets), consolidation scheme was applied to only 13 villages. The findings of these cases are: (i) possession of fragments and parcels had not been exchanged for the purpose of forming compact block in seven villages, (ii) in the second group of three villages, possession according to the block scheme had taken place partially, and (iii) in three villages possession had been fully exchanged as has been revealed from the survey.

In the second and third categories, where lands were partially or fully exchanged, most of the lands belonged to non-tribals. Out of these six villages, four are from pocket areas and two are from tribal talukas. Thus, out of 13 villages, the consolidation scheme was not successful in 10 villages as shown in categories (i) and (ii) above.

In the report of H.K.I., Kapoor Committee on 'Consolidation of the Holding in Gujarat State', it has been pointed out that the areas having one or more of the following characteristics were obviously unsuitable for implementation of the consolidation scheme:

1. areas having indulating and hilly terrain.
2. areas having disproportionately large varieties of soil.
3. areas where there is an insignificant problem of scatteredness.

4. area having a large percentage of tribal population or other inhabitants who are socially backward.

First, it seems that the above 10 villages where the consolidation scheme had not been taken up before the preparation of the Kapoor Committee's report and one or more of the above characteristics may be kept in view when the question of taking up tribal villages for introduction of the consolidation scheme arises in future. The feasibility of the scheme, the willingness of the landholders for implementation, etc., must be throughly examined while taking up a tribal village for the implementation of this scheme.

Secondly, the record of rights (in these 10 villages) was rewritten according to the consolidation scheme as if the possessions have all been exchanged according to the formation of blocks, and as such, block numbers, were shown in place of survey numbers and/or sub-divisions of survey numbers. However, the position on the ground was different in cases in which the landholders had not exchanged their possession.

This resulted in a lot of difficulties for the village officers concerned in doing crop inspection and keeping notes of the crops in the block numbers in the villages records. Since possession was not according to blocks in such cases, serious administrative difficulties were faced in day-to-day working of village officers.

In principle, the record of rights is the record of possession of land by an occupant. This is not observed under these conditions. The vital statistics of crops collected at various levels is also affected.

### *Record of Rights*

The tribal people are bound to their land by many and intimate ties. It is, therefore, necessary that the records of rights of tribal lands should be up-to-date and maintained correctly. The work of preparing the records of rights as far as the tribals are illiterate and ignorant of the implications of various enactments. The approach to this work should be a humane one rather than legalistic and should take full cognizance of tribal customs and traditions.

The records of rights in tribal areas were not found up-to-date due to following factors:

1. First, during the times of the erstwhile princely states, there was a practice of taking forced labour commonly known as *veth* from every landholder called *khatedar*. In order that a *khatedar* may not have to supply more persons for forced labour, he preferred to keep all his land in one *khata* only. This was one of the reasons why all tribal lands were entered in the name of the eldest male heir of the family. This practice of demanding forced labour does not at all exist at present. However, the custom of primogeniture persists and the heirs of a dead person maintain a joint *khata* in the name of the eldest brother, while separately cultivating their share of land for personal benefit. This is why the record of rights cannot be up-to-date in tribal villages.
2. Secondly, due to varying fertility of parcels of inherited land and the anticipated breach of Fragmentation Act referred to earlier, the names of all heirs are shown jointly against each parcel of land, which is actually sub-divided for the purpose of cultivation. Thus, the position in the records and on the ground differs.
3. On account of the compulsions of incurring debts for social ceremonies, maintenance in times of scarcity and in lean periods, many a tribals have no alternative but to alienate his land to a moneylender. However, due to ban on land alienation, he enters into concealed transaction with his creditor. Such transactions are not brought to the notice of revenue authorities and so land alienation of this kind are not reflected in the records of rights.
4. The programme of resurvey and revision survey have been undertaken in tribal areas. However, the survey staff has to ignore the existing portions of parcels of land separately cultivated by each heir, and set aside the provisions of the Fragmentation Act.
5. In tribal villages where consolidation scheme is implemented, tribals mostly do not exchange their lands as required for consolidation blocks. This creates an anomaly in the situation as the records of rights is prepared according to block scheme prescribed for this purpose (this point has been discussed earlier in Section V-B in detail.) As mentioned before, it seems appropriate to suggest that suitable steps may be taken to ensure that the record of right actually reflects the position on the ground.

## Compulsory Acquisition of Tribal Lands for Public Purpose

In all the large-scale irrigation projects, tribals in Gujarat have been the losers of their land as these projects are generally located in hilly and rocky tribal tracts. The tribal lands are compulsorily acquired and they are rendered almost landless and homeless. The fruits of irrigation go to the people living in downstream areas in the plains and they are usually the non-tribals.

### *Forest Land*

With the onrush of timber contractors who were permitted by the Forest Department to cut trees and/or prepare charcoal, the forests were opened up for exploitation by non-tribals. The demand for timber at higher prices than before also led the tribals to cut wood indiscriminately and sell to timber merchants and to others. In course of times, their age-old rights to cultivate forest land, to cut trees were restricted. Hunting could no more give them games to live by, and the changed circumstances compelled them to resort to new avenues of labour outside their habitat to sustain themselves to new avenues of labour outside their habitat to sustain themselves and their families after monsoon. The problems connected with the ownership of forest land by the tribals in general are complex, as revealed from the following points:

1. In the district of Dangs, the Gujarat government issued orders in 1970 conferring occupancy rights only on Dangis and not any outsider who might have obtained leases of certain lands either from the Dangis or from the Forest Department. This step was quite proper in the interest of the tribals who were the original occupants of the Dangs. However, the government had not placed any restriction on the extent of leased area for which occupancy rights could be conferred. This resulted in inequitable distribution of conferment of occupancy rights among the Dangis, because a person holding a big area of leased land became the occupant of larger areas, while a person holding a small area became occupant of smaller areas. Had the government put some ceiling limit on this, it would have become possible for more Dangi tribals to take advantage of having their own

land. Since it has become difficult to correct the situation at this point of time, it can be possible to help these landless tribals by giving them first preference in the distribution of jobs in the Forest Department, forest co-operatives, etc.

2. In order to regulate authorized and to curb unauthorized cultivation of forests land in all the areas other than Dangs, the Gujarat Government has issued various orders from time to time. The original orders issued in 1961 and 1964 were to grant occupancy rights of forests land to backward class persons whether cultivating forest lands in an authorized or unauthorized manner. Non-backward classes were then given occupancy rights of forests lands provided they cultivated authorizedly. However, they had no claim on forest lands if cultivated an unauthorized.
3. According to the order issued in 1972, the forest lands cultivated in an authorized manner by the cultivators prior to 31 December 1967 were permanently granted up to 8 acres including other lands which might have been occupied by them as per the customary rules. This order treated tribals and non-tribals on an equal footing and so it allowed non-tribals also to become occupants of forest lands cultivated by them in an unauthorized manner.
   The above mentioned concession to non-tribals has resulted in depriving chances to own forest lands by the needy landless tribals, and it is high time that the government may stop giving such concessions to non-tribals, specially respect of forest lands over which the tribals should have priority to become the occupants.
4. After merger of the erstwhile princely states and on the application of the Bombay Merged Territories and Areas (Jagir Abolition) Act, 1953, the forest areas remained as private forests of Jagirdars. The Gujarat government enacted the Gujarat Private Forests (Acquisition) Act, 1972, for acquisition of private forests which was not the property of the government. During the intervening period, the Jagirdars were only permitted indiscriminate cutting of trees in private forests and allowed unauthorized cultivation of forest lands to tribals and non-tribals alike. This resulted in a huge loss of trees and the forests become barren. The only way to make good the loss of these rich forests is to take up intensive

afforestation scheme without the slightest time lapse in planting saplings and rearing trees in the ex-private forests areas on priority basis.

The tribals of these areas should be attracted to take up afforestation work and get into forest labour and solve their unemployment problem at least on short-term basis.

5. A large number of intermediaries, contractors, etc. have been eliminated at present from operating in the forest areas. They are replaced by Forest Labour Cooperative societies. But even these cooperative societies have developed vested interests as they are governed by non-tribals, and the rich tribals working as office-bearers such as secretaries, etc. Unless the by-laws of these co-operative societies are changed or modified suitably in order to eliminate non-tribals and rich tribals from becoming members and/or from holding positions of power, the poor tribal members cannot be protected from exploitation.

## Legalizing Forest Land to the Tribals

As mentioned earlier, the tribals are cultivating the forest land out of their necessities and compulsion, of course as per government 'illegally'. The so-called encroachment of tribals in forest land was quite old. The tribals also had to pay fines for that. Sometime the receipts were given. Many tribals do not have receipt as they are not habituated to do so and there is no proper place to keep it safe.

Recently the government of Gujarat has announced to make such land 'legal', to those who have been cultivating since 1980. It is expected that total 2008 tribal farmers of 46 talukas of nine districts will be benefited. Total 65,950 tribal farmers will be getting land around half lakh hector land (Table 1). This shows the acuteness of forest land problems in the tribal areas. This is an appreciable measure of the Gujarat Government. But this issue is not without a problem. Some tribals have complained in the group meeting in a very aggressive manner. The poor tribals have no proof for proving their case. They do not have proper records. In many the forest officials have not given receipt for such illegal transactions.

The worrisome problem is that about the discrepancy in the government data. As per the government data total 54,784 tribals who are cultivating 39,750.590 hectares of land will be given the ownership rights (Table 2).

**Table 1**

*Beneficiaries of Forest Land Cultivators Among Tribals of Gujarat*

| Sr. No. | District | Taluka | Village | Farmer (Beneficiary) | Land (In Hect.) |
|---|---|---|---|---|---|
| 1. | Banaskantha | 2 | 92 | 1,744 | 1,284.390 |
| 2. | Sabarkantha | 8 | 198 | 3,059 | 2,526.49 |
| 3. | Panchamahal | 41 | 518 | 21,034 | 20,652 |
| 4. | Vadodara | 5 | 232 | 8,265 | 8,343 |
| 5. | Kheda | 2 | 25 | 1,092 | 980 |
| 6. | Bharuch | 5 | 313 | 5,110 | 6,294 |
| 7. | Surat | 5 | 80 | 511 | 1,733 |
| 8. | Valsad | 4 | 311 | 20,968 | 8,418 |
| 9. | Dang | 1 | 39 | 167 | 117 |
| | Total Declare in Public Meeting | 46 | 2008 | 65,950 | 50,651 |
| | Actual Total | 43 | 1808 | 61,950 | 50,347.88 |

**Table 2**

*Beneficiaries of Forest Land Declared by GOG based on Resolution Dt. 06–10–92*

| District | No. of Surveyed Persons | Area to be distributed (Heet.) |
|---|---|---|
| Banaskantha | 1,741 | 1,281.478 |
| Sabarkantha | 2,279 | 1,838.870 |
| Vadodara | 6,794 | 7,122.730 |
| Kheda | 790 | 760.040 |
| Panchmahal | 13,372 | 12,698.680 |
| Bharuch | 4,921 | 6,027.790 |
| Surat | 1,509 | 1,731.430 |
| Dang | 167 | 117.750 |
| Valsad | 23,211 | 8,171.780 |
| Total | 54,784 | 39,750.590 |

The Ahmedabad-based voluntary organization named Ekalavya Sanghathan, which is fighting for the tribal interest has opposed the move of the Gujarat Government on the basis that this will deprive 7,714 persons and around 10,600 ha land from their land rights.

However, the government has given three explanations for this discrepancy. First, as per the rules of the central government the land under the sanctuary does not include in the list as it was not legalized under the central rule. Secondly, the land of those persons who remained absent at the time of personal examination was not included in the list as it was not legalized under the Central rule. Secondly, the land of those persons who remained absent at the time of personal examination was not included in the list. Thirdly, some land can not be given as it is under the submergence.

## Alienation of Tribal Land: Action Plan

The loopholes mentioned in the preceding sections, both legal and otherwise, have resulted in alienation of tribal lands continuing unfettered. It is, therefore, felt that the Gujarat government will consider to undertake a special and independent legislation covering the following special features for prohibiting alienation of tribal lands for restoration of all categories of alienated lands:

1. Alienation should be strictly prohibited for all tribal lands wherever situated in the state, i.e. whether the areas are surveyed and settled or not, whether the areas are scheduled ones or not, and whether the lands are in tribal talukas/pockets or not. The necessity of issuing a government notification should be dispensed with.
2. Alienation of tribal lands will be allowed only for genuine public purposes like construction of school buildings, libraries, hospitals, dispensaries, roads, water sheds etc.
3. Provision will be made for restoration of tribal lands irrespective of the period during which they were alienated by removing bar of limitation keeping in view provision made by other state governments in their respective Acts.
4. Provision will to be made for treating admission of the tribals against their own interest as inadmissible evidence in any proceedings regarding tribal lands. Such provisions exist in the enactments.
5. In proceedings relating to tribal lands, provision will be made for an officer of the rank not below that of the Mamlatdar to be joined as a party so that rights of tribals can be safeguarded.
6. Provision for imposing penalty on non-tribal by way of imprisonment and fine will be made if the non-tribal gets

occupation of tribal land in contravention of legal provisions made in this context.

7. In case of tribal lands alienated to non-tribals, if the transfer has constructed a substantial structure on the land before the proposed enactment, provision will be made to validate the transfer if the transferee either makes available to the transferor an alternative holding of the equivalent value in the vicinity, or pays adequate compensation for rehabilitation of the transferor.
8. In proceeding regarding restoration of possession of tribal lands instituted by a tribal, provision may be made to the effect that no magistrate shall have jurisdiction under Criminal Procedure Code, 1973, in respect of dispute enjoyment in respect of the said land.
9. Provision may be made for prohibiting the attachment and sale of tribal lands in execution of the money-decree against a member of the Scheduled Tribe.
10. If the tribal does not agree to take back possession of the tribal land for any reason whatsoever (influence and pressure by others or his honesty etc.), provision may be made that such land should be vested in state government and subsequently may be allotted to a landless tribal or a tribal with marginal landholding.
11. Any document regarding transfer of tribal land should not be accepted for registration by the Registrar/Sub-Registrar except in cases in which specific permission is given by the state government or authority authorized by state government.
12. In tribal areas covered by scheduled area, if a non-tribal wants to sell his land it can be sold only to a landless tribal or tribal having marginal holding.
13. Likewise, for areas covered by tribal talukas/pockets, provision should be made that unless the contrary is proved, if a non-tribal is found in possession of a tribal land, it should be restored to the tribals under the presumption that he or his predecessor had acquired that land through transfer from tribal landholders. Such provision will be helpful in detecting concealed cases of transactions.
14. For transactions of transfer of tribal land between tribal transferor and non-tribal transferee that have taken place

before the coming into force of the proposed enactment regarding restoration of tribal lands (such transactions are not otherwise invalid under any law in force then), provision may be made for restoration of the land to the tribal transferor on payment of an amount equal to multiples of assessment as may be fixed or the amount of consideration paid by the non-tribal transferee, whichever is less, plus the value or improvements.

15. Provision may be made that for transfer of tribal land which has become invalid after the coming into force of the proposed enactment prohibiting alienation of tribal land, the consideration money paid by the non-tribal transferee to the tribal transferor should not be refunded.
16. Provision may be made for alienation of tribal lands from tribal to tribal in some special circumstances and such permission may be given only by the state government. The special circumstances, other than cases of transfer due to heirship and partition, in general may be: (i) In case the tribal family wants to give up forever the agricultural occupation and desires to settle elsewhere for non-agricultural occupation including trade, service etc. (ii) In case there is no direct heir to the tribal who desires to transfer his land by sale, gift etc. (iii) In case the tribal is old, infirm and unable to pursue agriculture and there is none in his family who can look after his land, (iv) The tribal purchase should not be rich and well-to-do, and must be personally engaged in agricultural occupation or agriculture labour. Moreover, a holding after the said transfer should not exceed the holding prescribed for a small farmer.
17. In the proposed legislation, a provision should be made for restoration of lands from the non-tribal who go back to the lands from the tribals on the above two counts by relaxing the period of time limitation. When this is done, tribals can be made deemed purchases and conferred occupancy rights when the lands are restored to them as tenants.
18. There is a provision in Section 70(b) of the Tenancy Act, allowing a person to apply to the *mamlatdar* whether he is or was a tenant. This requirement of obtaining the decision of the *mamlatdar* that a tribal is or was not a tenant of his land, has been taken advantage of by intelligent and tactful

landlords using fair and foul means and got possession of tribal lands. Also, there have been cases in which mutation entries in village forms have been effected indicating that tribal was not a tenant on the land and thereby his name as tenant was deleted and such entries were certified with the result that a tribal could not become a deemed purchaser. To overcome such difficulties, a provision should be made in the proposed legislation for restoration of lands to tribal concerned and they may be subsequently conferred occupancy rights as deemed purchasers.

19. One of the hurdles in restoration of the tribal land is that the names of non-tribals, probably those from whom tribals have borrowed money, are entered as tenants in the village records and subsequently they (non-tribals) become occupants of the land as deemed purchasers. Under the existing law, it is not possible to restore possession of such lands to the tribals in tribal areas which are treated as surveyed and settled, and where Section 73A of the Land Revenue Code is not applicable. The state may consider making some suitable enactment to cover such cases.
20. There are some tribals who have become occupants as deemed purchases under tenancy law, but they have not as yet been able to pay the installments of purchase price to their previous landlords, in order to compensate for the loss of land to the tribals to the fullest extent.

**The Following Points Call for Serious Consideration**

21. In the first instance, a tribal should be allotted equal land in exchange of the land compulsorily acquired instead of giving him compensation in cash.
22. The loss of living accommodation and facility in house/hut and breakable household materials which cannot be shifted should be fully compensated for when he is rehabilitated.
23. The amount of the award prices paid to him in case is so nominal that he cannot purchase adequate land for his living. This is why he should be given land in exchange, so that the chances of his losing the bargain on account of time lag in preliminary notification of acquisition and actually getting the award money do not arise.

24. On account of restrictions on alienation of tribal lands under Section 73A of the Land Revenue Code, it is almost impossible to make correct valuation of his land. In absence of any reliable method for this purpose, his lands are valued at a very low rate. It will be appropriate, therefore, that the sale statistics of old tenure lands in neighbouring villages or tracts may be utilized as a satisfactory yardstick for working out compensation of their lands.

# 9

# Scheduled Tribes and Their Health Situation

## An Analysis of Gujarat

**Binod C. Agrawal**

Over 50 years ago, Ghurye (1963) questioned the categorization of the Scheduled Tribes as against other Hindu castes done by British Administrators who referred them as 'The Aborigines'. Later in independent India, Scheduled Tribes have been referred to as *adivasis* by politicians and administrators. Now, Scheduled Tribes refers to themselves as *adivasis*. Ghurye (1963), in his book *The Scheduled Tribes* clearly brought out the confusion as who are and were Scheduled Tribes in the Indian civilization. It should be mentioned that there are references about inhabitants in remote and forest areas in the ancient literature of India as an integral part of the Indian Civilization. The confusion about who are Scheduled Tribes continued to haunt a large number of scholars, political leaders and administrators alike apart from lay persons, as it has taken a socio-political connotation having serious political ramification in independent India. It should be mentioned that the Scheduled Tribes and Hindu castes have been living in an interactive symbiotic relationships and remained inter-dependent on each other for variety of goods and services for time immemorial (Agrawal, 1977 and 1995).

The historical blunder was made by British colonial rulers who coined the term 'tribes' while taking census in pre-independent India and the same mistake was repeated for almost over 70 years that can be seen in the report of Census Commissioners from 1871 to 1931 who recorded tribal religion as 'Animism' and later as a 'Tribal Religions'. As early as 1891, J.A. Baines, the Commissioner of the Census of 1891, considered the distinction between tribal people who were Hinduized and those that followed their tribal form of religion as futile' (Ghurye, 1963: 2).

Hence, integration of Scheduled Tribes in independent India into the mainstream has been extremely complex and difficult task. '... given the varied conditions under which they (Scheduled Tribes) live in different parts of the country, and their different languages and distinct cultures' (Chandra, Mukherjee and Mukherjee, 2000: 106). Should a similar question be raised about whole of India?

Observations and a large number of field researches support the view that Scheduled Tribes in spite of their remote living continued to interact with rest of neighbouring Hindu and other religious groups. Not withstanding the intellectual discourse and controversy on the issue, it is suffice to state that the Constitution of India under Article 330 has recognized Scheduled Tribes as a separate social category who are considered socially, economically and technologically a deprived group. Hence, the Constitution of India enunciated provisions of reservation of seats in Centre, State and Union Territory apart from reservation in education and job and other facilities to uplift and bring Scheduled Tribes into mainstream.

The reason for raising the question is to emphasize that in case of healthcare, such a distinction between Scheduled Tribes and other caste and religious groups seem spurious given the universal health needs all across India be it the Scheduled Tribes, Hindu castes and the rest of the population. Within this backdrop, the effort in the paper will be made to examine the National Rural Health Mission (NRHM) and health needs of Scheduled Tribes and other Hindu castes in order to put forward a case of universal healthcare for all human beings living in India regardless of religion and such social categories.

## Scheduled Tribes of Gujarat

Scheduled Tribes of Gujarat inhabit 11 eastern districts of Gujarat adjoining three states Rajasthan, Madhya Pradesh and

Maharashtra having concentration of Scheduled Tribes on their borders. Therefore, some of the observations made for Gujarat are applicable to Scheduled Tribes of three neighbouring states. There has been rapid industrialization in several districts of Gujarat largely inhabited by Scheduled Tribes along with Hindu castes and other religious groups.

According to Census of India 2011, there are 8.91 million Scheduled Tribes comprising 14.8 per cent of the total population largely living in rural areas. There are 25 Scheduled Tribes in the state of Gujarat in which five are listed as most primitive tribes. These are Kotwalia, Kolgha, Kathodi, Siddi and Padhar (Upadhyaya and Pancholi, 2010). The other major Scheduled Tribes include Bhil, Dubla, Dhodia, Rathwa, Kokna, Varli, Gamit and Naika (Nayak). Bhil are the largest Scheduled Tribes comprising almost 46.01 per cent of the total Scheduled Tribes population. It was observed that the sex ratio among Scheduled Tribes is much higher than that of Gujarat State average (981 females per 1,000 male) and has improved since 2011. Further, Scheduled Tribes of Gujarat in search of work have been forced to move out of their rural habitat to industrial urban areas.

Exception apart, across India, Scheduled Tribes have lived in mixed habitations along with castes Hindu, other Scheduled Tribes and religious groups which will be now referred to as non-Scheduled Tribes in the paper. Scheduled Tribes across India have had continuous interaction with non-Scheduled Tribes and other Scheduled Tribes. Also, there has been continuous internal migration and displacement of Scheduled Tribes due to geo-political, economic and natural disasters from one region to another. Added to it has been flux of immigrants from other countries within India encroaching and occupying lands of Scheduled Tribes and non-Scheduled Tribes.

After Independence, an additional problem, for the displacement of Scheduled Tribes and non-Scheduled Tribes alike have been fast paced industrialization and to some extent urbanization. These forces have displaced, encroached and occupied land belonging to them without much environmental concern, opposition and objections by the non-government organizations even in the remotest and isolated regions of the country. This process has further brought Scheduled Tribes and non-Scheduled Tribes in close physical proximity, and has increased interdependence and social interaction.

This ongoing analysis tends to point out that both Scheduled Tribes and non-Scheduled Tribes by and large, share common problems and have almost identical health needs and depend on similar healthcare from available sources and services.

## National Rural Health Mission (NRHM) and Scheduled Tribes

In spite of health being a state subject, Central government has given a great deal of importance to health for all citizens of the country and felt the need to support state health programmes. It is especially true in case of Scheduled Tribes to bring about equitable and effective healthcare for Scheduled Tribes who mostly live in remote regions and hilly tracts of the country. The National Rural Health Mission (NRHM) aims to provide holistic and democratic health services to all rural inhabitants, including Scheduled Castes and Scheduled Tribes. In this context, Sharma (2014: 287) observed that 'NRHM has not achieved the stated goals in time and suffering from many bottlenecks'. Also, under NRHM there is no evidence to indicate that substantial additional funding, technical and institutional support has been provided to improve the health of Scheduled Tribes. At the same time, NRHM claims to provide accessible, affordable and accountable quality health services to rural population including Scheduled Tribes having concentration on 18 special focus states (Sharma, 2014: 290). Further, Sharma observed that 'rural and tribal population shows that for the rural poor the first place to be considered for health needs is the government hospital (in rural areas PHCs and CHCs are also called hospitals)'.

## Healthcare of Scheduled Tribes

In the remaining paper, an attempt has been made to discuss healthcare status of Scheduled Tribes of Gujarat based on secondary data and studies carried out by TALEEM Research Foundation.

Observations support the view that Scheduled Tribes have a strong urge and aspiration to achieve better standard of living thereby accepting rapid changes in their socio-economic life. The Scheduled Tribes of Gujarat have by and large accepted modern medical healthcare apart from existing health practices without significant improvement in their health in spite of state government efforts, provision of special fund allocation for their health and development.

Scheduled Tribes of Gujarat are suffering from high level of malnutrition especially young children leading to relatively higher degree of morbidity and poor maternal health. A large number of women are anaemic among the Scheduled Tribes. Their health status can be characterized as 'poor' though it is not because of lack of demand or availability of health services. Poverty and inadequate food intake coupled with environmental degradation are some of the major causes of poor health and related problems. Selected research findings on health of Scheduled Tribes have been drawn from two rounds of District Level Household Surveys known as DLHS-2 and DLHS-3 of Gujarat conducted during 2002–2004 and 2007–2008, respectively. Gujarat DLHS-2 and DLHS-3 provided state level estimates and progress of Reproductive and Child Health Programme/National Rural Health Mission (NRHM). Similarly National Family Health Survey-3 (NFHS-3) carried out during 2005–2006 yielded Gujarat state estimates on population health and socio-economic indicators. For understanding of Scheduled Tribes health situation the Scheduled Tribes data were segregated from the total Gujarat state level data and separately analysed. First hand health study conducted in 2012 has been incorporated in the paper and discussed.

## Health Situation in Gujarat: A Study

The first-hand study was carried out in five villages in Bharuch district during 26 July–30 August 2012. Both qualitative and quantitative methods were used for data collection which included interviews of 513 head of households of both sexes. Qualitative data were collected in 10 focus group discussions (FGD) and six case study supplemented by first-hand village observations. All five villages were part of agricultural land acquisition that was carried out by Gujarat Industrial Development Corporation (GIDC) from farmers during 2007–2009. The acquired land was allotted to various industries for setting up of factories to boost industrial production and economic development of Gujarat state (Anonymous, 2012).

In all five villages, Scheduled Tribes and non-Scheduled Tribes lived to in a multi-caste and multi-religious and formed an organic social mosaic of interdependence. Caste based spatial patterns of segregated living was clearly visible in each village in which Scheduled Tribes lived in a separate *falia* (ward) mainly on the periphery of the village. The pattern of social interaction, economic interdependence, participation in day-to-day socio-economic life, and participation in fairs and festivals seemed an established practice. The social hierarchy of Scheduled Tribes in political and economic activities was visible and was being followed in the village. Both Scheduled Tribes and non-Scheduled Tribes accept and follow generic social norms and broad values having far reaching policy implications for the healthcare of Scheduled Tribes (Anonymous, 2012).

The five villages under study represented microcosm of the macrocosm of rural Gujarat. As much as 90.6 per cent Scheduled Tribes and non-Scheduled Tribes claimed to be Hindu along with 9.4 per cent Muslim and others though Muslim population was largely concentrated in one village. No significant economic differences were observed between Scheduled Tribes and non-Scheduled Tribes who owned land or did not own land prior to land acquisition by GIDC. The distribution of Below Poverty Line (BPL) (35.7%) and Above Poverty Line (64.3%) households was not significantly different between them (Anonymous, 2012).

In this study, almost one-third or 33.3 per cent respondents were illiterate with little variation among villages. Almost nine out of 10 respondents lived in *pucca*/semi-*pucca* houses thereby showing marginal or no differences between Scheduled Tribes and non-Scheduled Tribes patterns of living. Almost all of them had access to major sources of drinking water through pipeline in their houses. All houses were electrified and seven out of 10 households had flush or pit toilet facility in the dwelling. The remaining used open field for defecation (Anonymous, 2012).

Like non-Scheduled Tribes, the Scheduled Tribes owned a large number of consumer goods like bed mattress, electric fan, electronic watch/wall clock and chair in their houses. In addition, Scheduled Tribes had acquired pressure cooker, television, telephone/mobile phone, scooter/motor cycle and some of them even owned refrigerator thereby showing Scheduled Tribes' eagerness to adopt and accept change like their counterpart non-Scheduled Tribes. One of the stimulations attributed for the acceptance of change and adoption of consumer products could be availability of disposable cash money received as compensation for selling land by GIDC. The important point to be emphasized is that Scheduled Tribes like non-Scheduled Tribes have also responded and accepted change in more or less similar way. Also, consumerism has increased for acquiring durable goods and means of transportation both among Scheduled Tribes and non-Scheduled Tribes (Anonymous, 2014). The brief profile of the households tends to support the view that little or no differences existed between Scheduled Tribes and non-Scheduled Tribes in five villages under study.

DLHS-2 and NFHS-3 studies of Gujarat recorded reduction in anaemia among pregnant Scheduled Tribes women (Table 1) and also increase in electricity connection in their households (Table 2). Same cannot be said about drinking water facility from taps, hand pumps and bore-well among Scheduled Tribes (Table 3). However, the condition of sanitation seemed to have not improved at all. Over 80.0 per cent of the households did not have toilet facilities that used open field for defecation (Table 4). Firewood remains the main source of cooking fuel for over 85.0 per cent households.

**Table 1**

*Anemia Among Scheduled Tribes Pregnant Women*

| *Prevalence of Anemia* | *DHLS-2 (15–44 years)* | *NFHS-3 (15–49 years)* |
|---|---|---|
| Mild | 27.7 | 46.5 |
| Moderate | 62.3 | 24.4 |
| Severe | 9.9 | 3.3 |
| Not Reported/None | 00 | 25.8 |
| Total Respondents | 160 | 358 |

*Source:* (Anonymous, 2014: 15)

**Table 2**

*Types of House and Electricity*

| *Type of House and Electricity connection* | *DLHS-2* | *DLHS-3* |
|---|---|---|
| Kaccha+Huts | 66.0 | 64.7 |
| Semi-pucca | 16.9 | 23.7 |
| Pucca | 17.0 | 11.5 |
| Electricity connection | 64.0 | 69.5 |
| Total No. of Household | 4,417 | 6,386 |

*Source:* (Anonymous, 2014: 7)

**Table 3**
*Sources of Drinking Water*

| *Source of Drinking Water* | *DLHS-2* | *DLHS-3* |
|---|---|---|
| Tap inside | 13.7 | 13.7 |
| Tap shared public | 10.0 | 8.0 |
| Hand pump-bore well | 54.4 | 51.0 |
| Protected well | 0.8 | 7.1 |
| Unprotected well | 17.2 | 15.1 |
| River/Pond/Streams/canal/Irrigation channel | 2.4 | 2.9 |
| Spring | 0.4 | 1.1 |
| Other | 1.0 | 0.9 |
| Total no. of household | 4,417 | 6,386 |

*Source:* (Anonymous, 2014: 7)

**Table 4**
*Type of Toilet Facility*

| *Toilet Facility* | *DLHS-2* | *DLHS-3* |
|---|---|---|
| Own Flush Toilet | 11.8 | 14.8 |
| Own Pit Toilet | 2.8 | 3.3 |
| Shared toilet/Public-community toilet | 3.3 | 0.2 |
| No toilet | 83.1 | 81.7 |
| Total No. of Household | 4,417 | 6,386 |

*Source:* (Anonymous, 2014: 7)

## Maternal Child Healthcare Services and Family Planning

Out of five villages surveyed in 2012 study, one village was predominantly Muslim. Hence, for the purpose of analysis of health services data of only four villages were taken into consideration. It was reported that over 50 per cent Scheduled Tribes and non-Scheduled Tribes were covered under various health schemes and had *Rashtriya Swasthya Bima Yojana* (RSBY) card without major differences between Scheduled Tribes and non-Scheduled Tribes. These villages had functional *Aanganwadi* and Integrated Child Development Scheme (ICDS) and were in operation. However, the utilization of ICDS services during pregnancy remained low as more than 25 per cent utilized the services. Similar findings were recorded in NFHS-3 (Table 5). Government health facilities like Primary Health Centre (PHC), Community Health Centre (CHC) and private doctors were available and utilized by Scheduled Tribes and non-Scheduled Tribes alike.

Three out of four respondents in the sample depended and preferred private doctors and private hospitals as compared to PHC and CHS services.

**Table 5**

*Utilization of ICDS Services During Pregnancy*

| *Pregnancy* | *NFHS-3* |
|---|---|
| No Service | 70.7 |
| Supplementary Food | 24.5 |
| Health Checkup | 20.3 |
| Health and Nutrition Education | 19.1 |
| Sample Size | 165 |

*Source:* (Anonymous, 2014: 13)

The child ever born to Scheduled Tribes women is a basic indicator of fertility. The average number of children born to a Scheduled Tribe woman was 2.9 which were higher than that of state average of 2.6 children born to a non-Scheduled Tribes woman supported by DLHS-2 and DLHS-3 studies (Table 6). At the same time, Infant Mortality Rate (IMR) was relatively higher among Scheduled Tribes (86.0) as compared to the State average of 49.7 among non-Scheduled Tribes as reflected in NFHS-3 survey (Table 7).

**Table 6**

*Mean Number of Ever Born Children, Son and Daughter*

| *Average Ever Born Children* | *DLHS-2* | *DLHS-3* |
|---|---|---|
| Children Ever Born/Total Fertility Rate | 2.8 | 2.9 |
| Son Ever Born | 1.4 | 1.5 |
| Daughter Ever Born | 1.3 | 1.4 |

*Source:* (Anonymous, 2014: 10)

**Table 7**

*Mortality Rate*

| *Rate* | *NHFS-3* |
|---|---|
| National Mortality Rate | 53.0 |
| Post-Neonatal Mortality Rate | 33.0 |
| Scheduled Tribes Infant Mortality Rate | 86.0 |
| Under 5 Mortality Rate | 115.8 |

*Source:* (Anonymous, 2014: 10)

Antenatal care services have had not improved among Scheduled Tribes and non-Scheduled Tribes alike. A marginal change in the status of institutional delivery was observed (Table 8). Important point to be mentioned is that necessity of institutional delivery had been felt and increased over a period of time. Similarly, breast feeding within two hours of child birth was reported to have increased both among Scheduled Tribes and non-Scheduled Tribes. Scheduled Tribes like non-Scheduled Tribes women were aware of diarrhoea and danger sign of pneumonia. So was the use of ORS for diarrhoea treatment (Anonymous, 2014).

**Table 8**

*Place of Delivery*

| *Place of Delivery* | *DLHS-2* | *DLHS-3* |
|---|---|---|
| Institutional Delivery | 32.4 | 34.6 |
| Home | 66.9 | 63.9 |
| Total no. of Women | 1,126 | 2,161 |

*Source:* (Anonymous, 2014: 11)

Family planning awareness among Scheduled Tribes and non-Scheduled Tribes was high. At least one method of family planning was known to both Scheduled Tribes and non-Scheduled Tribes. However, awareness about modern spacing methods was low. The use of modern family planning methods had increased over period of time though access to family planning services remained poor among Scheduled Tribe and non-Scheduled Tribes. No more than one-fourth of Scheduled Tribes women were aware of HIV/AIDS (Anonymous, 2014).

On the whole, little or no differences were observed between Scheduled Tribes and non-Scheduled Tribes health seeking behaviour (Anonymous, 2012).

## Conclusion

On the basis of limited analysis presented so far an argument has been advocated that differences between Scheduled Tribes and non-Scheduled Tribes health seeking behaviour, awareness and knowledge about healthcare reflected more or less identical behavioural patterns in Gujarat. Similar analysis should be carried out in other states of Western India and rest of the India. If the conclusion happened to yield similar results there is a need to review Scheduled Tribes health strategy planning afresh. It should be kept in mind that healthcare is a universal need for human survival within the country and elsewhere. In doing so, all efforts must be made to safeguard the interest of Scheduled Tribes and Constitutional obligations are fully met as proposed earlier by Agrawal (2015).

## References

Agrawal, Binod C. 'Interaction Between Tribes and Non-Tribes' in ed., S.C. Dube, *Tribal Heritage of India*, Vikas, New Delhi, 1977, pp. 118–140.

Agrawal, Binod C. 'Anthropology and Tribal Women Workforce in the Industrial Setting of India' in *Indian Tribes* (Health Ecology and Social Structure), R.C. Swarnakar (ed.), Printwell, Jaipur, 1995, pp. 253–258.

Agrawal, Binod C. 'Culture, Communication and Health in North East Region: An Anthropological Perspective'. In *Culture, Health and Development: The Situation among the Tribes of North-East India.* (eds) Singh, Narendra Kh. and Agrawal, Binod C., Concept, New Delhi, 2015, pp. 3–13.

Anonymous, Land Looser Survey of Dahej Survey. Ahmedabad: TALEEM Research Foundation (unpublished report prepared by Chandra Gupt Sanon), 2012.

Anonymous, Socio-Economic and Health Status of Scheduled Tribes in Gujarat: A Meta Analysis. Ahmedabad: TALEEM Research Foundation (unpublished report prepared), 2014.

Chandra, Bipin, Mukherjee, Mridula and Mukherjee, Aditya. *India After Independence*, 1947–2000, Penguin Books India, New Delhi, 1999.

Ghurye, G.S. *The Scheduled Tribes* (Third Edition), G.G. Pathare, Bombay, 1963.

Sharma, A.K. The National Rural Health Mission: A Critique, *Sociological Bulletin*, Vol 63, Number 2, 2014, pp. 287–301.

Upadhyaya, Chandrakant and Pancholi, Ravindra. Primitive Tribal Groups of Gujarat: A Baseline Survey, Ahmedabad: Tribal Research and Training Institute, Gujarat Vidyapith, Ahmedabad, 2010.

# 10

# A Comparative Study of Health and Nutrition

## Status of Kolgha, Varli and Kamar Tribes

**T.K. Vaishnav**

The Human Development Index of United Nations Development Programmes (UNDP) is mainly based on health, education and income-generating capacity. In a recently brought out Human Development Report, 2014, India is placed at number 135 among 187 countries on the basis of Human Development Index (HDI). In India, if we go state-wise, according to Human Development Index 2011–12, Kerala with 0.911 points is at the top, and Uttar Pradesh with 0.112 points is at the bottom. The state of Gujarat, is placed at number 10 with 0.477 points and Chhattisgarh is placed at no. 24 with 0.180 points. According to Global Hunger Index, 2013 report, India is at no. 63. In this report, we are even behind China, Sri Lanka, Nepal, Pakistan and Bangladesh. In the UNICEF Report 2013; it is shown that in India, 48 per cent of children in the age-group of 0–5 years are suffering from malnutrition. In China, this figure is at 10 per cent. In the United Nations Report on Trends in Maternal Mortality Estimates, 1990 to 2013, the rate of maternal death at the time of giving birth to a child, i.e. at the time of delivery, is more than 190 per one lakh deliveries in India. In the neighbouring countries like China, it is 32, in Sri Lanka it is 29, in Pakistan it is 170, in Bangladesh also it is 170. The facts revealed in all these reports simply indicate that there is a need for more awareness and greater dedication for promoting health and combatting malnutrition.

**Table 1**

*National and Regional Level Facts on Health and Nutrition among STs*

| S. No. | Details | India | | Gujarat | | Chhattisgarh | |
|---|---|---|---|---|---|---|---|
| | | Total Population | STs | Total Population | STs | Total Population | STs |
| 1. | Infant mortality | 57 | 62.1 | 50 | 86.0 | 71 | 90.6 |
| 2. | Under five mortality | 74.3 | 95.7 | 77.0 | 115.8 | 105.5 | 125.8 |
| 3. | Malnutrition % as per BMI | | | | | | |
| | 3.1 Children (upto 3 years) | 44.9 | NA | 47.4 | 60.9 | 52.1 | 77.8 |
| | *3.2 Female (15–49)* | | | | | | |
| | Under nutrition | 35.6 | 46.6 | 32.3 | 61.6 | 41.0 | 50.2 |
| | Over nutrition | 25.2 | 7.0 | 20.3 | 4.8 | 6.7 | 2.9 |
| | *3.3 Male (15–49)* | | | | | | |
| | Under nutrition | 34.2 | 41.3 | 28.2 | 49.5 | 31.8 | 41.5 |
| | Over nutrition | 18.6 | 6.6 | 15.4 | 2.6 | 6.5 | 0.8 |
| 4. | Anaemia (%) | | | | | | |
| | Female (15–49) | 56.2 | 68.5 | 55.5 | 74.2 | 57.6 | 74.0 |
| | Female – Pregnant (15–49) | 57.9 | NA | 60.8 | NA | 63.1 | NA |
| | Male (15–49) | 24.3 | 39.6 | 22.1 | 44.7 | 26.4 | 38.9 |
| | Children (0.5–5) | 78.9 | NA | 70.0 | 82.9 | 70.0 | 78.0 |
| 5. | Institutional Delivery (%) | 39 | NA | 53 | 21.3 | 14.0 | 3.9 |

*Source:* NFHS–3, 2005–2006 MOHFW.

In our country, the problems of health and malnutrition are worse than expected. In any society, the state of health is mainly affected by its socio-economic, cultural, geographical conditions as well as by biological reasons and also by the conditions of safe drinking water, sanitation and mulnutrition. We had the opportunity to study the socio-economic conditions as well as problems of health and nutrition of Varli and Kolghas of Gujarat in the year 1985; of Gamit, Chaudhari, Bhils and Patelias in the year 1983; of Gonds, Bhariyas, Baigas and Sahariyar of Madhya Pradesh in the year 1994–95; and of Kamars, Pahadis, Korwas, Bigas, Abujha, Madiyas and Birhors, etc. in Chhattisgarh in the years 1992 and 2005. Here an effort is made to present some facts related to health and malnutrition among Kolgha Primitive Tribe Group (PVTG) of Gujarat, Varlies, etc. and those of Kamar (PVTG) of Chhattisgarh as an illustration as well as to make some suggestions to bring about some improvement in health status and reducing malnutrition among these tribes.

## Introduction of a Tribe

### *Kolgha (PVTG)*

Kolgha, also known as Kolchas, is one of the most backward tribes of Gujarat. Since their main occupation is making of bamboo baskets, they are also known as tokre-koli. Their main habitation in Gujarat is in the talukas of Dharampur, Kaprada and Vansada in the district of Valsad.

The Kolgha men put on a small *dhoti* or a loin cloth; and wear turban on their head. The Kolgha women put on a small saree with a Kachhota style. They cover their bust with a blouse and put on a small *odhani* on the head. The main source of their income is collection of minor forest products, labour work and agriculture work. They mainly produce Nagli, Vari, Juwar, Tuwer, Urad and Kharsani. Their farm products are consumed in just three or four months of the year. They also make baskets from bamboo-chips.

The age of marriage among Kolghas was found to be 16–18 years for boys and 15–17 years among girls. There is a custom of dowry.

The Kolgha boys and girls, after their engagement, can stay together and have a family; but before the engagement of their children, it is compulsory for the parents to have an official marriage. The marriages among Kolghas can be held even by eloping, through an exchange method, etc. Often, the bridegroom stays permanently at his in-laws. The custom of remarriage among Kolgha girls is also rampant. There is a traditional panchayat system among Kolghas.

They mainly worship Dungar-dev (mountain-God), Baghdev (a tiger God), *Hirva dev, Kak-balia* (small-pox God), *Mawli Mata,* etc. Their main festivals are Holi, Deepawali, Dassehra, etc. They drink and dance to celebrate marriage and other festivals.

### *Varli*

In Gujarat, Varli tribe people mainly habitate in Valsad district. 'Varal' means a small piece of land. The people who farm on small piece of land are Varlis.

The men-folk usually wear a loin-cloth or a half-pant and cover their upper part of body with a jacket and put on turban on

**Table 2**

*General Statistical Information about Kolgha, Varli and Kamar Tribes (Year 2011)*

| *Sr. No.* | *Details* | *Kolgha (PVTG) (Gujarat)* | *Varli (Gujarat)* | *Kamar (Chhttisgarh)* |
|---|---|---|---|---|
| 1. | No. of Households | 14,222 | 59,293 | 6,700 |
| 2. | Population: | | | |
| | Total | 67,199 | 3,28,194 | 13,070 |
| | Male | 34,099 | 1,64,258 | 13,460 |
| | Female | 33,110 | 1,63,936 | 13,460 |
| 3. | Sex Ratio | 947 | 998 | 1,030 |
| 4. | Child Sex Ratio | 967 | 953 | 1,010 |
| 5. | Literacy Rate: | | | |
| | Total | 56.5 | 52.7 | 47.7 |
| | Male | 63.6 | 61.4 | 58.8 |
| | Female | 49.3 | 42.2 | 37.0 |
| 6. | Worker Participation rate | 51.4 | 46.7 | 62.2 |
| | – Main workers | 70.2 | 63.0 | 83.3 |
| | – Marginal Workers | 29.8 | 37.0 | 16.7 |

their head. The women wear a saree called *lugada*, usually red or blue in colour, up to their knees. They cover their bust with a blouse and also put on a small piece of cloth to cover the head. Their main occupations are agriculture, collection of minor forest products and labour work. They mainly produce Nagli, Vari, Juwar, Tuwer, Urad and Kharsani. They consume their farm products within 5–6 months of a year. For rest of the period, they buy foodgrains from market.

The marriage age among Varli boys is about 17 to 19 years and among Varli girls it is 16 to 18 years. After engagement, they stay together and when they earn enough money, they perform official marriage. There are prevalent customs of run-away marriages, mutual exchange marriages, remarriages, etc. Sometimes, a bridegroom stays with his in-laws permanently as *ghar-jamai*. Among Varli tribe, there is a tribe-panchayat.

They mainly worship Hirwadev, Narandev, Dharam dev, Chanda dev, Mawali Mata (Goddess), etc. Besides, they also worship Hindu Gods and Goddesses. Their main festivals are Holi, Diwali, Diwasa, Dussehra, Janmasthami, etc. They celebrate marriage and other festivals with drinks and dance.

**Table 3**

*Statistical Analysis of Surveyed Families*

| Sr. No. | Details | Kolgha, Dharampur, Gujarat | Varli, Dharampur, Gujarat | Kamar, Gariyaband, Chhattisgarh |
|---|---|---|---|---|
| 1. | Method of Study | Survey of Food, Quantity and medical test | Survey of Food, Quantity and medical test | Survey of Food, Quantity and medical test |
| 2. | Year of Survey | 1985 | 1985 | 1992 |
| 3. | Surveyed Village | 2. Girhara Bardoli | 2. Girhara Pipalser | 2. Kamar Dera Amzar |
| 4. | No. of Families | 77 | 82 | 50 |
| | Joint Families | 31 (40.3) | 34 | 15 (30) |
| | Seperate | 46 (59.7) | 48 | 35 (70) |
| 5. | No. of persons in surveyed families | 419 | 406 | 279 |
| 6. | Average no. | 5.6 (5.44) | 5 (4.95) | 56 (5.58) |
| 7. | Adolescents and adults | | | |
| | Male | 127 (30.01) | 125 (30.79) | 89 (31.90) |
| | Female | 114 (27.21) | 124 (30.54) | 93 (33.33) |
| 8. | Children (0.14) | | | |
| | Male | 86 (20.53) | 68 (17.75) | 48 (17.20) |
| | Female | 92 (21.95) | 82 (20.19) | 49 (17.56) |
| 9. | Average No. of children in each family | 2 (2.2) | 2 (1.88) | 3. (3.2) |
| 10. | Literacy | 3.68 (1985) | 4.22 (1985) | 4.5 (1985) |
| 11. | Sex Ratio | 967 | 1,050 | 1,036 |

Cont'd...

*... Cont'd*

| | | | | |
|---|---|---|---|---|
| 12. | Age at the time of marriage | | | |
| | Male | 16–18 | 16–19 | 17–18 |
| | Female | 15–17 | 15–18 | 16–17 |
| 13. | Birth rate | 52.5 | 51.7 | 55.56 |
| 14. | Death rate | 28.64 | 27.1 | 30.89 |
| 15. | Rate of increase in population | 23.9% | 24.6% | 15.43% |

*Source:* Survey Data.

### *Kamar (PVTG)*

In Chhattisgarh, a Kamar tribe is supposed to have been derived from Dev Dongar. The Kamar primitive tribe people mainly habitate in Gariyabandh, Menpur and Chhura talukas of Raipur district and Nagari Vikaskhand of Dhamtari district.

Their occupation is primitive agriculture work and making of baskets from bamboo chips. They hunt small birds and animals. They collect minor forest products like vegetable roots, Mahuda, Tendu leaves, Char, Salbij, Gond, Amla, Tikhood, Vaichandi, etc. and sell them. Due to prohibition on Bevara farming, now they have been engaged in steady agriculture work.

Those Kamars who habitate in hills are called 'Pahad-Patiya' and those habitating in forests are called 'Bunder-Jiwo'. Their main family names (gotras) are Netam, Markam, Marai, Kunjam, Sodhi, Jagat, etc. At the time of engagement or marriage, the boy-family has to give rice, *dal*, clothes, *haldi*, oil, jaggery, wine and some cash amount also to the bride's family. The marriage ceremony of Kamar tribe is performed in the presence of old persons of the tribe. They worship Kachana Ghurwo, Boodha dev, Takur dev, Boodhi Mai, Dharti Mata, (the mother earth), Pogari devta, Kul devta (the family Gods), Magar Mati (the dust from the place of ancestor) and Gata Dooma (the ancestors). Their main festivals are Navakhani, Dussehra, Diwali, Holi, etc. Their main folk dances are Karma, Sua, Diwali dance, Rahas, Bihavnucha etc. Similarly, their folk songs are Karma, Sua, Dadariya, Jash, Fag, Bhajan, etc.

**Table 4**

*Work-Force in Surveyed Families*

| *Sr. No.* | *Details* | *Kolgha (Dharampur, Guj.)* | | *Varli Dharampur Guj.)* | | *Kamar (Gariyaband, Chhattisgarh)* | |
|---|---|---|---|---|---|---|---|
| | | *Male* | *Female* | *Male* | *Female* | *Male* | *Female* |
| 1. | Working | 121<br>(56.86) | 120<br>(58.25) | 123<br>(62.12) | 125<br>(60.10) | 49<br>(64.96) | 92<br>(64.79) |
| 2. | Non-Working | 92<br>(43.19) | 86<br>(44.53) | 75<br>(37.88) | 83<br>(39.90) | 48<br>(35.04) | 50<br>(35.21) |
| | Total | 213<br>(100.0) | 206<br>(100.0) | 198<br>(100.0) | 208<br>(100.0) | 137<br>(100.0) | 142<br>(100.0) |

**Table 5**

*Land Holding Among Surveyed Families*

| *Sr. No.* | *Details* | *Kolgha (Dharmpur (Guj.)* | *Varli (Dharampur Guj.)* | *Kamar Gariyaband, Chhattisgarh* |
|---|---|---|---|---|
| 1. | Landless | 11 (14.3) | 11 (13.41) | 12 (24.0) |
| 2. | Marginal farmers (1–3 acres) | 53 (68.8) | 57 (69.51) | 28 (56.0) |
| 3. | Small farmers (3.5 acres) | 5 (6.5) | 8 (9.76) | 4 (8.0) |
| 4. | Medium farmers (5.10 acres) | 7 (9.1) | 3 (3.66) | 6 (12.0) |
| 5. | Big farmers (more than 10 acres) | 1 (1.3) | 3 (3.66) | – |
| | Total | 77 (100) | 82 (100) | 50 (100) |

**Table 6**

*Average Agriculture Product per Acre Among Surveyed Families (Kgms)*

| *Sr. No.* | *Produce* | *Kolgha (Dharampur, Gujarat)* | *Varli (Dharampur, Gujarat)* | *Kamar Gariyaband, Chhattisgarh)* |
|---|---|---|---|---|
| 1. | Nagli | 650 | 650 | – |
| 2. | Varli | 300 | 300 | – |
| 3. | Crude Crops | 500 | 600 | 800 |
| 4. | Juwar | 250 | 300 | – |
| 5. | Urad | 150 | 200 | 150 |
| 6. | Tover | 150 | 150 | – |
| 7. | Kharsani | 150 | 150 | – |

## Food Related Habits

### *Kolghas and Varlis*

The main food items among Kolgha tribe people is loaf made from *nagli* and sauce of chilly. Sometimes, they prepare vegetables and *dal*-rice also. They prepare food in the morning and evening but consume thrice a day, viz., morning, noon and night. In monsoon, when they do not have any foodgrains left, they also consume *mahuwa* flower, onions and raw vegetables from the forest. They do consume forest-grown vegetables, *kurdu, vasadi, tera* and other seasonal vegetables also. In non-vegetarian food, they consume fish, chicken, goat, pig, tortoise, turtle, guana, lizard, fox, hare and any kind of bird. But all these are available on few occasions only. They also consume wine prepared from mahuwa and jaggary.

### *Kamar*

The food for Kamar tribe people is rice, *pej, urad, dal* made from green bin, vegetable roots, kadukanda, kusum vegetables, other vegetables produced in forest area, vegetables from kitchen garden or from farms, fish, chicken, birds, rat and mouse, hare, etc. Adults eat twice a day whereas children and adolescents eat three-four times a day. They also consume liquor made from *mahuwa*.

Due to crops during monsoon, all the three tribes do get adequate quantity of foodgrains during winter; but the quantity gets reduced during summer and gets further reduced during monsoon. As a substitute, sometimes they consume roots available in forests or vegetables. The quantity available to them in respect of milk, oil, sugar, meat, fish, eggs and vegetables is much less than the prescribed quantity. Similarly, pulses are also consumed in lesser quantity.

All these three tribes get much inadequate quantity of calorie, proteins, carbohydrates, riboflavine, niacin, etc. Similarly, they get less quantity of vitamin A and vitamin C. Both Varli and Kolgha get adequate quantity of calcium and iron; but Kamar tribe gets it in inadequate quantity. The reason for this is obvious. Both Varli and Kolgha consume *nagli* (ragi) in their food and it is a great source of calcium.

## Daily Availability of Food Items

Only monsoon crops are available to tribals in winter. Shortage is felt in summer and more during monsson. Tribals use roots and leaves to compensate this shortage. Milk, oil, sugar, mutton, fish, egg and vegetables are found much less among tribals.

## Nutrients

Calorie, protein, carbohydrate, and riboflavin are available in less amount to all the three tribes. Vitamin A and C are found to be even lesser. Calcium and iron are found in sufficiencies among Varli and Kolgha, not among Kamar. Ragi being staple diet among Varli and Kolgha is the reason for this.

**Table 7**

*Availability of Food Items to ST Males (in grams)*

| | *Food items (grams)* | *Quantity (DRA)* | *Kolgha (Dharampur, Gujarat)* | | | *Varli (Dharampur Gujarat)* | | | *Kamar (Gariyaband, Chhattisgarh)* | | |
|---|---|---|---|---|---|---|---|---|---|---|---|
| | | | *Winter* | *Summer* | *Rain* | *Winter* | *Summer* | *Rain* | *Winter* | *Summer* | *Rain* |
| 1. | Food grain | 520 | 641.4 | 505.9 | 410.8 | 655.0 | 516.4 | 418.0 | 530.5 | 325.2 | 211.4 |
| 2. | Pulses (Dal) | 70 | 60.0 | 23.7 | 14.0 | 74.0 | 31.8 | 20.0 | 35.0 | 22.6 | 12.5 |
| 3. | Green vegetables | 125 | 21.2 | 6.5 | 53.7 | 28.4 | 14.6 | 60.0 | 26.2 | 20.1 | 50.2 |
| 4. | Other vegetables | 75 | 69.7 | 31.5 | 11.5 | 76.0 | 38.6 | 20.5 | 29.3 | 20.5 | 16.3 |
| 5. | Vegetable roots | 100 | 6.9 | 1.5 | 22.9 | 10.2 | 3.4 | 30.8 | 20.0 | 18.5 | 46.4 |
| 6. | Fruits | 30 | 8.8 | 15.3 | 10.4 | 11.2 | 20.7 | 16.2 | 6.4 | 15.8 | 8.2 |
| 7. | Meat, Fish & Eggs | 60 | 8.9 | 3.6 | 16.8 | 10.6 | 6.4 | 20.1 | 11.4 | 10.2 | 15.6 |
| 8. | Milk (ml.) | 100 | 6.6 | 6.4 | 6.8 | 7.4 | 6.0 | 8.6 | 4.3 | 4.0 | 4.2 |
| 9. | Oil | 50 | 4.6 | 3.4 | 3.8 | 4.8 | 3.2 | 4.0 | 3.1 | 2.9 | 2.8 |
| 10. | Sugar, Jaggery (*Gur*) | 35 | 7.3 | 6.2 | 3.1 | 7.6 | 6.6 | 3.2 | 4.8 | 4.2 | 4.0 |

**Table 8**

*Availability of Food Items to ST Females (in grams)*

| | Food items (grams) | Quantity (DRA) | Kolgha (Dharampur, Gujarat) | | | Varli (Dharampur Gujarat) | | | Kamar (Gariyaband, Chhattisgarh) | | |
|---|---|---|---|---|---|---|---|---|---|---|---|
| | | | Winter | Summer | Rain | Winter | Summer | Rain | Winter | Summer | Rain |
| 1. | Food grain | 440 | 446.0 | 399.8 | 325.1 | 455.0 | 411.4 | 330.0 | 390.4 | 283.6 | 210.5 |
| 2. | Pulses (Dal) | 65 | 45.4 | 21.2 | 12.4 | 51.6 | 21.8 | 15.6 | 28.1 | 20.8 | 12.3 |
| 3. | Green vegetables | 125 | 18.6 | 6.2 | 43.8 | 20.4 | 6.8 | 45.6 | 34.0 | 30.0 | 48.2 |
| 4. | Other vegetables | 75 | 56.2 | 26.4 | 10.2 | 60.4 | 26.8 | 10.8 | 26.6 | 19.0 | 16.8 |
| 5. | Vegetable roots | 75 | 6.2 | 1.3 | 19.3 | 7.1 | 2.0 | 20.2 | 13.0 | 12.4 | 31.0 |
| 6. | Fruits | 30 | 8.8 | 15.3 | 10.4 | 9.4 | 16.0 | 11.0 | 5.6 | 3.8 | 4.2 |
| 7. | Meat, Fish & Eggs | 60 | 8.6 | 3.4 | 16.3 | 8.8 | 4.6 | 17.0 | 8.3 | 6.8 | 12.4 |
| 8. | Milk (ml.) | 100 | 6.6 | 6.4 | 6.8 | 6.7 | 6.4 | 6.8 | 5.1 | 4.3 | 5.0 |
| 9. | Oil | 40 | 4.4 | 3.3 | 3.6 | 4.8 | 3.6 | 4.0 | 3.1 | 2.6 | 2.4 |
| 10, | Sugar, Jaggery (*Gur*) | 30 | 7.3 | 6.2 | 3.1 | 7.2 | 6.4 | 3.4 | 4.5 | 3.2 | 2.6 |

**Table 9**

*Availability of Nutrients to ST Males (in grams)*

| | Food items (grams) | Quantity (DRA) | Kolgha (Dharampur, Gujarat) | | | Varli (Dharampur Gujarat) | | | Kamar (Gariyaband, Chhattisgarh) | | |
|---|---|---|---|---|---|---|---|---|---|---|---|
| | | | Winter | Summer | Rain | Winter | Summer | Rain | Winter | Summer | Rain |
| 1. | Calorie | 3000 | 2820 | 2251 | 1749 | 2840 | 2262 | 1760 | 2656 | 2013 | 1547.5 |
| 2. | Protein | 70 | 70.6 | 53.9 | 37.7 | 73.8 | 57.6 | 39.8 | 59.9 | 50.2 | 35.2 |
| 3. | Fat | 22 | 10.6 | 9.1 | 7.2 | 11.4 | 9.8 | 7.6 | 8.2 | 7.6 | 4.0 |
| 4. | Carbohydrate | 493 | 586.5 | 483.2 | 364.5 | 592.4 | 494.0 | 370.6 | 498.6 | 461.3 | 344.8 |
| 5. | Calcium (mg.) | 500 | 1300 | 1200 | 1100 | 1380 | 1260 | 1150 | 465.5 | 386.2 | 311.4 |
| 6. | Iron (mg.) | 24 | 29.7 | 23.1 | 22.7 | 30.8 | 24.2 | 23.4 | 24.8 | 20.6 | 19.0 |
| 7. | Carotene (mg.) | 2400 | 304.3 | 270.7 | 1998 | 308.5 | 268.4 | 872.6 | 1376 | 834 | 1296.3 |
| 8. | Thiamin (mg.) | 1.2 | 20.0 | 1.5 | 1.3 | 2.1 | 1.6 | 1.4 | 0.9 | 0.8 | 1.0 |
| 9. | Riboflavin (mg.) | 1.5 | 1.0 | 0.8 | 0.7 | 1.5 | 1.1 | 0.9 | 1.0 | 0.9 | 1.0 |
| 10. | Niacin (mg.) | 16 | 12.7 | 7.1 | 5.3 | 13.2 | 7.6 | 5.7 | 9.6 | 9.2 | 8.8 |
| 11. | Vitamin C (Ascorbic Acid mg.) | 40 | 12.0 | 8.2 | 31.6 | 14.6 | 8.9 | 32.2 | 22.8 | 18.3 | 21.6 |

**Table 10**

*Availability of Nutrients to ST Females (in grams)*

| Food items (grams) | Quantity (DRA) | Kolgha (Dharampur, Gujarat) | | | Varli (Dharampur Gujarat) | | | Kamar (Gariyaband, Chhattisgarh) | | |
|---|---|---|---|---|---|---|---|---|---|---|
| | | Winter | Summer | Rain | Winter | Summer | Rain | Winter | Summer | Rain |
| 1. Calorie | 2400 | 2257 | 1838 | 1622 | 2268 | 1846 | 1636 | 2148 | 1810 | 1311 |
| 2. Protein | 65 | 63 | 47.3 | 36.7 | 66.2 | 50.4 | 39.4 | 49.2 | 40.8 | 36.5 |
| 3. Fat | 22 | 10.2 | 8.9 | 7.0 | 10.4 | 9.1 | 7.0 | 8.1 | 7.4 | 3.9 |
| 4. Carbohydrate | 400 | 479 | 426 | 308 | 482 | 431 | 320 | 399 | 378 | 278 |
| 5. Calcium (mg.) | 1000 | 1265 | 1183 | 1056 | 1272 | 1188 | 1065 | 428 | 364 | 282 |
| 6. Iron (mg.) | 32 | 28.2 | 22.9 | 21.6 | 28.6 | 23.3 | 22.0 | 20.1 | 17.8 | 16.2 |
| 7. Carotene (mg.) | 2400 | 293.6 | 264.7 | 1865 | 302 | 260.4 | 861.2 | 1238 | 765 | 1039 |
| 8. Thiamin (mg.) | 1.2 | 1.6 | 1.4 | 1.1 | 1.6 | 1.4 | 1.2 | 0.9 | 0.8 | 1.0 |
| 9. Riboflavin (mg.) | 1.4 | 0.9 | 0.7 | 0.6 | 1.0 | 0.8 | 0.7 | 1.0 | 0.9 | 1.0 |
| 10. Niacin (mg.) | 16 | 11.6 | 6.8 | 5.1 | 11.7 | 6.8 | 5.2 | 9.5 | 9.2 | 8.7 |
| 11. Vitamin C (Ascorbic Acid mg.) | 40 | 10.8 | 8.1 | 30.2 | 11.0 | 8.3 | 31.4 | 22.5 | 18.1 | 20.3 |

## Malnutrition

Comparatively, more children below five years of age are suffering from malnutrition. Likewise, more women, as compared to men, suffer from malnutrition.

**Table 11**

*Women, Men and Children Suffering from Malnutrition (Body Mass Index – BMI)*

| *Sr. No.* | *Details* | *Age* | *Kolgha (Gujarat)* | *Varli (Gujarat)* | *Kamar (Chhattisgarh)* |
|---|---|---|---|---|---|
| 1. | Women | 15–49 | 73.4 | 72.8 | 68.6 |
| 2. | Men | 15–49 | 69.8 | 69.2 | 62.4 |
| 3. | Children | 0–5 | | | |
| | Boys | | 77.6 | 77.4 | 72.8 |
| | Girls | | 77.8 | 77.6 | 73.4 |
| 4. | Children | 5–14 | | | |
| | Boys | | 75.4 | 74.8 | 70.6 |
| | Girls | | 75.8 | 75.2 | 70.3 |

**Table 12**

*Percentage of Women and Men who are Anaemic*

| *Sr. No.* | *Details* | *Kolgha (Gujarat)* | *Varli (Gujarat)* | *Kamar (Chhattisgarh)* |
|---|---|---|---|---|
| 1. | Women | 79.9 | 79.1 | 82.8 |
| 2. | Men | 60.8 | 60.4 | 63.4 |

Thus, more women are anaemic than men.

## Main Factors which Affect the Food and Nutrition among Tribals

- Geographical factors
- Economic factors
- Social factors
- Cultural factors
- Religious factors
- Social beliefs and customs
- Education

## Hygiene and Sanitation

Both sanitation and hygiene are important factors affecting health.

**Table 13**

*Percentage of Facilities for Drinking Water and Toilets in Residential Areas of Scheduled Tribes (2011)*

| *Details* | *India* | *Gujarat* | *Chhattisgarh* |
|---|---|---|---|
| Safe Drinking Water | | | |
| – in residential areas | 19.7 | 28.8 | 9.1 |
| – at far away place | 33.6 | 24.8 | 33.2 |
| Toilet | 22.6 | 24.3 | 14.8 |

## Morbidity Frequency among Tribals

Both in Gujarat and Chhattisgarh, many incidences of malaria, diarrhoea, typhoid, cough, coryza and cold, skin diseases, gonorrheal infection, liver pain, arthritis were found. There are more number of people suffering from sickle cell anaemia also.

## Health Services

Both in Gujarat and Chhattisgarh, we find fewer doctors and specialists PHCs and CHCs. Table 14 shows this:

**Table 14**

*Availability of Health Services*

| *Details* | *Required No.* | *Sanctioned Posts* | *In-Shortfall Position* | |
|---|---|---|---|---|
| Gujarat | | | | |
| 1.1 Doctors | | | | |
| (PHCs) | 358 | 342 | 242 | 116 |
| (CHCs) | 70 | – | – | 70 |
| 1.2 Specialists (CHCs) | | | | |
| – Paediatrician | 70 | 5 | – | 70 |
| – Gynaecologist | 70 | 5 | – | 70 |
| – Physicians | 70 | – | – | – |
| – Surgeon | 70 | 2 | – | 70 |
| Chhattisgarh | | | | |
| 2.1 Doctors | | | | |
| (PHC) | 403 | 365 | 170 | 233 |
| (CHC) | 84 | 82 | 9 | 75 |

*Cont'd...*

*...Cont'd*

| | | | | | |
|---|---|---|---|---|---|
| 2.2 | Specialists (CHC) | 336 | 328 | 24 | 307 |
| – | Paediatrician | 84 | 82 | 11 | 73 |
| – | Gynaecologist | 84 | 82 | 5 | 79 |
| – | Physician | 84 | 82 | 9 | 75 |
| – | Surgeon | 84 | 82 | 4 | 80 |

*Source:* RHS – 2012 Statistical Profile of ST in India, 2011.

## Suggestions

1. Adequate quality of food items and pulses, etc., considering their needs and culture should be made available to BPL families in Scheduled Area at low prices with special government subsidy.
2. In ashram-shalas, for the use of students, vegetables and fruits like papaya, guava, mango, amla, chikoo, etc. be grown.
3. In mid-day meals, the shortfall in vitamins A and C and calcium, protein, iron, etc. be compensated with use of ragi (Nagli), soyabean, groundnut, jaggery, cabbage, *amla*, etc.
4. More attention should be drawn towards the need of pure drinking water as well as to hygiene and sanitation. This can prevent diarrhoea, typhoid, malaria, jaundice, etc.
5. The shortfall of doctors in Scheduled Areas should be addressed to. The doctors, medical officers, para-medical staff appointed in Scheduled Areas should be provided with special incentive allowance; and additional facilities.
6. In revised guidelines issued by Ministry of Health and Family Welfare, Government of India, in 2012, there is a provision for one ayurvedic doctor and pharmacist along with allopathic doctor in a PHC. If this is followed in each PHC in Schedule Areas, the remote Scheduled Area people will get services of an ayurvedic doctor (Medical Officer, AYUSH).
7. There is also a need for increasing the frequency of mobile dispensaries in Scheduled Areas.
8. There is a need for more awareness for medical check-up of pregnant women, institutionalized delivery and immunization in Schedule areas.
9. Along with identification of sickle cell anaemia and other hereditary diseases, there is also a need for counselling and bringing awareness among the people.

# 11

# Educated Society vs. Dowry Custom in Meena Tribes of Rajasthan

## A Case Study

**Suman Meena**

In present time, the dowry has become a burning issue in the Indian society, its as level continuously increases at the unforeseen levels, among the Hindus of India. Mostly, in northern India dowry became a tradition. Dowry means to give gifts to bride at the time of her wedding. In recent years, it has become commonplace and is widely spread even in educated society and it increases as education level upgrades and jobs increases among people. Dowry is groom price at which he can be purchased according his qualifications by bride's parents. In the Indian society, working men's prices are fixed for their marriage. Young generation men also demand dowry to marry because it has become mentality of people that jobs with huge salary will make them to demand huge dowry. Indian society is a male dominant society and females depend on them for whole life; before marriage females depend on their fathers and brothers and after marriage depend on husband. Due to this dependence, they could not oppose the home violence because after marriage woman's home is husband's, not father home; there is commonly known words that 'a woman enter in husband's home in 'doli' and goes out from his home at 'sanati' only. In other words, a woman leaves husband's home when she dies not before and it is a custom very well followed still in Indian society.

Dowry is a social custom in Rajasthan, which is known for its traditional culture and customs. Dowry cases also increased continuously, according to Indian Penal Code (IPC), the homicide for dowry and dowry for deaths or their attempts come under Sections 302/304-B and cruelty by husband, and relatives come under Section 498-A (IPC) recorded that in 2012, 8,233 and 1,06,527 cases respectively during this year over all India. Torture (cruelty by husband or his relatives crime rate recorded 18.2 per cent at the national level whether Tripura reported highest crime rate 47.8 per cent and Rajasthan reported 12.5 per cent crime rate and 13,312 cases. Dowry increased the divorce problem in society which disturbed social system.

In Rajasthan, of the total population 13.5 per cent is Schedule Tribes, Meena caste's population is highest among all tribal castes. Education level in Meena tribes is higher in comparison to other tribes of Rajasthan. In Rajasthan economy, 50 per cent share is of service sector, whereas 80 per cent people engaged in organized sector would be from Meena castes. Meena people occupy in organized sector lowest to highest post, like peon to IAS officer. In spite of this, the dowry system is a social custom in Meenas. This community is divided in two parts – (1) *Zamindar* Meena, (2) *Chokidar* Meena.

The *Zamindar* Meena are traditionally engaged in agriculture sector for their livelihood and they claim themselves as Kshaṭriya equivalent to that of Rajputs. In the local socio-ritual hierarchy, they enjoy *a* clean caste status.

*Chokidar* Meena, who during the middle ages adopted fighting in armies, Britishers enforced them to report on choukis regularly to ensure that they do not indulge in any criminal activities. Therefore, they came to be known as *chokidar* Meena. *Chokidar* Meena mostly are inhabitant of Shekhawati region of Rajasthan state.

In Rajasthan, Meena tribes constitute in Jaipur, Dausa, Bandikui, Sawai Madhopur, Kota and Bundi, Bharatpur, Alwar, Karauli, Pratapgarh, Sikar, Churu and Jhunjhunu. The problem arise that the education level and salary oriented jobs in Meena tribes increases the problem of dowry, and mindset towards dowry changed by education level.

### *Objectives*

To determine whether education level changes the mentality of Meenas towards dowry custom. To find out dowry amount demanded according to salary grade pay in Meena society.

### *Hypothesis*

1. Higher education level reduced the dowry demand.
2. Increasing grade pay in jobs reduced the dowry demand.

### Literature Review

A another study also highlighted that there is a link between domestic violence and dowry demands; wife abuse has been found to be higher when a husband and/or his family believes dowry payments are inadequate (Banerjee, 1999; Bloch and Rao, 2002). Some studies highlight that 'Dowry Prohibition Act' failed because in this Act there are provisions that allows gifts to be given at the time of wedding thus providing a loop whereby the parties to a marriage can claim that transfers are gifts and not dowry. Moreover, according to the Act, since both giving and taking of dowry are illegal so, the family of a bride who is being harassed or abused over insufficient dowry and will implicate themselves by complaining (Basu, 2001; Diwan and Diwan, 1995; Shenk, 2007). Study of Caldwell, Reddy, and Caldwell also highlighted that educational and work opportunities for men increased, parents preferred that their daughters marry educated men with urban jobs, such men have higher and certain incomes that are not subject to seasonal variations and paid monthly; wives of such men will be free from drudgery of rural work (Caldwell; Reddy and Caldwell, 1983). According to Gangrade and Chander (1995) the dowry system as it is practised today has become an instrument of oppression and torture for the bride, her parents (Gangrade and Chander, 1991). Ghansham focused on 'Dowry Prohibition Act' in 1961 and this Act was future amended in 1985 to control this menace. Despite this Act, the 'give and take' phenomenon of dowry is practised widely throughout India, irrespective of caste and class (Ghansham, 2002).

Haveripeth explained in his study that persons participating in dowry related violence are mostly mother-in-low and siblings of the husband. He also focused on study of Gautam and Trivedi in which they found that in a majority of cases, the husband and the mother-in-law of the victim played a leading role in planning and execution of violence against the bride. These crimes took place in society due to socially structured expectations about dowry giving the inferior status of women and consequently the low bargaining power of the women and her parents, and the growing urban consumerism among lower and middle class sections of the society as well as the lack of effective legal sanctions against such crimes and dowry-related violence, bride burning are not peculiar to India and beside husband and his kin also join together in abusing the bride as dowry and related customs provide a good excuse to them for disgracing, insulting and even beating up women (Haveripeth, 2013). The qualities of bride also significantly affect the size of dowry in Bangladesh for example the dowry increases in tandem with age at marriage, and placing pressure on parents to marry their daughters early. This may be especially true if the bride suffers from other disadvantages in the marriage market such as lower social status or darker skin tones (Huq and Amin, 2001; Islam and Mahmud, 1996).

Lindenbaum explained in his study that the switch from bride price to dowry in Bangladesh was necessarily a result of the shortage of men *per se* but rather increased high quality of grooms (Lindenbaum, 1981). Narsimhan explained in his research study that sometimes the dowry provided by the parents of the bride is seen insufficient, and demands for supplement items continue long after the couple is married (Narsimhan, 1994).

According to Negi study, the dowry is a transfer of property from bride's family to that of the bridegroom at time of marriage (Negi, 1997). In modern times, dowry has taken a new form and according to this form, it has come to include cash, jewellery and household items, and appliances, vehicles and it is often open-ended in nature (Puri, 1999; Van Willigen and Channa, 1991). Paul explained in his study that dowry is a practice of giving material gifts, cash to bridegroom and his kin and continues as such after marriage (Paul, 1986). According to Sachdeva, the dowry system has increased due to various socio-economic conflicts with serious consequences. There are various incidents of bride burning and harassment, physical torture of newly-wed women, and various kinds of pressure tactics adopted by the husbands/in-laws pressurizing for more dowry have obligated the social reformers and the intelligentsia to many aspects associated with the institution of dowry (Sachdeva, 1998). Another reason for dowry demand is the feeling of mother-in-law that when she herself brought dowry from her marriage then why she shouldn't take dowry for her son. Therefore, this may be the reason for so many mothers-in-law resorting to violence on their daughter-in-law and they do not feel shy of indulging in it (Sarvanan, 2002). Singh explained in his study that the bride is helpless in her new home and physically so powerless, consequently, she cannot protest against the pain tactics or actions of other, and not many women have the courage to divorce their husbands on the ground of mental or physical torture since they have nothing to fall back upon in a traditionally and poorly developed country like India (Singh, 2005). People rarely adhere to the legal provisions of making lists of gifts exchanged and thus may not have basis for reclaiming property when faced with the situation. Suran (et al.), in the study 'Does dowry improve life for brides', found that in Bangladesh married females who paid dowry at marriage', and had a higher likelihood of reporting local violence compared to those who did not. In fact, paying no dowry is just protective and if not more so, in terms of controlling abuse as the largest dowry payments (Suran et al., 2004).

## Methodology

Primary data is collected to determine education level and mindset of people towards dowry custom, job grade pay of people and dowry amount demanded in Meena tribes. Data collected with help of structured questionnaire and the sampling collected technique purposive sampling. The collected data would be coded, classified and tabulated, analysed with help of simple statistical tools. Result would be presented through graph and pictograph technique. Hypothesis would test at 99 per cent level of significance by two tailed distribution. The secondary data is collected from government reports, research papers, articles, newspaper, etc. Information would be collected from 60 people at the basis of their education level and job grade pay. This information is collected from Jaipur city where Meena castes constitute highly.

## Findings/Discussion

Information of 60 people are collected and classified according to education level and grade pay and dowry demanded amount in tables. Simple correlation is used to find relation between education level and responses who accepted dowry or demanded dowry, relation between job grade pay and dowry amount demanded.

**Table 1**

*Education Level and Dowry Demands Response of the People*

| *Education Level* | *12th* | *Graduation* | *Post Graduation* | *Total* |
|---|---|---|---|---|
| Yes | 3 | 32 | 19 | 54 |
| No | 2 | 3 | 1 | 6 |
| Total | 5 | 35 | 20 | 60 |

*Source:* Primary Data

Spearman's rank correlation measure to develop relationship between education level and dowry demand in education group given ranking and measure the difference between actual and predicted ranking of dowry demanded by the education group respondents, that is denoted by *dj*, n is number of units or number of ranking. So, education level ranking in ascending order giving ranking post graduation level 1st rank and graduation level 2nd rank and 12th level given to 3rd ranking. Graduated people are the highest in Meena tribes because government jobs mostly require graduated candidate so, according to the response of these people is highest, it is given 1st ranking and 2nd ranking is given to post graduate people, 3rd ranking given to 12th standard people. Formula applied get +.5 correlation between both variables.

**Figure 1**

*People Demand Dowry in Meena Tribes*

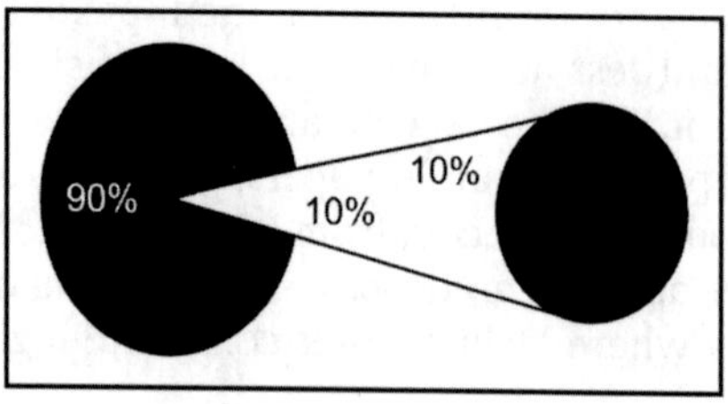


*Source:* primary data

It indicates that as education level of people increases the demand of dowry also increased in same ratio, master degree holder people highest replied: 'yes that they demanded dowry' only one among 20 refused that he/she not demanded. It is five per cent of master degree holders, while 95 per cent accepted that they demand dowry. It also finds that most of the people have graduation degree and 12th standard education level people are less than other people are.

**Table 2**

*Grade Pay and Dowry Amount in Meena Tribes*

| *Grade Pay (₹)* | *Dowry Amount (₹)* |
|---|---|
| 1,800 | 8,00,000 |
| 1,900 | 10,50,000 |
| 2,800 | 15,00,000 |
| 4,200 | 24,00,000 |
| 4,600 | 40,00,000 |
| 4,800 | 50,00,000 |
| 5,400 | 1,00,00,000 |
| 6,600 | 2,00,00,000 |

*Source:* primary data

**Figure 2**

*Grade Pay and Dowry Amount in Meena People*

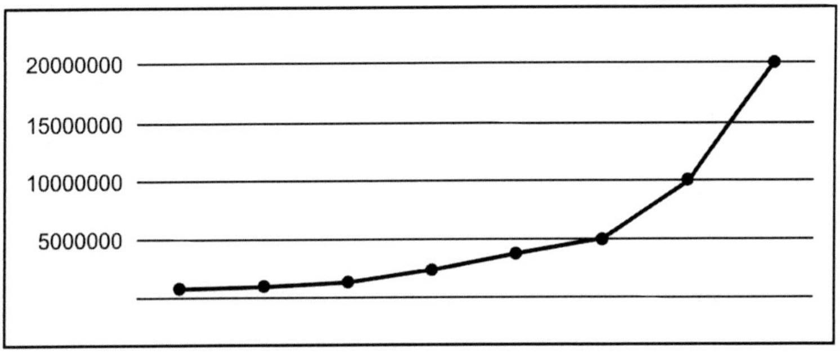


*Source:* primary data

This dowry amount is fixed by *zamindar* Meena while in *chokidar* Meena dowry amount is not fixed. As grade pay increases dowry amount which is demanded also increases. According to correlation calculation, there is a highly positive relationship between grade pay and dowry amount, +.99 correlation found. According to findings the hypothesis tested at the 99 per cent significance level of mean, one tailed test used-mean of sample – 18, sample standard deviation 14.53, and population size and mean are 60 and 20 respectively. T score test value find = –1.06,694, p value=0.1,430 which is less than the significance level 99, p value should be 0.1,990. Therefore, null hypothesis rejected and alternative hypothesis accepted that means there is no change in mentality of people to demand dowry while it shows that as education level increased the number of people demanding dowry also increased.

During the data collection, the people told that they face various problems to marry their daughters due to a high level of dowry amount. A widow women of *chokidar* Meena told that she was facing problem to marry her daughters because in *zamindar* Meena high dowry is demanded, she wants to marry her daughters to a government employed boy. There is a big competition to demand dowry because boys and their parents feel it upholds their status and standard in society that their son got huge dowry. Therefore, it has become a first deal between two parties to marry their children. In *zamindar* Meena marriage is decided but parents without asking the choice of girl and boy on the basis of dowry amount while in *chokidar* Meena first of all the choice is asked from both girl and boy and if they would like to marry, if they said yes then parents decide how much dowry amount would be given in marriage. Consequently, *chokidar* Meena are modern as compared to *zamindar* Meena. Another big difference in *chokidar* and *zamindar* Meena is dowry demand, *zamindar* Meena demand cash and vehicle, jewellery, etc. while *chokidar* Meena demand vehicle in dowry; *chokidar* Meena see qualifications of girls to get married to their sons. Although, in *chokidar* society also men dominate but not as much as *zamindar* Meena, in some cases love marriage is also accepted if both girl and boy love each other. Parents of girl want that their daughter's marriage should be in city and boy should have government jobs. The continued increase of demand of government servant for marriage indirectly increases the dowry amount in marriage market.

Girls' education has also increased but after for all the dowry amount is not reduced because boys do preparation government job to get huge dowry amount, so it became a style to upgrade their reputation in relatives and society. Education level could not help to reduce the difference between boys and girls.

This study is also similar to other studies which focus on dowry demanded as men's job standard increases and parents want to marry their daughters to high salaried and certain payment job. Therefore, government servant demand increases to marry girls or it has a direct relationship: demand of government jobs and dowry amount. Traditions and customs are constant. Therefore, in a developing country, education did not help to change the mentality of the people.

## Conclusion and Implications

It is concluded that dowry is a social custom and it became very difficult to change customs all of the sudden, practicing customs generates and strengthen unity, and cohesiveness among people. Many people give and take dowry only because their parents and forefathers had been practicing it. Until the time the younger generation gather courage to stop this practice and girls resist social pressure to take it, people will stick to this custom.

Meena tribes followed dowry customs significantly and demanded huge dowry. Everything is fixed according to job grade pay that to marry 1,800 grade pay men their parents have to pay ₹ 8 lakh dowry.

In this custom higher to lower offices of governments are involved. It is critical situation in zamindar Meena because young generation boy would marry a girl who does not have qualifications, which the boy wants but did marry. He did it due to family pressure or for dowry. Some cases found during study that either the man did marry another girl or filed divorce in court due to failure in creating mutual understanding between husband and wife. After all it is the loss of woman, and divorce destroys the life of children.

Education is not an effective factor in Meena tribe to change their mentality or counter social evils; consequently it would create fears to give birth to girl child. It would induce people to practice foeticide of girls. Because this amount will be increased continuously in future. Really it is a big issue for society and state. Dowry would affect the education of girls because parents will save money for their marriage to pay dowry amount because in India marriage is a necessary task for girls to live in society, people taunt the parents if they did not do marry their daughters at the early age. If girls did not marry then it became a big issue in society. In this 21st century Indian society, also a male-centred society, no caste far from this custom whether government have taken various step to stop dowry but still failed. There should be a change in Dowry Prohibition Act's provisions, which allows giving gifts to the bride at the time of marriage. Gift value should be considered in money value and this value should be fixed, because it became an inevitable custom in society without strict laws it could not be controlled. Court also should interfere in this custom and court marriage should be compulsory for each and every society and there should be maintained a menu of materials with their bills which are given to the bride at the time of marriage. It would be helpful to handle dowry cases in court and claiming dowry amount. It also helps to judge a dowry case legal or illegal. Court marriage will also reduce the child marriage problem. Government employed boys also should be banned if giving and taking dowry, if he/she indulge in this then he/she should be terminated at the time. It will create fear among people of losing their jobs. This step would help to reduce this problem significantly. There should be a committee to check the women's status at her husband's home, from newly married ones to those with 10 years of marriage because after that intensity of demand for dowry comes down. After marriage, it should be compulsory for the couple to appear in court and give their signatures, to prove that there is no conflict in their married life and everything is running smoothly.

## References


Banerjee, Kakoli. 'Gender Stratification and Marriage Market in India', *Journal of Family Issues*, Vol. 20, No. 5, 1999, pp. 648–676.

Basu, M. *Hindu Women and Marriage Law: From Sacrament to Contact*, Oxford University Press, Delhi, 2001.

Bloch, Francis and Rao, Vijayendra. 'Terror as a Bargaining Instrument: A Case Study of Dowry Violence in Rural India', *American Economic Review*, Vol. 92, No. 4, 2002, pp. 1029–1043.

Caldwell, J.C. Reddy, P. and Caldwell, P. 'The Causes of Marriage Change in South India', *Population Studies*, Vol. 37, 1983, pp. 343–361.

Proceedings of 11th International Business and Social Science Research Conference, 8–9 January 2015, Dubai, UAE.

Diwan, P. and Diwan P. *Dowry and Protection to Married Women* (3rd ed.), Deep and Deep Publications, New Delhi, 1995.

Gangrade, K.D. and Chander, H. 'The Dowry System in India', in S. Sewell and A. Kelly (eds) *Social Problems in the Asia Pacific Region*, pp. 260–263, *Encyclopedia Britannica,* Chicago, 1991.

Ghansham, D.M. Female Foeticide and the Dowry System in India, Townsville International Women's Conference, James Cook Univ, Australia, 2002.

Haveripeth, P.D. Causes, and Consequences of Dowry Menace in India: A Criminological Perspective, *RIJS*, Vol. 2, No. 2. (www.rierc.org), 2013.

Huq, Lopita and Amin, Sajeda. Dowry Negotiations and the Process of Union Formation in Bangladesh: Implications of Rising Education, Unpublished Manuscript.

Islam, M. Mazharul and Mahmud, Mamum 1996, Marriage Patterns and Some Issues Related to Adolescent Marriage in Bangladesh, *Asia-Pacific Population Journal,* Vol. 11, No. 3, 2001, pp. 27–42.

Lindebaum, Shirley. 'Implications for Women of Changing Marriage Transaction in Bangladesh', *Studies in Family Planning*, Vol. 12, No. 11, 1981, pp. 394–401.

Narsimhan, S. 'India: From Sati to Sex Determination', in M. Davis (ed.), *Women and Violence*, Zed Books, London, 1994, pp. 43–52.

Negi (C.F. Saravanan, S., 2002). Violence against Women in India: A Literature Review, Institute for Social Studies Trust, 1997.

Paul, M.C. *Dowry and Position of Women in India: A Study of Delhi Metropolis*, Inter-India Publications, New Delhi, 1986, p. 9.

Puri, D. Gift of a Daughter: Change and Continuity in Marriage Patterns among Two Generations of North Indians in Toronto and New Delhi, Unpublished Ph.D. Thesis, University of Toronto, 1999

Sachdeva (1998), C.F. Sarvanan S. (2000). Violence against Women in India: A Literature Review/Institute of Social Studies Trust.

Saravanan, S. *Violence Against Women in India: A Literature Review*, Institute of Social Studies Trust (ISS), 2002.

Suran, L. and S.H. and Choudhry, K. Does Dowry Improve Life for Brides? A Test of the Bequest Theory of Dowry in Rural Bangladesh, Population Council Research Division, *Working Paper Series No. 195,* 2004.

Shenk, M.K. Dowry and Public in Contemporary India, *Human Nature*, Vol. 18, 2007, pp. 242–263.

Singh, J.P. Dowry in India: Search of Social Identity, *The Eastern Anthropologist*, Vol. 58, No. 2, 2005, pp. 199–200.

Van Willigen, J. and Channa, V.C. 'Law, Custom and Crimes against Women: The Problem of Dowry Death in India', *Human Organisation*, Vol. 50, 1991, pp. 360–377.

# 12

# Tribal Education in Western India

## Issues and Implications

**Tattwamasi Paltasingh**

Education contributes immensely in human resource development and in economic development, which has been well recognized by research studies, the national policies of education and the Five Year Plans. Development of the government policy in the subsequent years, perceptions about education for tribal and measures taken by the government to address the situation – all these need to be considered with seriousness. The 93rd constitutional amendment has made education a fundamental right. Free and compulsory education for all children up to the age of 14 years was envisaged in the national policy on education, 1986, which was modified in 1992. A number of policies and programmes have been launched and separate thrust has been entrusted in different Five Year Plans. It is commonly comprehended that the society with higher percentage of literates has higher levels of development.

Universal elementary education has become a constitutional obligation of the state and a fundamental right of children with the enforcement of the RTE Act in 2009. The Act lays down rules and guidelines for minimum standards in providing free and compulsory primary education. Despite the several ambiguities and criticisms that limit or restrict the rights of children, the effective implementation of the RTE Act and the principle of the National Curriculum Framework (NCF, 2005) are still awaited across the regions. The Act is expected to be useful particularly to the children of marginalized communities like the SCs and the STs. The poor performance of ST community with respect to many developmental indicators including education and literacy is a matter of concern. Translating these guidelines into policy decisions and suitable implementations is an essential task. The future approach for education needs to reflect these issues with seriousness and commitment. There has to be dialogues with the Centre, state and local bodies on policy and implementation of quality Primary education among the ST children. This is important in order to bring genuine state accountability towards the deprived children, especially for the ST communities. With the help of available data, the paper is therefore intended at understanding the status of tribal education in India with a special focus on western India and to what extent the governments at the Centre and in the states are taking initiatives and applying their implementation strategies for the improvement of ST education.

The sizeable ST population in the different states assumes significance both in terms of socio-economic and political processes defining the context of developmental intrusion. The history of vulnerability and prolonged marginalization of the STs along with their present socio-economic conditions in terms of work-participation, education, health, livelihood etc. obstruct their inclusion in all developmental activities undertaken by the state. The imbalanced progress among various social groups is clearly evidenced in western states of India, where a large number of ST population reside. They need to be a productive partner in the development process (Joshi, 1998). Education plays a pivotal role in ensuring inclusive growth. Primary education plays a major role in economic development, as the return to primary education is the maximum followed by secondary and higher education (Tilak, 2007). Special attention should be directed towards education as a mechanism of achieving as well as a component of inclusive growth, which is also recognized by the Planning Commission in different Five Year Plans (Planning Commission, 2006, 2011). However, the efficiency and equity effects of education depend upon the level of both quantitative and qualitative expansion of schooling. Indian education system is stratified and there is clear reflection of hierarchical ideology based on caste, tribe, class and gender (Velaskar, 1992). Since elementary education has the highest impact on generation and distribution of income, there is a greater need for expansion of elementary education particularly in less developed regions and among marginalized population.

**Table 1**

*Literacy Rate of All Social Groups and ST Population (1961–2011)*

| *Year* | *All Social Groups* | | | *ST* | | | *Gap in Literacy (Total and ST)* |
|---|---|---|---|---|---|---|---|
| | *Male* | *Female* | *Total* | *Male* | *Female* | *Total* | |
| 1961 | 40.4 | 15.35 | 28.3 | 13.83 | 3.16 | 8.53 | 19.77 |
| 1971 | 45.96 | 21.97 | 34.45 | 17.63 | 4.85 | 11.30 | 18.15 |
| 1981 | 56.38 | 29.76 | 43.57 | 24.52 | 8.04 | 16.35 | 19.88 |
| 1991 | 64.13 | 39.29 | 52.21 | 40.65 | 18.19 | 29.60 | 22.61 |
| 2001 | 75.26 | 53.67 | 64.84 | 59.17 | 34.76 | 47.10 | 18.28 |
| 2011 | 80.89 | 64.64 | 72.99 | 68.53 | 49.35 | 58.96 | 14.03 |

*Source:* Census-Various Years

As shown in Table 1, in the years 1961, 1971, 1981, 1991, 2001 and 2011; the literacy rates of STs were 8.53 per cent, 11.30 per cent, 16.35 per cent, 29.60 per cent, 47.10 per cent and 58.96 per cent respectively. The gaps found in the literacy rate between the STs and all social groups was 19.77 per cent, 18.15 per cent, 19.88 per cent, 22.61 per cent, 18.28 per cent and 14.03 per cent, respectively, in these Census years. Despite many efforts the gaps remain noticeable in all the decades with some variations (MTA, 2013). The trend of enrollment of the tribal at different stages of education shows that there is a steady decadal rise. When compared with the Scheduled Castes (SCs) and the general categories, the growth of Scheduled Tribe enrollment is most steady. The gap between Scheduled Tribes and the other social groups in terms of access to school education has narrowed down, especially during the past decade. However, the gap still remains significant and it is a matter of concern. Region specific analysis of literacy status can reveal the issues pertaining to ST education and help in identifying the gaps and take policy measures. A comparative analysis of STs with their literacy status as well as the influencing factors in each of the selected states of western region is presented.

## Tribal Education in Western India

Socio-economic development among the tribes is not uniform. It can vary from one region to another region; between one tribe to another tribe; and even among different tribal sub-groups (Paltasingh and Paliwal, 2014). Education is one of the most important developmental indicators among any social group. In this section, the situation of tribal education in the western part of Indian states, including Gujarat, Madhya Pradesh, Maharashtra and Rajasthan is reflected. There is substantial concentration of tribal population in all these states. With regard to population size, the tribal population constitutes 21.08 per cent in Madhya Pradesh, 9.35 per cent in Maharashtra, 13.47 per cent in Rajasthan, and 14.75 per cent in Gujarat to the total population of India. The analysis of total Scheduled Tribes population in all these four states explains that percentage of total Scheduled Tribes population has increased in all states during 2001–11, except in Gujarat where it has not recorded any change between these two Census years. These four states are among the top five thickly populated tribal states of India. However, in the ranking of the literacy rate of ST population, Gujarat occupies 17th position with 62.5 per cent tribal literacy, MP occupies 29th rank with 50.6 per cent literacy, Maharashtra occupies 15th position with a literacy rate of 65.7 per cent, and Rajasthan occupies 25th position with 52.8 per cent literacy rate among the STs (Census, 2011). Hence, the ranking in terms of density of ST population and ranking in ST literacy rate in these states depict a wide variation. The literacy rate of STs in India and the four western states, namely Gujarat, Madhya Pradesh, Maharashtra and Rajasthan is lower than the literacy rate of all social groups in these states during last three decades (Table 2).

**Table 2**

*Literacy Rate of Total and ST Population (India/Western India: 1991–2011)*

| *Sr. No.* | *Country/ State* | *Literacy Rate-1991* | | *Gap in Literacy Rate* | *Literacy Rate-2001* | | *Gap in Literacy Rate* | *Literacy Rate 2011* | | *Gap in Literacy Rate* |
|---|---|---|---|---|---|---|---|---|---|---|
| | | *Total* | *ST* | | *Total* | *ST* | | *Total* | *ST* | |
| | INDIA | 52.2 | 29.6 | 22.6 | 64.8 | 47.1 | 17.7 | 73.0 | 59.0 | 14.0 |
| 1 | Gujarat | 61.3 | 36.4 | 24.9 | 69.1 | 47.7 | 21.4 | 78.0 | 62.5 | 15.6 |
| 2 | Madhya Pradesh | 44.7 | 18.4 | 26.3 | 63.7 | 41.2 | 22.6 | 69.3 | 50.6 | 18.8 |
| 3 | Maharashtra | 64.9 | 36.8 | 28.1 | 76.9 | 55.2 | 21.7 | 82.3 | 65.7 | 16.6 |
| 4 | Rajasthan | 38.6 | 19.4 | 19.2 | 60.4 | 44.7 | 15.8 | 66.1 | 52.8 | 13.3 |

*Source:* Registrar General of India, Census, 1991, 2001, 2011.

The gap in the literacy rate between total population and ST population has consistently reduced in each decade in India and in each of these four states. However, in India, there is still 14 per cent gap in literacy rate between the total population and STs, despite several initiatives with schemes and provisions. States like Gujarat and Maharashtra have the literacy rate among STs more than India with 62.5 per cent and 65.7 per cent literacy, respectively. Among the tribal dominated states in western region, Madhya Pradesh and Rajasthan are having lower literacy rates i.e. 50.6 per cent and 52.8 per cent, respectively, than the country's literacy rate (58.96%) for ST population (Census, 2011). Both these states require additional efforts to increase the literacy level and make it comparable at least with the national level.

**Table 3**

*Male and Female Literacy Rate of All Social Groups and STs – Selected States*

| *Sr. No.* | *Country/ State* | *All Social Groups* | | | | *ST* | | | |
|---|---|---|---|---|---|---|---|---|---|
| | | *Male* | *Female* | *Total* | *Gender Gap* | *Male* | *Female* | *Total* | *Gender Gap* |
| | India | 80.89 | 64.64 | 72.99 | 16.25 | 68.53 | 49.35 | 58.96 | 19.18 |
| 1 | Gujarat | 85.75 | 69.68 | 78.03 | 16.07 | 71.68 | 53.16 | 62.48 | 18.52 |
| 2 | Madhya Pradesh | 78.73 | 59.24 | 69.32 | 19.49 | 59.55 | 41.47 | 50.55 | 18.08 |
| 3 | Maharashtra | 88.38 | 75.87 | 82.34 | 12.51 | 74.27 | 57.02 | 65.73 | 17.25 |
| 4 | Rajasthan | 79.19 | 52.12 | 66.11 | 27.07 | 67.62 | 37.27 | 52.80 | 30.35 |

*Source:* (As per 2011 Census), Office of the Registrar General and Census Commissioner, India.

There is a huge gap between the male and female literacy rate in all the four states, and the highest gap is found in Rajasthan (Table 3). Along with other educational indicators, regional and gender disparities are noticeable in enrollment and retention. Due to special measures adopted by several state governments in the past decade, the rate of decadal growth of enrollment of girls at the national level as well as at state level have been higher, but gender disparities still persist in both retention and enrollment. The gender gap is more prominent among the ST students in all these four states. The subsequent section has concentrated on the literacy and educational issues of the ST children in each of the states in western region with specific focus.

## Status of ST Education and Literacy in Gujarat

The Scheduled Tribe population of Gujarat as per 2011 Census constitutes 14.75 per cent of the total population of the state. The state has registered 19.2 per cent decadal growth of the Scheduled Tribe population during 2001–2011. There are 32 notified Scheduled Tribes in the state. The major Particularly Vulnerable Tribal Groups (PTGs) in the state includes Kathodi, Kotwalia, Padhar, Siddi and Kolgha. There are 26 districts in Gujarat (now 33) and the tribal population is largely concentrated in Dangs, Panchmahal, Banaskantha, Surat, Bharuch, Valsad and Vadodara districts. Among the tribal dominated states in western region, nine districts of Gujarat are with more than 25 per cent of ST population and the range of the literacy rate of Scheduled Tribes in these districts is between 53.8 per cent in Dahod and 74.6 per cent in Navsari district (Census, 2011). The Scheduled Tribe populations in Gujarat migrate to other districts and states due to lack of sustained employment opportunities. Scarcities of water in some tribal regions affect the agricultural and allied activities adversely (Paltasingh and Paliwal, 2014). Tribal groups migrate to other districts and cities, especially during November to May as agricultural labourers, brick kiln workers, sugarcane cutters, mill workers and construction workers. The process of educational development has some positive impacts and the disadvantaged tribal groups have benefitted from various government initiatives in the tribal districts. However, the disparity still persists with 19.18 per cent gender gap in literacy rate among the STs at the national level and 18.52 per cent in Gujarat. The educational needs and problems of tribal communities are to be appropriately identified. The efforts to enhance their educational status need to be done with participation and as per their requirement.

### *Initiatives for Promoting ST Education*

Dictionaries in Dangi and Bhili dialects are developed for the ST students. A local language glossary in Dangi has been prepared and distributed in schools for classes I-IV in Dang district.

Similarly a local word glossary in *adivasi* dialect has been prepared for class I-IV in Banaskantha district and circulated in schools. The Vidyasahayaks were given training on the use of these dictionaries. Gujarat government has also initiated work for preparation of Teaching Learning Materials (TLMs) in tribal languages. The TLMs developed include flash cards for different languages and also cards for simple mathematics. However the print materials and the word vocabularies in the tribal languages for primary classes developed by the initiative of Tribal Welfare Department and other agencies were used rarely as supplementary reading materials in the schools. Children need to be encouraged to use these materials with genuine interest (Paltasingh, 2014). Lot more efforts are required for developing tribal language and education. Special attention should be given to the migrant ST students as dislocation adversely affects their education and learning process.

## Status of ST Education and Literacy in Madhya Pradesh

There are 50 districts in the Madhya Pradesh and the tribal population is largely concentrated in Jhabua, Mandla, Surguja, Bastar, Dhar, Khargone, Khandwa, Ratlam, Betul, Sconi, Balaghat, Hoshangabad, Raigarh, Bilaspur, Durg, Rajnandgaon, Raipur, Morena and Chhindwara districts. The Scheduled Tribe (ST) population of MP as per 2011 Census constitutes 21.08 per cent of the total population of the state. The state has registered 25.2 per cent decadal growth of the Scheduled Tribe population during 2001–2011. There are forty-six notified Scheduled Tribes in the state. The major Particularly Vulnerable Tribal Groups (PTGs) in the state includes Abujh Marias, Baigas, Bharias, Hill Korbas, Kamars, Saharias and Birhor. Among the tribal dominated states in western region, Madhya Pradesh has the maximum number of districts (18) with more than 25 per cent of ST population and the range of the literacy rate of Scheduled Tribes in these districts is between 32.4 per cent in Alirajpur and 62.7 per cent in Seoni district. The district-wise percentage of total Scheduled Tribes population of Madhya Pradesh indicates that ranking of districts have not changed much over the period of last three decades. The districts of Alirajpur, Jhabua, Dindori, Barwani and Mandla retain the top five ranks in 1991, 2001 and 2011. In the similar way Datia, Morena and Bhind occupy the last three places throughout the three decades. From the comparative analysis of number of literates and literacy rates, it is revealed that Madhya Pradesh (MP) has lower literacy rates among the total and in rural as well as urban population than in India during 2001 and 2011. The quality education in MP remains a question. In remote and inaccessible areas, absenteeism among teachers and students for longer duration is noticed by Ramachandran and Naorem (*EPW*, 2013)

### *Initiatives*

In Madhya Pradesh, teachers' handbooks called Bridge Language Inventory (BLIs) have been prepared in three tribal languages, viz. Gondi (Shahdol and Betul district), Kuduk, (Raigarh) and Bhili (Dhar district). Training was given to identified teachers for use of BLIs in classroom transaction. The teaching-learning package called 'Dham Dhama Dham' was translated into Gondi and supplementary reading material 'Kopal' was developed for tribal children. The class I textbook 'Bharati' has been translated into tribal languages. Supplementary TLM for tribal children has been developed in Jhabua district using local cultural practices, i.e. folk tales, songs, proverbs, riddles to make the learning process interesting. Teachers from the tribal dominated regions are also trained to use the supplementary materials.

There are other schemes like Antyodaya Anna Yojana and mid-day meals, though not exclusively introduced for ST community, but has made substantial contribution in the form of food security to the parents as well as the children of under-privileged families including SCs and STs. Despite poor outreach, inadequate infrastructure and poor quality of food, these schemes have contributed in increasing the enrollment and attendance among the students in tribal dominated districts (Jain and Shah, 2005). A lot more is to be done with only 50.6 per cent ST literacy rate in Madhya Pradesh, which depicts the lowest literacy rate in the western region.

## Status of ST Education and Literacy in Maharashtra

The Scheduled Tribe (ST) population of Maharashtra as per 2011 Census constitutes 9.35 per cent of the total population of the state. The state has registered 22.5 per cent decadal growth of the

Scheduled Tribe population in 2001–2011. There are 36 districts in the Maharashtra state and the tribal population is largely concentrated in the western hilly districts of Dhule, Nandurbar, Jalgaon, Nashik and Thane (Sahyadri Region) and the eastern forest districts of Chandrapur, Gadchiroli, Bhandara, Gondia, Nagpur, Amravati and Yavatmal (Gondwana Region). There are 47 notified Scheduled Tribes in the state. The major Particularly Vulnerable Tribal Groups (PTGs) in the state include Katkaria (Kathodia), Kolam and Maria Gond. Among the tribal dominated states in western region, four districts of Maharashtra have more than 25 per cent of ST population and the range of the literacy rate of Scheduled Tribes in these districts is between 59 per cent in Dhule and 68 per cent in Gadchiroli district (Census, 2011).

Maharashtra has witnessed imbalanced development with regard to communities and regions. The main source of livelihood of STs in Maharashtra includes agricultural activities, wage labour, animal husbandry and dependency on forest products (Chattopadhyay and Durdhawale, 2009). Migration issue is very much evident among the STs. Landless tribes such as Katkaris and Dhor usually migrate to other districts for a period of six to eight months and get informally employed in brick kilns, sugarcane fields, mills, etc. They are accompanied by their children while migrating, for which the schooling gets affected. There is a need, therefore, to address the issue of sustainable employment opportunities in tribal areas. School teachers in inaccessible and tribal dominated areas of Amravati, Nandurbar, and Godchiroli find it difficult to converse in Marathi with Korkus, Bhils, Madiasand Gonds. There is a need to appoint local teachers with knowledge of both tribal dialect as well as Marathi in regular as well as in ashram schools.

### *Initiatives*

In Maharashtra, tribal language dictionaries have been developed. Language resource groups have been set up for Bhili, Pawara, Madia, Gondi, etc. Bridge material for ST students has been developed in Dhule district. These initiatives are not sufficient. Transportation is one of the major problems for teachers and students to come to the schools regularly. Community and school linkage need to be strengthened for better attendance and enrollment.

## Status of ST Education and Literacy in Rajasthan

Rajasthan is characterized by sharp variances in terms of topography, livelihood, patterns of settlement and social identity. The state does not have significant manufacturing industries or employment source. Agriculture and animal husbandry are the major sources of livelihood in rural Rajasthan. The economic class distinction in terms of income and resources is discrete. In such a situation ensuring universal education and making it relevant for all sections of society remain crucial. There are 33 districts in the Rajasthan and the tribal population is largely concentrated in Banswara, Dungarpur, Udaipur, Chittaurgarh and Sirohi districts. The Scheduled Tribe (ST) population of Rajasthan as per 2011 Census constitutes 13.47 per cent of the total population of the state. The state has registered 30.2 per cent decadal growth of the Scheduled Tribe population during 2001–2011. There are twelve notified Scheduled Tribes in the state. The major Particularly Vulnerable Tribal Groups (PTGs) in the state include Seharias.

Among the tribal dominated states in western region, Rajasthan has six districts with more than 25 per cent of ST population and the range of the literacy rate of Scheduled Tribes in these districts is between 32.9 (Sirohi) and 66.6 per cent (Dausa). The education of the girl child, especially among Scheduled Tribes and Scheduled Castes, is one of the core challenges in Rajasthan. It is important to address the socio-economic needs of the scheduled tribe population, giving them options for skill training and livelihood.

### *Initiatives*

In the Scheduled Areas, the state is taking initiative for skill development to enable the STs to offer employment opportunities through promoting training for vocational skills. Education Guarantee Scheme (EGS), initiated at Madhya Pradesh, is being extended to other states including Rajasthan to bridge the gap in literacy among the social groups. However, such scheme has partially addressed the need of the under-privileged STs. The state had started the Rajiv Gandhi Elementary Education and Literacy Mission to facilitate education in a mission mode. Para teachers (both male and female), identified by the community, are appointed for teaching at the primary school of the village. These teachers are given training by NGOs and District Institutes of Educational Training (DIET). This is to ensure that people with limited educational backgrounds can teach to the lower grade students. Evening schools are set up and 'Shiksha Karmi' in the local school is required to teach in addition to the responsibility at day schools (Jain and Kumar, 2013). This arrangement is meant for the children who are unable to attend schools during normal school hours, especially those who help their parents or accompany their parents for work. In difficult access areas or in the areas with scattered population, the 'Rajiv Gandhi Swarn Jayanti Pathshalas' scheme is in operation. These initiatives are positive steps for enhancing educational status; however, some of these are not sustainable with change in governance and lack of interest among the community members and parents as they are too occupied with their daily wage and livelihood issues.

## Issues and Challenges

Education is not just a medium for economic development; it can also contribute in promoting self-confidence and courage to face new challenges. Despite many development agendas, there are several areas which require serious attention. There are still a large number of schools which do not have minimum infrastructure, adequate number of teachers. While there has been increase in enrollment and decline in the percentage of out-of-school children across gender and social categories, tribal children still lag behind. They need focused attention in both enrollment and retention. From various large surveys, macro and micro studies, it has been broadly recognized that the socio-economic conditions and loss of livelihood among the STs have constrained the process of balanced development resulting in more deprivation among the STs (Xaxa, 2012). A large proportion of children from disadvantaged section are not able to complete even the initial years of primary schooling. This has been a scenario across Indian states. Persistent social inequalities based on caste, class and gender have been acknowledged as major causes of educational deficiency among children coming from deprived background (Dreze, 2003; Velaskar, 2005). Regular school attendance is a problem in the tribal areas even with reasonable infrastructure and student enrollment. This is pertinent in many tribal dominated districts of Gujarat (Paltasingh, 2014). A state like Madhya Pradesh has the lowest attendance rate among the ST students. The problem of teacher absenteeism as well as issues of quality teaching persists in many schools located in tribal areas. Teachers' efficiency in delivering quality teaching is one of the most important factors that can influence in motivating the students and their learning outcome (Pandey et al., 2010). The two states of western India, i.e. Gujarat, and Maharashtra have higher literacy rate than India, whereas the other two states – Madhya Pradesh and Rajasthan – still lag behind the national literacy rate. Gender issues play a very important role in Rajasthan due to customary practices, child marriage and labour related issues, which affect the enrollment and retention. With regard to economic indicators, both Maharashtra and Gujarat are relatively more developed compared to the other two states – Rajasthan and Madhya Pradesh. However, such economic development is not translated much to enhance the literacy status of ST community. Along with enrollment rate, issues of drop out, attendance and retention raise critical questions.

### *Drop-out Issues*

Issues pertaining to school drop-out are one of the critical indicators, which reflect the lack of educational development. This further indicates the inability of a given social group to complete a specific level of education. There is regional variation among the school drop-outs. Even the variation is noticed in the same region which is caused by many factors.

**Table 4**

*Drop-out Rates Among General and ST Students*

| *Sr. No.* | *India/ States* | *Classes I-V* | | *Classes I-VIII* | | *Classes I-X* | |
|---|---|---|---|---|---|---|---|
| | | *General Students* | *ST Students* | *General Students* | *ST Students* | *General Students* | *ST Students* |
| | India | 27.0 | 35.6 | 40.6 | 55.0 | 49.3 | 70.9 |
| 1 | Gujarat | 25.7 | 48.0 | 46.7 | 70.2 | 57.9 | 77.6 |
| 2 | Madhya Pradesh | 29.5 | 37.1 | 30.7 | 36.1 | 51.1 | 64.6 |
| 3 | Maharashtra | 20.3 | 21.1 | 25.9 | 44.4 | 38.2 | 69.8 |
| 4 | Rajasthan | 50.6 | 49.4 | 53.3 | 64.0 | 68.5 | 79.3 |

*Source:* Statistics of School Education 2010–2011

Dropout rates are very high among the tribal students (Table 4) – 35.6 per cent in Classes I to V; 55 per cent in Classes I to VIII; and 70.9 per cent in Classes I to X in 2010–11, which is considerably higher than the all India figures for other/general students. Among the four states of western region with tribal dominated places, three states – Gujarat, Madhya Pradesh and Rajasthan – surpasses India's drop-out rate (35.6%) for Classes I-V showing the rate as 48 per cent, 37.1 per cent and 49.4 per cent, respectively. Drop-out rate for Maharashtra is 21.1 per cent, which is less than India's drop-out rate (Statistics of School Education, 2010–2011). From the analysis of India and western states, it has been revealed that out of every 100 ST students who entered Class-I, only 45 could complete Class VIII in India, in Gujarat only 30 students could complete, in MP only 64 could complete Class VIII, in Maharashtra 56 students could complete, in Rajasthan 36 students could complete Class VIII grade. The comparative data for all categories is indicating that Gujarat has the highest dropout rate, followed by Rajasthan, Maharashtra and Madhya Pradesh (Statistics of School Education, 2010–2011). In the recent years available statistics show that the government efforts, especially through SSA interventions drop-out rates have come down. The rate has drastically declined during 2012–13 and 2013–14. This can be considered as a positive step. There is also decline in the number of out-of-school children, as can be seen from the statistics of the Ministry of Human Resource Development in different years. However, the gap between different social groups including the STs, still remain noticeable giving scope for debates and discussions.

The tribal boys share the economic responsibilities in the family at an early age, which compel them to discontinue their studies. Early marriage of both girls and boys, make them responsible at household domain (Deshmukh, 2004). Despite government initiatives schools are located in inaccessible hilly areas without proper transport facility. Parents are reluctant to send their young children to ashram schools where they would be staying away from the family. In addition to this there are areas where higher grades in ashram schools and block level schools are not prevalent. Seasonal migration and temporary drop-outs during the harvesting season and during festivals are also noticed in tribal areas. Girls are required to help their mothers in the household and often look after their younger siblings. Educational needs of the children often take a back sit due to the financial constraints of the parents to run the house. Medium of instruction in schools which is different from the tribal dialects and low level of education of the parents play a role in access to schooling. Many such factors are responsible for the disadvantaged situation among the ST students. The influencing factors could have different intensity and region-specific variations. Appropriate initiatives are required for alleviating these issues. Poverty, lack of basic school infrastructures, lack of involvement in teaching-learning process and many related factors add on to the existing situation.

## Schemes for ST Education: From Planning to Implementation

Government has made a number of initiatives to facilitate the STs. This section presents an interface of the government policy and scheme for educating the tribal children of India and their actual impact on them. There have been schemes with convergence approach. For instance schemes like establishing and strengthening of ashram schools, establishing and strengthening of hostels, vocational training in tribal areas, post-matric scholarship, and pre-matric scholarship are inter-linked. Though these schemes are centrally sponsored schemes, there could be variations in expenditure as per the requirement of the states and tribal communities. Ashram schools in TSP Areas are set up with a central assistance to the states and Union Territories on 50 per cent and 100 per cent basis, respectively. Total 14 Tribal Research Institutes (TRIs) have been set up in different states of India. Gujarat, Madhya Pradesh, Maharashtra and Rajasthan are included in this category. These institutes are engaged in providing expertise and inputs to the state governments, conducting research and evaluation studies, documentation, conduct of training, seminars and workshops. Museums exhibiting tribal art and culture are also maintained in some of these institutes.

Vocational Training Centres in Tribal Areas are facilitated with an aim of upgrading the skills of the tribal youths in various traditional/modern vocation depending upon their educational qualification. These centres can enable them to gain suitable employment or enable them to become self-employed. There is also a provision of strengthening education among Scheduled Tribe girls in low literacy district. The scheme primarily envisages the running and maintenance of hostels linked with schools running under Sarva Shiksha Abhiyan or other schemes of the Education Department. Where such schooling facilities are not available, the scheme has a provision for establishing a complete educational complex with residential and schooling facility. In addition to this there is facility for providing coaching for disadvantaged ST aspirants to enable them to successfully compete in examinations for jobs/admission to professional courses. Grant-in-Aid facility has been extended to voluntary organizations working for welfare of Scheduled Tribes. Post-Matric Scholarship for Scheduled Tribe students has been introduced with an objective to provide financial assistance to students belonging to Scheduled Tribes pursuing post-matriculation and other recognized courses in recognized institutions. There is a provision to upgrade the merit of ST students by providing them remedial and special coaching in Classes IX to XII which can help reducing deficiencies in various subjects. Students with disabilities are also eligible for Reader Allowance in different categories (Ministry of Tribal Affairs, 2011).

Schemes are planned with good intentions, but there are many gaps in the implementation and allocations of Scheme for Education of ST children (Ramachandran et al., 2007). In budgetary allocations, no special priorities for tribal development are specified. Such allocations are not clearly reflected and there seems to be no rationale behind deciding the priorities in Tribal Development. The relevant and practical requirements of tribal people need to be considered while deciding the schemes for their development. Allocations for TSP are too scarce in relation to their socio-economic backwardness. In addition to this, the implementation is too slow and stagnant, which has been reflected in the underutilization of small funds by the Tribal Welfare Department.

The trend of sanctioning ashram schools without scrutinizing the infrastructural amenities and facilities is a major problem. Many of the ashram schools are in a gloomy condition, where the students can hardly get any motivation for further study. Prior to the sanctioning of ashram schools, a thorough examination of the integrity and efficiency of the agency, availability of the required infrastructure including drinking water, building, playground etc. should be carried out. Education of tribal children is affected due to inadequate infrastructure and poor quality teaching (Jojo, 2013). More number of good residential schools with proper infrastructure and quality teachers should be promoted. The coverage of the schemes and incentives continues to be scarce. There is also no monitoring procedure for the implementation and efficacy of these programmes. The reflection on achievement and target oriented planning can help determining future strategy with appropriate budgetary allocation and involvement of the relevant stakeholders (NCF, 2005). Schemes and incentives can always facilitate the development of the marginalized STs. However, these schemes should be effectively implemented with more pragmatic approach. The benefits of development as well as the gaps between the STs and other communities remain and sincere efforts should be to bridge this gap.

## Recommendation and Conclusion

The analyses on educational scenario in India and specifically in western region have revealed that the tribals lag behind in all the indicators of education. Undoubtedly the government has made concentrated efforts to develop the educational status by increasing the number of schools, teachers and infrastructures. But such efforts to improve the educational status are either not sufficient or not appropriate to fulfil the requirement of educational needs among the STs. More serious efforts starting from planning to implementation is required. It is clearly mentioned in the National Policy, 1986, and the National Curriculum Framework that the problems of inequality need to be addressed not only through plans and schemes, but also through design of appropriate curriculum which can be imparted through proper pedagogic practices. Designing polices, for the marginalized community like the STs is an important task. Giving equal rights along with enhancing capabilities of people and also eliminating obstacles from the lives of people can give them the opportunity and freedom to live the desired life (Sen, 2005).

With regard to tribal development inter-sectorial convergence, an essential component is missing. Skill development, education, employment and such issues are correlated, but many schemes are implemented in isolation. Awareness of Tribal Development

Schemes among the tribals is less or absent (Paltasingh, 2014). There is lack of departmental representatives at the community and village level to identify the gaps. It is important to reach out to tribal through folk culture, literature, pamphlets, cultural programmes, etc. Undernourished children should be looked after through provision of nutritional food. Mid-day meal should not be a routine activity of the school; rather it should be served ensuring the quantity and quality. Proper infrastructure and amenities can make the learning atmosphere more interesting. In the inaccessible areas, teachers should be provided accommodation and transport facility should be extended to the ST students.

There has been continued imbalance in power relationships between the STs and the privileged non-STs. Such situation has expedited to maintain the hegemonic control of the dominant over the subordinate. The unequal status is evident in the language policies of many states of India where local language has been introduced as medium of instruction among the tribal populations of the respective states. Education policies and practices of the specific state have also been found to maintain and strengthen a hegemonic social order by the dominant groups. Such process has largely alienated the socio-culturally subordinated tribal/indigenous learners. Inequality in the schooling system should be viewed from multiple perspectives at different contexts. The influence of the larger society and the social norms within the school, the attitude and behaviour of teachers and lack of involvement and indifferent approach of parents and community members can influence the ongoing dominant practices (Ramachandran, 2013).

The curriculum should be formed in such a manner that it can appreciate the tribal/indigenous outlook and sustain it as an active component of their identity, not hampering the collective consciousness (Xaxa, 2011). There are evidences that the state has availed much from the tribes while denying them to be the participant and stakeholders of development of the specific regions. The status of tribal community, including the children, continues to remain ignored. Tribal communities in many regions of India communicate with their own mother tongue. But official/regional languages are used for teaching-learning process in most of the states. These are that tribal children find it difficult to follow the regional language especially at primary level of schooling. Promoting Multi-Lingual Education (MLE) has been acknowledged in many research reports and documents considering the low literacy and high drop-out rates affecting the overall learning achievements and quality education among the tribal children. The educational policies should move away from its remedial model and accommodate structural and critical perspectives that seek social transformation rather than creating unstable situation. Such an approach would make tribal education relevant, inclusive as well as responsive to the socio-political and economic needs of the community.

## References

Census of India, 2011, 2001, 1991, 1981, 1971 and 1961, Registrar General of Census, Government of India, New Delhi.

Chattopadhyay, A. and Durdhawale, V. Primary Schooling in a Tribal District of Maharashtra: Some Policy Relevance. *Journal of Education Administration and Policy Studies,* Vol. 1(5), 2009, pp. 70–78.

Deshmukh, B.A. *Tribal Education*, Sonali Publications, New Delhi, 2004.

Dreze, J. 'Patterns of Literacy and their Social Context,' in Das V. et al. (ed.). *Oxford Handbook of Indian Sociology*, Oxford University Press, New Delhi, 2003.

Jain, J. and Shah, M. Antyodaya Anna Yojana and Mid-Day Meals in MP, *Economic and Political Weekly,* 26 November 2005, pp. 5076–5088.

Jain, A. and Ashok Kumar. A Survey of Government Polices to Improve the Primary Education in Rajasthan, *International Journal of Education and Psychological Research,* Volume 2, Issue 3, 2013, pp. 133–142.

Jojo, B. Decline of Ashram Schools in Central and Eastern India: Impact on Education of ST Children, *Social Change*, 2013, 43(3): pp. 377–395.

Joshi, V. *Tribal Situation in India: Issues in Development*, Rawat, Jaipur, 1998.

Ministry of Human Resource Development, The Right of Children to Free and Compulsory Education Act (2009). New Delhi, 2010.

MTA. 2011–12 and 2012–13. Annual Report. Ministry of Tribal Affairs, Government of India, New Delhi.

National Council of Educational Research and Training, *National Curriculum Framework (NCF) 2005.* New Delhi, 2005.

National Curriculum Framework, Position Paper, National Focus Group on Problems of Scheduled Castes and Scheduled Tribes Children, NCERT, New Delhi, 2007.

Pandey, P., Sangeeta, G. and Venkatesh, S. 'Public Participation, Teacher Accountability and School Outcomes in Three States', *Economic and Political Weekly,* Vol xlv(24), 2010, pp. 75–83.

Paltasingh, T. Assessment of Available Facilities for Primary and Upper Primary Education in Tribal Areas in Gujarat; Report submitted to NUEPA and MHRD, New Delhi, 2014.

Paltasingh, T. and Paliwal, G. 'Tribal Population in India: Regional Dimensions and Imperatives', *Journal of Regional Development and Planning,* Vol. 3, No. 2, 2014, pp. 27–36.

Planning Commission. Towards Faster and More Inclusive Growth: An Approach to the 11th Five-Year Plan, Government of India, New Delhi, 2006.

Planning Commission. Twelfth Five Year Plan: 2012–17, Volume III, Government of India, New Delhi, 2011.

Ramachandran, V. and Naorem, T. What it Means to be a Dalit or Tribal Child in our Schools: A Synthesis of a Six-State Qualitative Study, *EPW,* xlviii(44), 2013, pp. 43–52.

Ramachandran, V., Mehrotra, R. and K., Jandhyala. Incentives in Elementary Education. Do they make a difference?, *Journal of Education Planning and Administration,* 11(2), 2007, pp. 141–153.

Sen, A. Human Rights and Capabilities, *Journal of Human Development,* Routledge, Vol. 6, No. 2, July 2005, pp. 151–166.

Statistics of School Education, GOI, Ministry of Human Resource Development, Bureau of Planning, Monitoring and Statistics, New Delhi, 2012.

Tilak, Jandhyala B.G. Inclusive Growth and Education: On the Approach to the Eleventh Plan, *Economic and Political Weekly,* 22 September 2007, pp. 3872–77.

Velaskar, P. 'Unequal Schooling as a Factor in the Reproduction of Social Inequality', *Sociological Bulletin,* Vol. 39, Nos. 1 and 2, 1992, pp. 131–146.

Velaskar, P. 'Educational Stratification, Dominant Ideology and the Reproduction of Disadvantage in India', in Dahiwale, S.M. (ed.) *Understanding Indian Society: The Non-Brahmanic Perspective.* Rawat, Jaipur, 2005, pp. 196–220.

Xaxa, V. 'Tribes and Development: Retrospect and Prospect', in D. Nathan and V. Xaxa (ed.) *Social Exclusion and Adverse Inclusion: Development and Deprivation of Adivasis in India,* Oxford University Press, New Delhi, 2012.

Xaxa, V. *The Status of Tribal Children in India: A Historical Perspective.* IHD and UNICEF, New Delhi, 2011.

# 13

# Attitudes of Parents of Scheduled Tribes and Non-Scheduled Tribes towards the Education of their Children

## With Reference to Gujarat State in India

**J.C. Patel**

In the traditional Indian society education was not open to everybody but was ascribed to a certain caste. As such the parents had no choice in deciding what education should be given to their children. It was decided by the community by custom. In the modern urban and industrial era in education, the parents have a choice. They are free to educate their words as they like. And most of the time children spend with their parents at home. As such the influence of the family as they socialize with young is very great. In fact, parents are important socializing agents of the children.

The parents of children are found to have varied opinions about education, occupation, religion, values, attitudes and modernist etc. so it is necessary to study the parents of the students as an important factor influencing the achievement and aspiration of children towards education.

Formal education is the institution through which a society socializes its younger members. Education shares the responsibility for the socialization of the young with other agencies such as the family, the kin-group and the peer group. Among the agencies responsible for the socialization of a child in the early years, the family and the school are most important. Parents and teacher share the responsibility for the proper upbringing of children in equal measure. Family is the most important agent to contribute in the developing social responsibility.

The purpose behind interviewing parents in this study were to find out parents' view regarding the goals of education, the role of the student and their social attributes and values. In this regard, the focus of the parents' social backgrounds have been described.

## Objectives

The study focuses on differentiation between Scheduled Tribe and Non-Scheduled Tribe education, occupation, religion, values, attitudes and modernism, etc. and finds out the achievement and the aspiration of education of their children.

## Methodology

This study is empirical as well as descriptive analytical and comparative. It aims to explain who gets more education and how. The sample selection was identified by three important variables, population, education and region, and then 1,074 parents from Scheduled Tribe and 462 from non-Scheduled Tribe were selected as sample. There were found some differences between Scheduled Tribe and non-Scheduled Tribe regarding the occupation, service. Type of house, physical facilities school of children, expenditure towards, expenditure towards education, tuition fees, problem in admission, etc.

**Table 1**

*Education Level of Head of the Family*

| *Education status of head of the family* | *ST* | | *Non-ST* | | *Total* | |
|---|---|---|---|---|---|---|
| Illiterate | 272 | 25.33% | 66 | 14.29% | 338 | 22.01% |
| Primary | 161 | 14.99% | 73 | 15.80% | 234 | 15.23% |
| Upper Primary | 113 | 10.52% | 79 | 17.10% | 192 | 12.50% |
| Secondary | 159 | 14.80% | 72 | 15.58% | 231 | 15.04% |
| Higher Secondary | 86 | 8.01% | 44 | 9.52% | 130 | 8.46% |
| Graduation | 48 | 4.47% | 17 | 3.68% | 65 | 4,23% |
| Post-Graduation | 4 | 0.37% | 5 | 1.08% | 9 | 0.59% |
| Not applicable | 231 | 21.51% | 106 | 22.94% | 337 | 21.94% |
| Total | 1,074 | 100.00% | 462 | 100.00% | 1,536 | 100.00% |

The education level of head of the family is the most important factor that contributes to the level of education among children. Therefore, we have attempted to study the level of education of the head of the family.

Comparing ST with non-ST, it is found (Table 1) that the proportion of illiterate person is more among ST. The proportion of illiterate is higher among ST as compared to non-ST. At the same time, the proportion of head with post-graduation qualification is higher among non-ST as compared to ST.

Occupation is mainly dependent on the level of education. Because of lack of education, ST are more engaged in agriculture and labour work. Such type of work also affects the education of their children.

**Table 2**

*Main Occupation of the Head of the Family*

| *Main occupation of head of the family* | *ST* | | *Non-ST* | | *Total* | |
|---|---|---|---|---|---|---|
| Cultivation and allied agriculture | 351 | 32.68% | 166 | 35.9% | 517 | 33.66% |
| Agricultural wage labour | 102 | 9.50% | 7 | 1.52% | 109 | 7.10% |
| Self-cultivation wage labour | 30 | 2.79% | 13 | 2.81% | 43 | 2,80% |
| Non-Agricultural wage labour | 226 | 21.04% | 72 | 15.58% | 298 | 19.40% |
| Cultivation and farm labour | 1 | 0.09% | 2 | 0.43% | 3 | 0.20% |
| Artisan/Independent work | 119 | 11.08% | 70 | 15.15% | 189 | 12.30% |
| Shop/Business | 22 | 2.05% | 48 | 10.39% | 70 | 4.56% |
| Govt. employment (Grade I and II) | 18 | 1.68% | 4 | 0.87% | 22 | 1.43% |
| Govt. employment (Grade III and IV) | 52 | 4.84% | 10 | 2.16% | 62 | 4.04% |
| Academic | 19 | 1.77% | 3 | 0.65% | 22 | 1.43% |
| Private employment | 36 | 3.35% | 1 | 2.38% | 47 | 3.06% |
| Professional (e.g. doctor/lawyer) | 6 | 0.56% | 6 | 1.30% | 12 | 0.78% |
| Factory worker | 0 | 0.00% | 1 | 0.22% | 1 | 0.07% |
| Housewife | 36 | 3.35% | 21 | 4.55% | 57 | 3.71% |
| Unemployment | 26 | 2.42% | 16 | 3.46% | 42 | 2.73% |
| Others | 7 | 0.65% | 1 | 0.22% | 8 | 0.52% |
| Not ascertained | 23 | 2.14% | 11 | 2.38% | 34 | 2.21% |
| Total | 1,074 | 100.00% | 462 | 100.00% | 1,536 | 100.00% |

From Table 2, it is evident that the proportion of labour work is more among ST, whereas the proportion of business and trade is more among non-ST.

The environment at house, amenities available at house, etc. creates impact the educational performance and social environment.

**Table 3**

*Type of House of Respondents*

| *Type of House* | *ST* | | *Non-ST* | | *Total* | |
|---|---|---|---|---|---|---|
| *Pucca* house with very good condition | 179 | 16.67% | 12 | 26.41% | 301 | 19.60% |
| *Pucca* house with less space for all family member | 182 | 16.95% | 88 | 19.05% | 270 | 17.58% |
| Semi-*Pucca* | 298 | 27.75% | 145 | 31.39% | 443 | 28.84% |
| Huts | 87 | 8.10% | 15 | 3.25% | 102 | 6.64% |
| *Kutcha* (mud walls, floor and thatched roof) | 322 | 29.98% | 92 | 19.91% | 414 | 26.95% |
| Not ascertained | 6 | 0.56% | 0 | 0.00% | 6 | 0.39% |
| Total | 1,074 | 100.00% | 462 | 100.00% | 1,536 | 100.00% |

Looking at the position of house (Table 3), the proportion of *pucca* houses is more among non-ST. So, it can be said that even today ST people live in *kutcha* houses. It shows their economical condition.

**Table 4**

*Availability of Ration Card*

| *Ration Card Facility* | *ST* | | *Non-ST* | | *Total* | |
|---|---|---|---|---|---|---|
| APL | 351 | 32.68% | 222 | 48.05% | 573 | 37.30% |
| BPL | 608 | 56.61% | 196 | 42.42% | 804 | 52.34% |
| Other | 12 | 1.12% | 8 | 1.73% | 20 | 1.30% |
| None | 81 | 7.54% | 34 | 7.36% | 115 | 7.49% |
| Do not know/Not answered | 2 | 0.19% | 1 | 0.22% | 3 | 0.20% |
| Not ascertained | 20 | 1.86% | 1 | 0.22% | 21 | 1.37% |
| Total | 1,074 | 100.00% | 462 | 100.00% | 1,536 | 100.00% |

The proportion of BPL Card is more among ST than non-ST which presents the picture of their economical condition (Table 4).

**Table 5**

*Type of School Management*

| *Management Type* | *ST* | | *Non-ST* | | *Total* | |
|---|---|---|---|---|---|---|
| Fully government | 544 | 50.65% | 209 | 45.24% | 753 | 49.02% |
| Government aided | 63 | 5.87% | 24 | 5.19% | 87 | 5.66% |
| Fully private | 161 | 14.99% | 95 | 20.56% | 256 | 16.67% |
| Do not know/Not answered | 7 | 0.65% | 5 | 1.08% | 12 | 0.78% |
| Not applicable | 279 | 25.98% | 122 | 26.41% | 401 | 26.11% |
| Not ascertained | 20 | 1.86% | 7 | 1.52% | 27 | 1.76% |
| Total | 1,074 | 100.00% | 462 | 100.00% | 1,536 | 100.00% |

The proportion of getting education through private schools is more among non-ST because they take care for getting good education (Table 5).

**Table 6**

*Results of Respondent's Children in the Last Two Classes*

| *Results of Children* | *ST* | | *Non-ST* | | *Total* | |
|---|---|---|---|---|---|---|
| Very Poor | 6 | 0.56% | 2 | 0.43% | 8 | 0.52% |
| Unsatisfactory | 28 | 2.61% | 10 | 2.16% | 38 | 2.47% |
| Satisfactory | 121 | 11/27% | 52 | 11.26% | 173 | 11.26% |
| Good | 486 | 45.25% | 204 | 44.16% | 690 | 44.92% |
| Very Good | 88 | 8.19% | 54 | 11.69% | 142 | 9.24% |
| Do not know/Not answered/No opinion | 6 | 0.56% | 1 | 0.22% | 7 | 0.46% |
| Not ascertained | 339 | 31.56% | 139 | 30.09% | 478 | 21.12% |
| Total | 1,074 | 100.00% | 462 | 100.00% | 1,536 | 100.00% |

**Table 7**

*Visit to School in Past 12 Months*

| *In Past 12 months-gone to Child School* | *ST* | | *Non-ST* | | *Total* | |
|---|---|---|---|---|---|---|
| Yes | 391 | 36.41% | 196 | 42.42% | 587 | 38.22% |
| No | 420 | 39.11% | 143 | 30.95% | 563 | 36.65% |
| 11 times | 1 | 0.09% | 0 | 0.00% | 1 | 0.07% |
| Do not know/Not answered | 1 | 0.09% | 0 | 0.00% | 1 | 0.07% |
| Not applicable | 219 | 20.39% | 105 | 22.73% | 324 | 21.09% |
| Not ascertained | 42 | 3.91% | 18 | 3.90% | 60 | 3.91% |
| Total | 1,074 | 100.00% | 462 | 100.00% | 153 | 100.00% |

Comparing the results of the last two years, it is seen that the proportion of very good is less among ST while it is more among non-ST (Table 6).

The parents go to school for celebrations in school during the past 12 months. Among non-ST, the frequency is more (Table 7). This shows their awakening towards education.

In expectations towards education, the highest ambitions are found among non-ST parents (Table 8).

**Table 8**

*Aspirations of Children*

| *Level of education of child want to be* | *ST* | | *Non-ST* | | *Total* | |
|---|---|---|---|---|---|---|
| Primary | 18 | 1.68% | 4 | 0.87% | 22 | 1.43% |
| Middle | 44 | 4.10% | 22 | 4.76% | 66 | 4.30% |
| Higher secondary | 107 | 9.96% | 47 | 10.17% | 154 | 10.03% |
| Any degree | 417 | 38.83% | 170 | 36.80% | 587 | 38.22% |
| MBBS | 20 | 1.86% | 21 | 4.55% | 41 | 2.67% |
| BE | 19 | 1.77% | 6 | 1.30% | 25 | 1.63% |
| Teacher | 73 | 6.80% | 32 | 6.93% | 105 | 6.84% |
| Any other | 76 | 7.08% | 29 | 6.28% | 105 | 6.84% |
| DK/NA | 272 | 25.33% | 122 | 26.41% | 394 | 25.65% |
| 999 | 28 | 2.61% | 9 | 1.59% | 37 | 2.41% |
| Total | 1,074 | 100.00% | 462 | 100.00% | 1,536 | 100.00% |

In respect to entrustment of work at home, the proportion is found to be more among ST (Table 9). Looking to this, it can be said that ST children are entrusted petty works.

**Table 9**

*Child's Assistance for Any Work at Home*

| *Child work at home* | *ST* | | *Non-ST* | | *Total* | |
|---|---|---|---|---|---|---|
| Yes | 458 | 42.64% | 176 | 38.10% | 634 | 41.28% |
| No | 434 | 40.41% | 204 | 44.16% | 638 | 41.54% |
| Not applicable/No child | 178 | 16.57% | 79 | 17.10% | 257 | 16.73% |
| Not ascertained | 4 | 0.37% | 3 | 0.65% | 7 | 0.46% |
| Total | 1,074 | 100.00% | 462 | 100.00% | 1,536 | 100.00% |

Compared to ST students, non-ST are more regular at school whereas less regularity is seen among ST (Table 10).

**Table 10**

*Child Regularity in School*

| *Child work at home* | *ST* | | *Non-ST* | | *Total* | |
|---|---|---|---|---|---|---|
| Yes | 662 | 61.64% | 297 | 64.29% | 959 | 62.43% |
| No | 157 | 14.62% | 36 | 7.79% | 193 | 12.57% |
| Not applicable/No child | 3 | 0.28% | 0 | 0.00% | 3 | 0.20% |
| Not ascertained | 252 | 23.46% | 129 | 27.92% | 381 | 24.80% |
| Total | 1,074 | 100.00% | 462 | 100.00% | 1,536 | 100.00% |

Looking to the proportion of PTA/VEC/SMC membership, it is more in non-ST (Table 11). They have awakening for having knowledge regarding the education work of the school.

**Table 11**

*Membership of PTA/VEC/SMC*

| *Child work at home* | *ST* | | *Non-ST* | | *Total* | |
|---|---|---|---|---|---|---|
| Yes | 41 | 3.82% | 33 | 7.14% | 74 | 4.82% |
| No | 667 | 62.10% | 249 | 53.90% | 916 | 59.64% |
| Do not know | 47 | 4.38% | 30 | 6.49% | 77 | 5.01% |
| Not ascertained | 319 | 29.70% | 150 | 32.47% | 469 | 30.53% |
| Total | 1,074 | 100.00% | 462 | 100.00% | 1,536 | 100.00% |

**Table 12**

*Aspiration Regarding Job Choice of Child*

| *What your child wants to become* | *ST* | | *Non-ST* | | *Total* | |
|---|---|---|---|---|---|---|
| As per his/her wish/luck | 125 | 11.64% | 44 | 9.52% | 196 | 11.00% |
| Female: nurse, Male: studying up to Higher Secondary Level | 4 | 0.37% | 0 | 0.00% | 4 | 0.26% |
| Military | 7 | 0.65% | 1 | 0.22% | 8 | 0.52% |
| Software Engineer/Job in a Private company | 15 | 1.40% | 4 | 0.87% | 19 | 1.24% |
| Clerk/Peon | 1 | 0.09% | 0 | 0.00% | 1 | 0.07% |
| Lawyer/Magistrate | 0 | 0.00% | 2 | 0.43% | 2 | 0.13% |
| Chartered Accountant | 1 | 0.09% | 1 | 0.22% | 2 | 0.13% |

The proportion of development is less among the tribal areas. The wind of change has begun after the advent of non-tribals but they could not understand this wind of change because strong exploitation of them has taken place in the first phase of development. They remained silent. There are three reasons for their silence. The planning was self-centred. New history and lack of knowledge of economic factors. To strengthen such tribal communities, modern viewpoint should be accepted with the spirit of development of all. They can feel about these factors.

In India, efforts and attempts for their economic development were done after Independence. The reasons being backwardness on the one hand and getting minerals from these areas on the other, roads were made to get minerals and minerals were excavated. Rules were made by the administrators for this purpose. This class of the society is fully clever. The tribals are unfamiliar to them. They do not have any idea of this new system. Non-tribals take full benefit because of this. As a result dissatisfaction and distrust has been created among the tribals. Here education plays an important role but certain disturbing factors have come up in the education system.

While discussing the tribal development, we can field that there are several areas which are extremely backward but they are efficiency oriented. We can't find any large dissimilarity among all these people.

This condition is found to be different in the rural and urban areas. Here, high, middle and low classes are found mainly two classes high and low are found in the rural areas. The tribals come in the lower class mainly in cities and towns in the rural areas sometimes there can be only this class. Non-tribal people mainly live in cities and towns. They are in the high and middle classes. Sometimes they go to the villages and form a new high class there. This matter becomes difficult mainly among tribals because there are two blockades against them: blockade of knowledge and socio-psychological blockade. They are unfamiliar with the lifestyle of the cities. They do not have enough knowledge regarding rules and regulations, administrative procedure, economic system based on exchange.

Education is an important factor for development but for the tribals, language and socio-psychological factors turn out to be blockades. Moreover, social values, hand life, dresses may also turn out to be blockades.

1. In household, the proportion of English knowing members is more among non-ST. In the household, tribals still speak

their dialect although the government does nothing to give importance to their dialect.

2. The proportion of illiteracy is more among tribals compared to non-tribals.
3. People engaged in the occupation of labour are seen more among tribals.
4. Looking at the position of houses, 38 per cent more *kutcha* houses are seen among tribals.
5. There are more number of BPL card holders among STs. The difference of 24 per cent is seen between ST and non-ST.
6. The proportion of modern things of household is more among non-ST. Similarly, non-ST neighbours have more education compared to ST ones.
7. The proportion of getting education in private schools is more among non-STs. The approach towards school of ST respondents is proportionately less positive.
8. When we think of the result of the children, good result is found less among STs. Non-ST parents visit the school and they hold membership in various committees. This proportion is seen less among STs.
9. ST children are engaged more in various household chores. As a result, a difference is found between them in respect to school regularity.

## References

Adiseshiah, M.S. and Ramanathan, S. Educational Problems of Scheduled Castes and Scheduled Tribes in Tamil Nadu, Madras Institute of Development Studies, Madras, 1974.

Ananda, G., *Educating Tribals*, Commonwealth, New Delhi, 2000.

Bernard, H. Russell, *Social Research Methods*, Sage Publication, Los Angeles, 2013.

*Census of India 2001*. Government of India.

Dubey, S.M. *Study of Scheduled Caste and Scheduled Tribe College Students in Assam*, Dibrugarh University, Dibrugarh, 1974.

George, E.I. *Educational Problems of the Scheduled Caste and Scheduled Tribe College Students in Kerala*, Kerala University, Trivandrum, 1975.

Gore, M.S., Desai, I.P. and Chitnis, Suma. Papers in Sociology of Education in India, National Council of Educational Research and Training, New Delhi, 1967.

Gore, M.S., Desai, I.P. and Chitnis, Suma. *Field Studies in the Sociology of Education*, NCERT, New Delhi, 1970.

Mehta, Arun C. Analytical Report, 2006–07, Elementary Education in India, National University of Educational Planning and Administration, New Delhi.

Sachidananda. Education Among the Scheduled Castes and Scheduled Tribes in Bihar (College Students). Patna: A.N.S. Institute of Social Studies, 1974.

Shah, B.V. and Thaker, J.D. Scheduled Caste and Scheduled Tribe College Students in Gujarat: A Research Study, Sponsored by ICSSR, New Delhi, Dept. of Sociology, S.P. University, 1977.

Shah, B.V. Field Studies in the Sociology of Education, Study Report, National Council of Education Research and Training, New Delhi, 1969.

Shah, Ghanshyam. *Tribal Education in Gujarat*, Centre for Social Studies, Surat, 1985.

State Report, 2008–09, Elementary Education in India, National University of Educational Planning and Administration, New Delhi.

Vyas, N.N. and Choudhary, N.D. The Dropouts in a Tribal Situation, Tribal Research Institute and Training Centre, Udaipur, 1970.

# 14

# Tribal Identity Issues in Western India

**Ashok Chaudhari**

I, on behalf of Adivasi Ekta Parishad, thank you for inviting me in this seminar at this historic place Gujarat Vidyapith, established by Mahatma Gandhi. The seminar on 'Adivasi Situation in Western India and Issues of Development' has a national and international importance because we all are facing the crisis and threat to our existence.

In 1992, the Earth Summit was held at Rio-de-Janeiro in Brazil wherein political, religious and social leaders and experts from different schools and nations had participated in this thought process to save mother earth. During this Summit, around 400 *adivasi* representatives from 68 countries had thoroughly discussed for three days and expressed their feelings and views regarding basis of tribal identity issues.

## Uniqueness of *Adivasi* Culture

1. Most practical culture, respecting all while recognizing their differences, equality with all, respecting nature and animals, treating all humans with respect.
2. Sustainable community-based economy model, sustainable development with inclusive positive and constructive approach, community-based mechanism, traditional appropriate technology.

3. Role of biodiversity and respecting human values.
4. *Adivasi* knowledge (technical, agricultural, medicine plants, art, handicrafts and historic experiences).
5. *Adivasi* lifestyle and values like: simplicity, openness, love, tolerance, non-violence, purity of heart, cooperation, freedom, equality and harmony.

### Current Status of *Adivasi* Communities

1. Risk of losing cultural identity.
2. Lack of integrating *adivasi* cultural values in current development/education model which vanishes creativeness and talents.
3. Extraction of minerals and natural resources, using *adivasi* communities for disruptive development, leading class based differentiations in society.
4. Dispossession and marginalization of *adivasi* communities from their land, water and forest.
5. Disruption of their socio-political institutions.

### Future Challenges for *Adivasi* Communities

1. Cultural identity
2. Modern economic dependence, class and community-based discriminations, structural violence
3. Violation of human rights
4. Corporate and state repression

### Road Map of Preserving Plants/Nature/Animal/Human

1. Strengthening educational system
2. Respecting cultural identity and *adivasi* empowerment
3. Respecting Nature
4. Accepting sustainable development models with respect for biodiversity and human values.

After discussion, we have presented our indigenous perspective and relationship with the environment. The roots of our perspective lie in the symbiotic relationship to the earth, based upon a delicate balance between its living parts. We are only care-takers of our mother earth. And therefore, each generation is responsible to ensure the survival of its seventh generation. This basic law was the driving force behind the development of our culture and values which reflects in our socio-political and economic institutions. In our clan system, decision-making process is based on consensus and division of labour based upon needs, ability to contribute and share the social cohesion as well as respect for life. Respect for people and for the earth is linked together in orderly system for people to survive and care for future generation. We have also stated the contrast between indigenous perspective and dominant perspective that is sacred versus secular relationship to the earth, collective interest and responsibility versus individual interest and responsibility and the way we consider the life of the planet as a gift of creator or resources to be used. We also consider that utilizing the organic matter of the earth should be viewed as a sacred circle of the life for a linear growth for human satisfaction. Out traditional economies have been disrupted constantly by development schemes and introduction of cash crops production for exchange. These have lead to dispossession and have marginalized us from our land base and created dependency for us.

## Adivasi Ekta Parishad

The situation of *adivasis* in western India is not much different than one in other parts of the country. The formal economic, social, political and legal systems are based on the concept of property, the individual and the written word whereas *adivasi* economy and institutions are informal and based on the concept of resource that is to be used according to needs of the community. Even their identity centres around common property resources though more than 80 per cent of the *adivasis* depend on forests and lands as an important part of their livelihood. This pattern of modern development has created ecological degradation and land alienation, displacement and declining employment among *adivasis*.

Parallel to Rio-Summit, Adivasi Ekta Parishad had been formed in Maharashtra by *adivasi* activists and within two years it has been expanded in western India, i.e. Maharashtra, Dadra Nagar Haveli, Gujarat, Rajasthan and Madhya Pradesh. It is an ideological process and is focused on raising awareness on sustainable development to keep alive Mother Earth and *adivasis*. Since then the programmes are: (1) Protection and regeneration of natural resources, i.e. land, water and forest. (2) Preserving and promoting diverse cultures, i.e. respecting different cultures and encouraging tribal communities to preserve their culture, knowledge, art-craft and dialects as a human heritage. After Rio Summit, we have organized 22 annual cultural festivals, hundreds of youth camps and formed the village-level committees to implement different constructive activities in western India. Political leaders of major parties have participated in this process of awareness-raising among *adivasis* and non-*adivasis*.

Mahatma Gandhi had long back written a book *Hind Swaraj* and cautioned us about western industrial revolution and warned us against limitless greed of mankind. He also said that mother earth has enough for our need but not for everybody's greed. In his views, mother earth is for all creatures and we are the guardians of them.

During our freedom struggle, Gandhiji initiated 18 constructive programmes, i.e. (1) Communal harmony (2) Abolition of untouchabilty (3) Liquor prohibition (4) Khadi (5) Gramodhyog (6) Village sanitation (7) Nai Talim education (8) Adult literacy (9) Women empowerment (10) Health education (11) Regional languages (12) National language (13) Economic equality (14) Welfare of farmers (15) Welfare of labourers (16) *Adivasi* welfare (17) Leprosy eradication (18) students. Unfortunately, it has never become an agenda of mass movement in our country.

After his assassination, we have undermined his views regarding nation building and development. We have adopted the western model of development wherein industrialization is in a centre and therefore the over exploitation of natural resources becomes inevitable. We have degraded forests, destructed land by so-called green revolution, over consumption of natural resources through extraction of minerals and polluted air and water with toxic waste. In the era of globalization and privatization, the people's sovereignty on the natural resources has been overlooked and ecological imbalances occurred. The private economic structures are dominating the political systems. Pandit Nehru's Panchshil Principles have been eventually forgotten and the development schemes for *adivasis* have miserably failed to achieve its desired objectives and goals as expected by our planners. These have created insecurity and unrest among the marginalized societies, including *adivasis*. It has also reduced the democratic space and constitutional rights of the people.

To address these issues, comprehensive, integrated and nationwide joint efforts are required. During this period, we are organizing and also participating in different forums and try to develop a nationwide consensus regarding alternative development model and promoting Gandhian way of life and Gram Swaraj which is obviously a traditional *adivasi* way of life which includes simple life, minimum use of natural resources and self-reliance and self-governance of the rural communities. We are also trying to have linkage with the different organizations and networks like ICITP (Adivasi Sanghmam), Adivasi Vikas Parishad, Ekta Parishad and MMP (Mines, Minerals and People) for future actions. The issues that emerged due to new economic policy are as under:

- *Adivasis* are losing control over natural resources such as land, water and forests that are basic to their existence. This has impoverished them, degrading their culture and threatening their very survival.
- Changes in lifestyle brought by the increase in the spread of mass media, particularly television, the expansion of market forces and accompanied by the growing middle class among *adivasi* communities are adversely affecting the simple, non-consumerist and inclusive lifestyles of *adivasi* communities and their culture.
- With mechanization, there is growing unemployment among *adivasi* youths and women.

## Conclusions

To protect and conserve the natural resources and *adivasi* interests, I feel that:

- *Adivasi* leaders, activists, concerned intellectuals and citizen's groups must get together to present alternative development model which would place *adivasi* world view comprising the celebration of life and nature, collectivity and cooperation in the centre. The collective effort is needed to question the public interest which is the motive force behind all industrialization and infrastructure development projects under the banner of liberalization and globalization.
- Philosophical and social values are embodied in *adivasi* culture as expressed in songs and other literature. This needs to be highlighted thorough various media to all the societies to counter the present trend towards consumerism.

- In terms of economic strategy, it should be based upon the principle of convergence of local resources to meet the local need rather than for outside regional, national or global markets.
- Several charters, conventions and declarations of United Nations bodies can be used to generate awareness about the conditions and rights of *adivasi* communities.

In this seminar, I would like to share the experiences and ground realities in different parts of the country. During two days of discussions, we hope that consensus will emerge for (1) common minimum programme for protecting and regenerating natural resources. (2) Protection of *adivasi* culture and heritage (3) Reduce the miseries of common man, including *adivasis*, and (4) programme for sustainable development.

# 15

# Role of Civil Society in Tribal Development

**Kanubhai Vasava**

Tribals mostly live in the forest. They know the secrets of the forest. The life of tribals was not anthropocentric rather they referred to all animals and plants as human beings. Earlier, they practised shifting agriculture and when faced with shortage of grains they used flowers, fruits, barks, etc. of trees. For instance, they prepared vegetables as well as liquor out of flower of Mahuda. Similarly, oil was obtained from seeds, bread (*rotlo*) out of seed of mango. They possessed the knowledge of using different parts of plants for preparing food as well as medicine. The monarchy prevalent earlier preserved the traditional lifestyle of tribals. It were the British who intervened in this traditional lifestyle of tribals for the first time. In the long run, this intervention eroded the traditional lifestyle of tribals which was based on preservation of environment. A life without art is akin to that of an animal. Tribal life is full of various kinds of arts. Many arts of tribals are still not known to the world. It can also be said that the world does not consider tribal art as art. It may be this reason for the widespread belief that tribals are generally wild in nature and akin to animals.

Many people consider tribals as devoid of any religion whereas many others have fixed labels of different religions on them. Many tribals have started considering these labels as their religion. Tribals do accept what they find good in the other cultures in the world. They also have made changes in their lifestyle based on their understanding of civilization. These changes have been labelled as 'religion' of the tribals. A major reason for this phenomenon can be the fact that there is no written scripture of the tribals and there is hardly any chance of any such scripture to be prepared. It is difficult to do so because the religion of tribals is too vast and it is a living religion. Nature is one religion for the tribals. Nature allows development of different arts. In fact, almost all religions of the world are connected to nature in some or the other way and religion is evolved from nature itself. Tribal religion is based on the changing behaviour of the natural world. But now the natural behaviour has become dependent on the behaviour of the human beings. Because of this, tribal culture too has now become dependent on human behaviour. Now literacy is spreading slowly among the tribals. Because of this literacy, many tribals have become professionals (in the modern connotation of the term) such as teachers, doctors and businessmen. They have become conscious of the world around them. They have started feeling the external power exerted over their own culture. They seek to counter such external pressures in a non-violent ways.

They are eager to present their culture in front of the wider world, their points of view is wide and large, there while is a widespread negative belief in the world regarding tribal life and culture. Such beliefs are results of complete or partial knowledge about the tribal life and culture. Educated tribal youths now seek to counter such false beliefs about the tribal culture. After so many decades of Independence, tribal world still has not come out in the wider society or it has not been allowed to come out. Looking at history one finds that whether it is the fight against the British or the question of establishing an integrated India, the tribal kings or leaders have never been taken into confidence. No effort was made to know or understand their desires or anxieties. Their territories have either been annexed through state legislation or through armed forces attack. Tribal revolutionaries have never been given the opportunity to present their culture. Because of this, the tribal society continues to be at the receiving end of such oppressive external forces. Nowadays we see an emergence of lot of new organizations among the tribals. There are also many activities happening which are akin to uprising against the dominant repressive order. These uprisings still have not found their adequate expression in the larger world but their importance cannot be ruled out. In the year 2015, the ninth annual state-level gathering of World Tribal Community took place in Vyara taluka of Tapi district in Gujarat on 9 August 2015. Huge numbers of tribal population came for this gathering. Although the mainstream media of Gujarat took no notice of the event, it was noted by most of tribal and non-tribal intelligentsia in Gujarat. This is not the first time that this kind of activity took place among tribal population nor is it the first time that tribals are carrying out any movement. The history of protest movement among tribals dates back to 1793 when Umedsinh Vasava of Rajpipla started a protest movement against the king of Rajpipla for the unsatisfactory administration. During the independence movement, most of the tribal movements were against the British rule, against the oppression and repression of the tribal population, and for social and religion reform. After the Independence, major reasons of tribal movements have been: social awareness, reforms, land-water-forest rights, conservation of forests, rehabilitation, conservation of tribal heritage, autonomous rule for tribals, and equal participation in resources and other rights. These movements have picked up momentum now and as educated tribal population too started participating in them so they have become important movements. I consider three movements which have happened in the recent past to be of immense importance: (1) movement for environment conservation and rehabilitation which took place in 1990 (and non-tribal population too participated in large numbers); (2) movements led by Ashokbhai Chaudhari and his colleagues in 1992; and (3) Gujarat Autonomy movement led by Chhotubhai Vasava in 1995. These movements have had a major impact on tribal population and this impact movements, there are three kinds of movements which are going on among the tribals: (1) Conservative Movement, (2) Revisionist Movement, and (3) Political Movement. Out of the three, this paper focuses on the revisionist movement. Research on tribal population has been going on since the British era in India. Researches which took place during the British era basically focused on finding characteristics of tribals so as to fix their identity. It was an exercise in identification and classification. Among such research work, a unique work is that of Verrier Elwin. Post-Independence, for next five decades, almost till 1990, most of the researches were done with the framework of 'development thesis' in mind. After 1990, development-oriented research work decreased in number and simultaneously tribals too started researching their own community and culture. After the Narmada Bachao Movement, educated tribals turned their research attention to their own community. One can find a new perspective in such research works. Tribals got a bad press in the research work carried on during the British era and they have not forgotten that insult. Development-oriented researches were carried out solely with the aim of bringing 'development' in the tribal areas which rapidly devolved into destruction of the environment and the tribal cultural and geographical world. Many among the tribal population too participated in such destructive activities. From 1930 CE to 2006 CE, 18 committees were formed for the development of tribal community and these committees have recommended several recommendations for development among tribals. Government as well as non-tribal people believe that the fundamental needs of tribal population are education, health, road and transportation. According to them, the major problems of tribals are poverty, low level of education, unemployment, etc. So, as a solution to the problem of education, we see the proliferation of various kinds of schools and allied infrastructure in tribal areas: basic education schools, residential schools, secondary schools, hostels for boys and girls, Eklavya Model Schools, Saraswati Cycle Scheme, Book Bank Scheme, etc. They also believe that the way to development of tribals is possible only through dairy industry, electricity, roads, dams, etc. In contrast to such researches, the one carried out by tribals themselves shows different problems for the lack of development. These are as follows: Tribals believe that if they start following Hindu or Christian or any other religion, they will lose their own identity as tribals. They believe that the prevalent model of development is destroying the environment. The destruction of environment will automatically result into the destruction of tribal identity. They firmly believe that tribal identity is linked to the preservation of the environment. They believe that they have the traditional ownership over the natural resources and this ownership is being overlooked by the state and the resources are being destroyed rapidly in the so-called development. They firmly believe that the government as well as the mainstream society has denied the inherent rights of tribals throughout the history. The kind of development envisioned by the government is going to destroy the tradition as well as the region of the tribals. The development model pursued by the government is forcing a new identity on the tribals that of being uneducated, poor, sick, anti-development, etc. The communal property of tribals such as water, land, forest and its minerals are being looted by the government for the benefit of some special people in the mainstream society. Industrialization, urbanization and foreign capital have resulted into the destruction of the environment. Capitalism has led to the destruction of self-sufficient society. Now under capitalism, the ownership over the means of productions has concentrated in the hands of a particular class and everybody else has been reduced to the status of labourers. External forces in the form of market have invaded the tribal society in a major way resulting into the change in lifestyle. This changed lifestyle has resulted into the emergence of health issues among the tribal society. Their reading of the Indian Constitution has made them aware that they have been denied the rights which they are entitled to as the original inhabitants of the country. The condition of tribals has deteriorated further in the wake of liberalization, privatization and globalization in the country post-1991. These concerns make it clear that tribals are not opposed to the idea of development but they are certainly opposed to the current model of development pursued by the government and the industrial-capital class of the society. The development of the tribals cannot take place by taking away their land. Their very identity is linked to their land. All the problems started the day land was started to be seen as a resource for earning money. Huge tracts of lands were usurped from the tribals by the government as well as the non-tribal people in the name of development. After 1965, government ownership over forests came into effect with the express motive of preservation of forests. This led to numerous controls over the tribal life in the name of preservation of forests. In this scheme of things, the rights of tribals which were linked intricately with the forest were not even spared a thought. From that time, forest turned to be of commercial importance only and forests were made bereft of human life. Tribal rights over the forest as well as over the land were snatched away. So, this is the reason for the lack of development among them is different from those given by the government and non-tribal people. There are many reasons which are responsible for tribals' interest in researching their own community and culture. It is not as if the idea for this kind research came out of the blue to the tribal people. This 'turn' took place after a long period of thinking and contemplation. Many young people from tribal community went for higher education and in the process they came in contact with different branches of learning and research. Their critical faculty developed and they started looking at things critically and intellectually. In this process of higher education they also came in contact with the research work done on tribal communities as well as constitutional measures and rules made for the tribals by the government. During this period, many non-tribal researchers also started looking at the tribal community through a new perspective. For instance, the research works of Bhagwandas Patel, Vidyut Joshi, etc. gave inspiration to tribal youths to look at their own community through a new perspective. It was also the period when government also started formulating new policies for tribals with the express objective of bringing development at their doorsteps. These policies failed miserably and tribals started losing hope with the government as well as their own leaders. New ideas and perspectives among the tribal youths led to the formation of organizations such as Adivasi Ekta Manch and periods such as Adilok. Both of these played a major role in raising consciousness among the majority of the tribal youths. Due to spread of education, many youths also took up law courses and they became experts in legal rules and regulations. Because of all these, researches based on surveys or development models came to a halt and new researches started happening on the question of identity. Historical accounts were looked at again critically and this has led to the process of construction on new history of the tribals. Higher education and such kind of researches made tribals aware of thc fact that they have been cheated thoroughly by the state as well as majority of the non-tribal researchers. Educated tribals started looking critically as well as with doubt at the relationship of non-tribals or the government or different religions with the tribal community. These doubts also led them to doubt their own community. This led them to look at their own community in a different way and they started a process of critical understanding of their own community. On the other hand, government made many such policies whose benefit to the tribals was dependent on their maintaining their tribal identity. This led some tribals towards preserving their tribal identity with a new sense of urgency. There is an understanding in the educated tribal community today that tribal histories as have been written in the past by non-tribal researchers and scholars have represented tribal community in bad light. So, they believe that a new history of the tribal people needs to be written and this can be done by tribal people only. Only such kind of a history can bring out their life and culture in true light. They also believe that only such kind of a history can bring those tribal people who has lost their faith in their community and culture back into the fold. During the course of their research, tribal researchers have come into contact with their own different branches of knowledge. Different fields of knowledge such as tribal economics, tribal sociology, tribal mathematics, tribal jurisprudence, tribal environment studies, etc. have set forth a new standard of tribal knowledge system. Today, tribal youth have understood that fight against the society or government cannot be won by arms but rather by knowledge. So, tribals have committed themselves to create a new field of knowledge which will keep human being in the centre. Their project is epical in proportion. They aim to bring about unity in the entire human society where any and every individual can come as a human being, devoid of any hierarchy. They want to raise their values to the philosophical level. These concerns can bring them out of petty issues. In this exercise, they aim to deconstruct the markers of their own identity and re establish it only after thorough critical examination of such markers. Keeping all these grand questions in mind, they are demanding the re-establishment of their own self-sufficient system. They are demanding the establishment of autonomy and self-rule in administration and also the implementation of constitutional safeguards given to them. They also seek to bring out sweeping changes in attitude of others towards tribals, tribals' attitude towards others and change in the beliefs of others regarding the tribal society. Today's educated tribal youth thinks about the entire humanity. The human behaviour pattern and lifestyle prevalent today in the society is such that can it destroy the very existence of humanity. Educated tribal youths have understood that it not a question merely of the tribal community. They emphasize that if today's problems have relevance only for the tribal community, then there is no need for them to fight. But if we pause to think what would happen once all the tribals are destroyed from the earth, then who will be next to be destroyed. It is this concern which has inspired them to fight prevalent problems in the society. They have started linking their life with the natural surroundings around them. Many tribal youths have started writing and they want their voices to be heard. They wish to examine their own life which can be used to create a new history. Tribals have a unique folk culture which encompasses their natural, social, religious and political life. Out of this life one can get the expression of the primal human society. Their life and literature carries the most primal culture of humanity in the world. Today many tribal youths come together and examine whether their thoughts and ideas are true or not. They examine whether their ideas are for the well-being of entire humanity or not. They also guide and show correct path to those youths who have been attracted towards the false promises of commercial society. It has often been asked how to live in literature. The answer to this question seems to be answered here. The creative community desires for the establishment of Adivasi Sahitya Akademi (tribal literature academy). Such academy becomes a place for discussion and deliberation over tribal literature. There should be comparative studies of tribal literatures as well as tribal and non-tribal literature. Such an academy should encourage such literature for tribal community which it deems to be beneficial even when such a literature may be considered to be trivial by the mainstream academy. There should be literary interpretations from the tribals' point of view. It should also examine all literatures which are passed as tribal literature to examine their claims of tribal literature. The academy should also examine the researches carried out on tribal community by non-tribals and see if there are fault-lines in such researches. It should preserve and make available those works of tribal literature which are on the verge of extinction. This will be the biggest gift of the academy for the future generations. Through this academy, tribal creative writers would be able to produce works which preserve and present community values, principles of life, dreams, aspirations, and emotions of the tribal community. Culture is constituted by both the society as well as literature. So, in this way, tribal literature will be beneficial to the development of human society as well as culture. Tribal literature will act as a conduit to understand the interpersonal emotions of the tribals, their life secrets, and their way of looking at life and also living a fulfilling life. A social form will rise out of tribal literature. This literature will hold the mirror to the entire society which will also reflect the non-tribal society and culture. Tribal literature will become a vehicle of social reform. A new international social consciousness will emerge out of such literature which will create a new world society. Out of this literature one will get to know intimately the history, archaeology, religion, psychology, linguistics, performing arts, literature, etc. of the tribal community. This literature will create a lively picture of tribals' intimate emotions such as happiness, sadness, intimacy, love, hope, despair and also their traditions. In short, such literature will bring out the vivid colours tribal community. This will become a vehicle from which the tribals' identity and pride will emerge.

# 16

# Issues and Development of Tribal Communities of Tribal Sub Plan

## Legislation Can do Away Historic Injustices

**Mahender Jethmalani**

### *Adivasi's* Charter of Demands for 2015–16 Union Budget to do away Historic Injustices

The *Adivasi* population in India is (10.5 crore), which is about 8.6 per cent of the total population of country. There are 705 groups identified across 30 states as *adivasis* and 75 groups as Particular Vulnerable Tribal Groups (PVTG) spread in 17 states. The *adivasis* are the most marginalized and disadvantaged section of society due to their exploitation and isolation. They lag behind in every aspect of human development and economic indicators (Annexure-I). The history of marginalization of *adivasis* goes long back to the colonial period. The Government of India has also admitted about historic injustices done to *adivasis*. It is also a fact that the *adivasis* have faced displacement and deprivation to facilitate various developmental projects such as setting up of industries, mining operations, construction of big dams, etc. According to some estimates close to 10 million *adivasis* have been displaced and lost their livelihoods on account of such developmental activities undertaken in the country. All these developments led to a large scale alienation of land from tribes to non-tribes. This has also resulted in violent reactions in some pockets of tribal belt. Unfortunately, despite constitutional protection and earmarked budgets they continue to remain among the poorest, as the legal acts and economic packages have not been implemented as envisaged to get the desired result.

Briefly speaking, persistent problems, land alienation, indebtedness; forest rights, involuntary displacement and improper rehabilitation, shifting cultivation, poor utilization of government funds, and poor governance (poor delivery of government programmes) for the *adivasi* have by and large remained unattended, and need immediate redressal through facilitating policy framework and budgetary resources under Tribal Sub-Plan (TSP) with participatory approach for accountable and transparent governance.

## BJP's Manifesto Commitments for Tribal Development

The Manifesto of present party in the Union Government has promised that 'tribal development will be one of the focus areas' and will have 'comprehensive, all-encompassing long-term strategy to empower tribals and ensure their welfare. The goal would be to ensure tribal development while preserving the unique identities of this community. The manifesto also suggests 'following the principles of *samajik nyay* (social justice) and *samajik samrasata* (social harmony). This social justice must be further complemented with economic justice and political empowerment in the context of tribal issues and commitments.

The Union Government must focus and initiate concrete steps for undoing injustice on *adivasis* and mitigate the development gaps through legislative policy and committed budgetary resources over next years. Steps should be taken to create an enabling ecosystem of equal opportunity – for education, health and livelihood. Highest priority should be accorded to tribal security for their land and forest resources, security of their cultural identity and also security, especially protection, and prevention of atrocities against STs.

## Status of TSP Implementation, Budget Utilization for *Adivasi* Development

Tribal Sub-Plan (TSP) was started with the objective of addressing the multitude of deficiencies confronted by tribals in various spheres. The idea was to channelize funds and benefits from the general sectors in the Central Ministries/Departments towards the development of Scheduled Tribes (STs), at least in proportion to their share in the total population. Yet, as the 12th Five Year Plan noted, even after more than three decades since it started, the implementation has not been up to the mark. The outlay under TSP should be 8.6 per cent out of total plan outlay, but in the year 2012–13, it was 4.04 per cent, the revised estimates of 2013–14 suggest expenditure around 4.63 per cent and the Budget estimates for 2014–15 is 5.63 per cent and the Budget estimates for the year 2015–16 is 4.29 per cent (Annexure II). Besides, the budgetary allocation under TSP for the development of *adivasis* is never fully utilized (Annexure-III), the percentage expenditure under TSP is around 90 per cent of budget outlay. The non-fulfilment of TSP guidelines and non-utilization of budgetary outlay under TSP has been observed ever since TSP was launched. One of the reasons for non-fulfilment of the TSP norm is that so far there has been no legal requirement on the Union Ministries and Departments to fulfil the stipulated norms and target as the recommendations of Planning Commission do not have any constitutional legitimacy. Only 25 to 28 (Ministries and Departments) have been reporting plan expenditure earmarked for tribals after Narender Jadhav Committee recommended for proper implementation. Therefore, it is high time the Union Government must show its strong resolve for *adivasi* development by converting the TSP guidelines into legislation for non-divertible, non-lapsable, and earmarked funds should benefit the *adivasis* people and development of infrastructure in Scheduled Areas.

## Planning of TSP

- *The planning process of TSP should encourage all ministries and departments to:* identify the additional difficulties/challenges confronting STs' socio-economic developmental challenges in their sectors of concern, and the measures could be taken by them to address those special difficulties/challenges of STs, and the planning process should arrive at 'quantum of additional resources required for such special measures'. These additional resources devoted for the special measures for STs should then be reported under TSP.

  In this regard it is recommended:
- *Enact legislation on TSP:* that provides for earmarking of Plan allocations for STs in proportion to their share in the total

population at national level, to ensure effective implementation of TSP by all ministries. Andhra Pradesh is the pioneer state in the country to have passed the 'Andhra Pradesh Scheduled Castes Sub-Plan and Tribal Sub-Plan (Planning, Allocation and Utilization of Financial Resources) Act. No 1 of 2013 for the effective implementation of Scheduled Caste Sub Plan (SCSP) and Tribal Sub Plan (TSP)'.

- *Specific concerns of tribal women:* should be identified and accounted for, while planning the schemes and programmes across sectors. They face challenges distinct from tribal men and non-tribal women. These should be adequately addressed while planning programmes to be reported in TSP.
- *Set up a nodal body in each Ministry for TSP:* A unit should be set up in every Ministry for proper implementation, supervision and monitoring of the strategy. It should act as the nodal agency within each ministry and department to recognize the specific disadvantages faced by tribals in their respective sectors and suggest how the policies/guidelines/programmes of the ministry can be made more responsive to the specific needs of the group. Further, wherever needed, this unit can help conceptualize new schemes for the tribals and improve the coverage of schemes in the tribal areas.

## Proper Utilization of the Budget of Ministry of Tribal Affairs (MoTA) for Good Governance

The Ministry of Tribal Affairs (MoTA) was set up in 1999 with the objective of providing more focused approach on the integrated socio-economic development of the Scheduled Tribes (STs), in a coordinated and planned manner. The Ministry is the nodal Ministry for overall policy, planning and coordination of programmes for development of STs. All the programmes and schemes for tribal development are implemented with the help of the union departments, state departments, UT administrations, NGOs, and institutions of the local self government. The schemes and programmes focus on three crucial aspects of integrated development of tribal population namely: infrastructure, community and personality development.

1. There is an urgent need to make systemic changes in the way MOTA and Tribal Departments function; their approach must change from simply spending their own budget through

narrow departmental schemes to knowledge-based advocacy with other concerned Ministries/Departments.

2. MoTA is not able to spend even the limited budget allotted to it. Table 1 shows the budget estimate, revised estimate and actual plan expenditure for the previous year along with the budget estimate for 2014–15.

Plan and non-Plan allocation for the Ministry of Tribal Affairs and expenditure incurred during the last five years is given in Table 1.

**Table 1**

*Budgetary Provision and Expenditure for Tribal Affairs – Union Budget*

(Rupees in Crores)

| *Year* | *BE Budget* | *RE Revised* | *AE Account* | *% of AE against BE* |
|---|---|---|---|---|
| 2011–12 | 3,740.01 | 3,740.01 | 3,638.71 | 97.29 |
| 2012–13 | 4,108.00 | 3,115.55 | 3,072.63 | 74.80 |
| 2013–14 | 4,295.94 | 3,896.05 | 3,820.88 | 88.97 |
| 2014–15 | 4,497.96 | 3,850.00 | – | 85.61 |
| 2015–16 | 4,792.19 | – | – | – |

*Source:* Demands on Grants, Ministry of Tribal Affairs, GOI.

3. Looking at backwardness among *adivasis* and isolation, the Union Government should take measures to fully utilize the budget and enhance the budget outlay for the year 2015–16 to ₹ 10,000 crore for providing direct welfare benefits 8.6 per cent *adivasi* people.

## What Affects the Schedule Areas is Poor Governance

Apart from poor utilization of funds under TSP and also by MOTA, tribals have also suffered because of the poor quality of governance. Programme delivery and various services has deteriorated due to shortage of staff, and also, the fact that in tribal areas, where government servants are reluctant to work, it is a pity that massive vacancies exist in tribal regions in the face of acute educated unemployment in the country, and health care services is example as revealed by NRHM-14.

## *A Systemic Change is Needed for Governance*

The MOTA should give sufficient attention to the important problems of the tribals on the plea that many of these subjects, such as land alienation, displacement, and PESA, have not been allotted to it. Even then the Ministry should play a more proactive role in addressing these issues by pursuing with the concerned Ministries, therefore MOTA should establish a separate monitoring mechanism/body like National Tribal Development Authority (NTDA) to bring out the evidences about the poor implementation of acts for the protection of tribals' concerns and poor delivery of schemes in the tribal areas and take up the issues with the sectoral Ministries and the states to improve their policies and implementation for tribal development. There should be strong policy framework for *adivasis.*

## Policy Framework for *Adivasi*

There should be a facilitating policy framework for the *adivasi's* concerns for development to fill up the gap between *adivasis* and mainstream society. The Ministry of Tribal Affairs must pass The National Policy for Tribal (*adivasis*) with nationwide debate that should be the basis for future visions for the 8.6 per cent population of the country. Besides, the national acts passed for the protection, justice, development and welfare of *adivasis* should be implemented in true letter and spirit. The Ministry of Tribal Affairs (MoTA) must play a proactive role to monitor and review the status of implementation of acts and it must coordinate with the entire department for better implementation of all the acts and policy provisions.

## Revisit the Implementation of FRA

The recent FRA-2006 Act (Forest Rights Act), The Schedule Tribes and Other Traditional Forest Dwellers (Recognization of Forest Rights) Act, 2006, to do away historic injustice on *adivasis* to confer the land and forest resources rights for survival is a welcome step but unfortunately, the verification process for conferring the land entitlement defeats the purpose of the Act. Till October 2014 (from the year 2006, in all the states), total number of claims for land entitlements submitted by (IFR Individual Forest Rights) *adivasis* is 38.72 lakh and only 38.68 per cent forest land cultivators have been distributed land deeds; 44 per cent land claims have been rejected and 17.39 per cent land claims are still to be decided. The MOTA should issue direction to the state governments to re-verify the rejected claims and for the verification process; provisions of PESA (Panchayat Extension in Schedule Areas) should be employed, giving Gram Sabha to verify the claims. The process of conferring the Community Forest Right (CFR) should be expedited, so far 27.58 per cent out of total 97,579 CFR received have been distributed.

### *Demand for Development Forest Land under FRA*

The Union Government should also announce a financial package for the development of forest land conferred on forest land cultivators for enhancing the land yield through modern techniques like micro-irrigation, soil improvement, quality seeds, fertilizers, and animal husbandry for increasing family income.

The scheme titled 'Tribal Forest Dwellers Empowerment Scheme of NSTFDC' launched last year (National Schedule Tribes Finance and Development Corporation) for economic development of FRA beneficiaries, given land rights under FRA-2006, provides concessional financial loans with 6 per cent interest. The FRA beneficiaries should be provided subsidy for the development of land yield, as the poor tribals can hardly afford the loans.

## Specific for Human Development of *Adivasis*

### *Addressing the Malnourishment and Healthcare among Tribal Women and Children*

As most of the field-based survey reports and NFHS-3 survey finding reveal that tribal children and women are inter-generationally malnourished. High prevalence of wasting in this group is of particular concern MoTA (2013). Around 77 per cent of children belonging to ST category are anaemic, including 26 per cent who are mildly anaemic, 47 per cent are moderately anaemic and above 3.3 per cent are severely anaemic. ST children fare worst compared to all social groups, as far as 'any anaemia' prevailing among them is concerned.

Hence, special attention needs to be paid to ensure for them adequate access to nutrition-related programmes (viz., the ICDS, mid-day meal scheme, and public distribution system for foodgrains). The Union Government should initiate and devise a scheme for providing additional foodgrains through Public Distribution System (PDS) to tribal families, besides additional milk supplement to the malnourished women, girls, children and lactating mothers. Gujarat provides milk supplement under 'Dudh Sanjivini Yojna' to students. The milk supplement with 200 ml. fortified milk contains 3 per cent fat, 24 gm carbohydrate, 7 gm protein, vitamin A 500 IU and vitamin D 40 IU. The Union Government should initiate such scheme for highly malnourished children and women and lactating mothers with such scheme.

### *Healthcare Services Needs Improvement*

The problem is compounded by the fact that 'in spite of the efforts of the government, these tribal areas continue to suffer from poor maternal and child health services and ineffective coverage under national health and nutrition programmes' (MoTA, 2013). The Rural Health Infrastructure in Tribal Areas (NRHM-2014, as on 31 March 2014) of NRHM data shows that the basic health infrastructure such as the Sub-Centres, Community Health Centres (CHCs), Public Health Centres (PHCs) and others fall short of the requirement in the tribal areas Annexure IV. Shortage of Health care providing Human resource like doctors at PHCs (Primary Health Centres) and CHC (Community Health Centres) is 1,466 and 397 respectively, Besides, the post of Pediatricians for providing child care services is vacant 365, likewise posts of obstetricians and gynaecologist is 437 vacant in tribal areas.

The shortage of healthcare human resources has detrimental impact on the health status of tribals in general, women and children in particular. The MoTA must take up the issue of vacancy of healthcare with respective state government and Union Ministry of Health for improving the governance of healthcare services in the Schedule Areas.

### *Women's Ownership over Forest Resources*

*Adivasi* women have traditional knowledge and wisdom for management of the forestry resources for their sustainable utilization for their survival and nutrition. There should be policy framework for according priority to ownership rights of natural resources with capacity building in alternate livelihoods: (i) upgrading of traditional knowledge and skills and revitalizing them in areas where they have been lost; (ii) introduction of new knowledge and technologies to support women's access to expanded markets; and (iii) women's unmediated access to collective or individual ownership of resources, including land, housing and finances. This last is seen as a means to empower women and increase their economic security for better provision of food and nutrition of the young and not so young *adivasi* women and men.

### *Mechanism for Marketing of Minor Forest Produce (MFP) through Minimum Support Price (MSP) and Development of Value for MFP*

The Budget outlay for Mechanism for Marketing of Minor Forest Produce (MFP) through Minimum Support Price (MSP) and Development of Value for MFP is ₹ 317 crore. This is the only scheme for STs for which there is substantial increase in the outlay in BE 2014–15 compared to 2013–14 (₹ 122 crore). This is a welcome scheme for Minor Forest Produces gatherers. The Budget outlay should be enhanced to help the MFP gatherers as the most of gatherers are tribal women. This will certainly help tribal women to have more remuneration.

## Human Resource Development and Empowerment through Education

### Enhancing the Welfare Measures

The drop-out rates among the tribal students is very higher at each level as shown in the below table. There are several schemes run by Union and respective state governments for promoting the education level among the ST students but the benefits provided under these schemes are very meagre in amount with economic ceiling criteria to access the benefits. As the Union government provides scholarship benefits at pre-matric and post-matric level, there is need to provided financial assistance from the Union government at primary level as well. The amount being provided as scholarship should be enhanced to assist the students as in context of prevailing rates. Besides, income criteria for eligibility to access the benefits under these schemes should be removed.

Presently, under the pre-matric scholarship schemes parent annual income should be less than ₹ 2 lakh and under the post-matric scholarship scheme the income level is ₹ 2.5 lakh, in the present circumferences the parent's annual income ceiling should be removed for the most disadvantageous groups like *adivasis*.

There should be financial support to parents for education at primary level as the literacy level among the *adivasis* is very low and drop-out rate is very high. To retain the *adivasis* children to gain the education and skills, the financial assistance at primary level in form of foodgrains for attending the schools for 80 per cent school days should be provided.

**Table 2**

*School Drop-out Rates (DoR) (in %)*

| | *ST* | *All* | *Gap* |
|---|---|---|---|
| Classes I–V | 35.6 | 27 | 8.6 |
| Classes I–VIII | 55 | 40.6 | 14.4 |
| Classes 1–X | 70.9 | 49.3 | 21.6 |

*Source:* Statistics of School Education 2010–11

### *Suggestion for Enhancing the Financial Support*

| *Scheme* | *Present* | *Should be Changed to* |
|---|---|---|
| Post-matric scholarship for scheduled tribes students | The maintenance allowance for hosteller is between ₹ 380 to ₹ 1,200 p.m. and for day scholars from ₹ 230 to ₹ 500 p.m. depending upon the level of courses | The maintenance allowance for hostellers should be enhanced to ₹ 2,000 and for day scholars ₹ 1,000 p.m. in the prevailing rates of commodities |
| Pre-matric scholarship for ST students studying in classes IX and X | Scholarship @ ₹ 150 per month for day scholars and @ ₹ 350 per month for hostellers, for a period of 10 months in a year. | Scholarship of ₹ 150 p.m. is a meagre amount to take care of daily needs of a student, therefore the scholarship amount should be enhanced to ₹ 500 p.m. for day scholar and ₹ 1,000 p.m. for hostellers |

### *Schemes for Educational Development and Empowerment of STs*

1. Provision of Anganwadi Centre (AWC) in every habitation of STs with a qualified and well trained teacher.
2. High quality residential schools from Class VI to XII, one each for ST girls and ST boys, should be set up in each of the blocks (Taluk level) in the Scheduled Areas of the country for quality education.
3. Strengthening the delivery of scholarship schemes as under:
   (a) Post-Matric Scholarship Scheme
   (b) Overseas Scholarship Scheme

(c) Coaching and Allied Scheme
(d) Scheme for Upgradation of Merit
(e) Rajiv Gandhi National Fellowship
(f) Top Class Education
(e) Educational Loans for ST students for full time professional and technical courses provided by the National Scheduled Tribes Finance and Development Corporation.

There should not be any income criteria of family to access the scholarship for categories which are so educationally backward.

## Development of PVTG (Particular Vulnerable Tribal Groups)

The PVTG, of 75 such groups some of them are rare group and less in numbers, are the most vulnerable section among Schedule Tribes. It becomes very essential to allocate adequate funds from central sector/centrally sponsored and state plan schemes for the socio-economic development of PVTGs. The PVTGs should be provided with opportunities for livelihood within their surrounding socio-cultural environment vicinity with 'Conservation-cum-Development CCD', besides focusing on the basic amenities of housing, drinking water, education and economic upliftment, electricity supply and free healthcare services.

## Sharing of Benefits from Resources

As tribal belt is endowed with natural and mineral resources and the tribal people have suffered the displacement and land alienation for extraction of mineral resources for the development. Therefore, the profits of all natural resource-based commercial activities in tribal areas, including mining and power generation, should be taxed at higher rates and revenues thus collected should be shared between the union, state and local government bodies so as to ensure its utilization for the benefit of *adivasis*.

## Schemes for Economic Development and Empowerment of STs that should be included in a Meaningful TSP

1. Effective machinery for preventing non-tribals from buying or occupying or possessing any land of STs – effective

machinery for strict implementation of the Schedule Areas Land Transfer Regulations/Acts existing in some states (and to be introduced in other states)

2. Irrigation for all unirrigated, but irrigable lands of STs through micro-irrigation, drip irrigation and lift irrigation, the Union budget should address the irrigation issues of tribals, as the most of catchment areas is in tribal areas but command areas is in the plains.
3. Union Government should create Tribal Land Bank. The land should be procured with each year's unspent budget under TSP and MoTA. The land should be distributed for livelihood purpose among landless tribal's cooperative, those who have lost the land for the development process.
4. The tribal youth should be provided skills and income generating assets, implements and vehicles like auto rickshaws and taxis for livelihood.
5. Massive skill development programme along with all necessary resource-related, finance-related, management-related and market-related linkages.
6. A massive programme of housing for all ST families and provision of all essential facilities like drinking water, electricity supply, roads, sanitation and space for keeping their animals in all ST localities/habitations.
7. Strengthening the working of National Scheduled Tribes Finance Development Corporation (NSTFDC) and National Scheduled Castes Finance and Development Corporation (NSCFDC) and their state counterparts and Tribal Marketing Federation (TRIFED, State Tribal Development Cooperative Corporations) and other such national and state level organizations set up for marketing of tribal produce and collections.
8. For enhancing the livelihood opportunities, the Union Government should initiate Integrated Livestock Development Programme by supporting the breeding, feeding and management services at the doorsteps of the dairy farmers in their vicinity and these services be provided through 'Integrated Livestock Development (ILD) Centres'. Each of these ILD centres will be operated by *a* local educated unemployed

youth and will cover about 5–6 villages within a radius of 5–8 km. This will improve the breed of milch animal, enhance milk yield, address the nutrition issue and also provide employment to educated youth.

- There is a need to improve the access of tribals to justice. Data by the National Legal Services Authority (NLSA) shows that the many cases concerning STs are still pending. In this regard there is a need to strengthen the NLSA by earmarking budgetary outlays for the same and address the issues of staff shortages.
- Measures to strengthen the implementation of the Biological Diversity Act need to be put in place.
- When designing the schemes for tribals, there is a need to pay special attention to developing schemes in the areas of agro-forestry and animal husbandry, as these are crucial sectors for the group.

## Van Bandhu Kalyan Yojana

The government launched for the welfare of tribals, Vanbandhu Kalyan Yojana with initial allocation of ₹ 100 crore. The Van Bandhu Kalyan Yojana launched in Gujarat in 2007 with 10-point definite agenda focusing with outcome oriented intervention and planning, participation of local communities and also rigorous monitoring of tribal areas schemes. The 10-point agenda includes vision of: (1) poverty removal, (2) mainstreaming (PVTG), (3) education, (4) shelter, (5) health care, (6) drinking water, (7) irrigation, (8) basic facilities, (9) urban development and (10) skill development for migrant families.

The Van Bandhu Kalyan Yojna also includes implementation in mission mode, time bound and outcome orientation, involvement of every implementing department, experts and professional for capacity building. The Union Government's Van Bandhu Kalyan Yojana seems to supplement the gaps by providing assistance to voluntary organizations, TRIFED, research and training, vocational training, national commission for STs, monitoring and evaluation, fellowship, assistance to ASSAM, etc.

The Union Government should follow the Gujarat Van Bandhu Kalyan Yojana and to achieve the same outcome by allocating the Ten point agenda, also known as Chief Minister's

Agenda at state level, it should be Prime Minister's 10-Point Agenda at the Union level

The budget outlay should be enhanced by multifold to get the desired result at national level as per the TSP guidelines.

## Annexure I

*Development Indicators for Adivasis and Others/All*

| *Indicators* | *Year* | *Adivasi* | *Other/All* |
|---|---|---|---|
| Literacy Rate | 2011 | 59 | 73 |
| Literacy Rate among Women | 2011 | 49.4 | 64.6 |
| Poverty, Source: NSSO, 2011–12 | 2011–12 | | |
| | Urban | 24.1 | 13.7 |
| | Rural | 45.3 | 25.7 |
| Infant Mortality Rate | 2005–06 | 62.1 | 48.9 |
| < 5 Mortality Rate | 2005–06 | 95.7 | 74.3 |
| Women with BMI<18.5 (%) | 2005–06 | 46.6 | 29.3 |
| Women with Anaemia (%) | 2005–06 | 68.5 | 51.2 |
| Household Access to Sanitation (Latrine) | 2011 | 22.6 | 46.9 |
| Open Defecation | 2011 | 49.8 | 74.7 |
| Households having Drinking water Facility | 2011 | | |
| | within Premises | 19.7 | 46.6 |
| | Near the Premises | 46.7 | 35.8 |
| | Away from Premises | 33.6 | 17.6 |
| Main Source of Drinking Water | Treated Tap water | 53.82 | 65.46 |
| | Un-treated Tap water | 19.58 | 21.62 |
| | Uncovered Well spring | 26.6 | 12.92 |
| Assetless Houses | 2011 | 37.3 | 17.8 |
| Employment Status in Rural Areas (2009–10) | Self-employed | 44 | 47.4 |
| | Labourers | 46.5 | 40.4 |
| | Others | 9.5 | 12.2 |
| Employment Status in Urban Areas (2009–10) | Self-employed | 23.3 | 34.7 |
| | Labourers | 38.4 | 39.7 |
| | Casual labourers | 21.1 | 13.4 |
| | Other | 16.9 | 12.1 |

*Source:* Census, 2011, NFHS-3, India Human Development Report, NSS Report

## Annexure II

*Utilization of TSP Budget*

| *Particulars of Total Plan and Share of TSP (₹ in Crore)* | | | | | | | |
|---|---|---|---|---|---|---|---|
| | *2012–13* | *2013–14* | *2013–14* | *2014–15* | *2014–15* | *2014–15* | *2015–16* |
| | *(AE)* | *(BE)* | *(RE)* | *(IB)* | *(BE)* | *(RE)* | |
| Total Union Plan Budget | 4,13,625 | 5,55,322 | 4,75,532 | 5,55,322 | 5,75,000 | 4,67,931 | 4,65,277 |
| Allocation under TSP | 16,723.73 | 24,598.39 | 22,030.47 | 30,726.07 | 32,387 | 20,536 | 19,980 |
| % of TSP | 4.04 | 4.43 | 4.63 | 5.53 | 5.63 | 4.39 | 4.29 |
| Due to TSP in percentage | 8.6 | 8.6 | 8.6 | 8.6 | 8.6 | 8.6 | 8.6 |
| TSP as per | 35,571.75 | 47,757.69 | 40,895.75 | 47,757.69 | 49,450 | 40,242 | 40,013 |
| Guideline should be Dental Under TSP | 18,848.02 | 23,159.3 | 18,865.28 | 17,031.62 | 17,063 | 19,706 | 20,033 |

*Source:* Compiled from Statement 1,16 and Expenditure Budget Vol. I, Union Budget of various years.

## Annexure III

*Status of Utilization of TSP Budget and Unspent Budget*

| | *Budget Estimates ₹ in Crore* | *Revised Estimates ₹ in Crore* | *Actual Expenditure ₹ in Crore* | *Utilization Against Outlay in %* | *Shortfall Utilization ₹ in Crore* | *Shortfall in Utilization %* |
|---|---|---|---|---|---|---|
| 2012–13 | 21,710 | 18,721 | 20,184 | 93% | –1,526.01 | 7.03 |
| 2013–14 | 24,598 | 22,030 | 22,039 | 90% | –2,568.42 | 10.44 |
| 2014–15 | 32,387 | 20,536 | | 63% (RE) | | |
| 2015–16 | 19,980 | | | | | |

*Source:* TSP Statement for 2013–14, 2014–15 and 2015–16.

Marginally reduced contribution by the Union Government in BE 2015–16 vis-à-vis RE 2014–15 is on account of enhanced devolution of Union taxes to state as recommended by the Fourteenth Finance Commission (FFC). Consequent to the acceptance of the FFC award, Plan outlay of the Union has come down. However, to keep the budget for such programmes unchanged, states are to contribute from their enhanced resources. It is estimated that any shortfall in SfSP/TSP on account of FFC award will be made up by the states from their enhanced resources. Therefore, the total resources available for SCSP/TSP will remain unaffected.

## Annexure IV

*Rural Health Infrastructure in Tribal Areas (NRHM-2014)*

*Rural Health Infrastructure in Tribal Areas (NRHM-2014), (As on 31 March 2014)*

| *Sr. No.* | *Particulars* | *Required* | *Sanctioned* | *In Position* | *Vacant* | *Shortfall* |
|---|---|---|---|---|---|---|
| 1. | Health Workers (F) ANM at Sub-Centres in Tribal Area | 26,949 | 32,500 | 35,600 | 3,124 | 1,219 |
| 2. | Health Workers(F) ANM at Sub-Centre and PHC – In Tribal Area | 30,844 | 37,677 | 40,145 | 3,498 | 1,727 |
| 3. | Health Workers (M) ANM at Sub-Centres in Tribal Areas | 26,949 | 17,534 | 12,380 | 5,973 | 15,714 |

*Cont'd...*

*...Cont'd*

| | | | | | | |
|---|---|---|---|---|---|---|
| 4. | Health Assistant (Female) LHV/at PHCs in Tribal Area | 3,895 | 2,653 | 2,107 | 647 | 1,946 |
| 5. | Health Assistant (MALE) at PHCs in Tribal Area | 3,895 | 2,125 | 1,679 | 624 | 2,606 |
| 6. | Doctors at PHCs in Tribal Area | 3,895 | 5,177 | 4,218 | 1,466 | 701 |
| 7. | Surgeon at CHCs in Tribal Area | 979 | 539 | 146 | 397 | 823 |
| 8. | Obstetricians and Gynaecologist at CHC in Tribal Areas | 979 | 616 | 184 | 437 | 795 |
| 9. | Physician at CHCs in Tribal Areas | 979 | 502 | 125 | 384 | 854 |
| 10. | Pediatricians at CHC in Tribal Areas | 979 | 495 | 145 | 365 | 834 |
| 11. | Total Specialists at CHC in Tribal Areas | 3,916 | 2,149 | 600 | 1,570 | 3,316 |
| 12. | Radiographer at CHC in Tribal Areas | 979 | 656 | 375 | 331 | 628 |
| 13. | Pharmacist at PHC and CHCs in Tribal Areas | 4,874 | 4,293 | 3,193 | 1,313 | 1,807 |
| 14. | LAB Technicians at PHCs and CHCs in Tribal Areas | 474 | 3,093 | 2,624 | 812 | 2,279 |
| 15. | Nursing Staff at PHCs and CHCs in Tribal Areas | 10,748 | 9,008 | 8,842 | 2,018 | 3,899 |
| | Total Healthcare Staff in Tribal Areas | 1,25,734 | 1,19,017 | 1,12,363 | 22,959 | 39,148 |

*Source:* NRHM – National Rural Health Mission (2014).

# 17

# Making Sense of Implementation of PESA in Gujarat

## Some Observations

**Binoy Acharya**

I am thankful to Prof. Vidyut Joshi for asking me to write about the implementation of PESA in Gujarat on the occasion of International Day of the World's Indigenous People, 9 August. This is written deriving lessons from experience of capacity building of Panchayat Raj Institutions (PRIs) and participation in various official and non-official consultations during last 20 years. The title, 'Making Sense', is borrowed from the Vishvajit Pandya and Majumdar's article on Jarawa tribe in Andaman Island (*EPW*, No. 44, 3 November 2012).

The Panchayat (Extension in Schedule Area) Act, 1996 provides an opportunity for decentralized governance in tribal areas (Schedules V and VI) 'in consonance with the customary law, social and religious practices and traditional management practices of community resources', U/S – 4(b). In the past 20 years, there have been very little efforts by the government to implement it. This paper seeks to find out why in Gujarat PESA has not received much importance despite a large section of its population are Bhil tribes with a purpose to draw attention of policy-makers and senior administrators.

On 7 January 2011, a regional workshop on PESA was organized at Udaipur which was presided by Hon'ble Minister,

MoPR, GoI, Dr C.P. Joshi. Gujarat was represented by five Zila Panchyat Pramukhs for the tribal districts, respective DDOs. The author was nominated by the Government of Gujarat to participate as an NGO representative. This consultation provided a new perspective. All the Zila Panchayat Pramukhs from the PESA districts in their deliberation made it clear that they do not want to be governed by the customary law. They further made it clear that they no more practice the Bhil customary law in their present day transactions. There might be some socio-cultural Bhil tribal practices, but are limited to the personal sphere of life and not linked to public life. The real representation of this view can be questioned, but this view is predominant the state. In our interaction with the sarpanches in the PESA area, there has been eagerness to know the provisions and the implementation process. When the elected sarpanches know that in the Scheduled Areas the Gram Sabha or the panchayats at the appropriate level have the right over planning and management of minor water bodies, management of minor minerals, including lease and auction, ownership over minor forest produce, control over money lending, etc. they feel a sense of empowerment. It is evident that they are in favour of decentralization of management over natural resources, minor forest products and minor mineral. The Bhil tribal traditional customs does not come in the process of devolution.

Recently in a review meeting on PESA between the MoPR, GoI and Department of Panchyati Raj, Government of Gujarat, (30 January 2015), the author had the honoured privilege to participate. Besides, the secretaries and other senior level officials, selected PRI representatives from PESA area were also present. On the issue of implementation of 4(d) of the Act, ('every Gram Sabha shall be competent to safeguard and preserve the tradition and customs of the people, their cultural identity, community resources and the customary mode of dispute resolution') there was a presentation on behalf of Rajasthan Government on the implementation of conflict resolution keeping with the community traditions. The PESA rules of Government of Rajasthan (2011, Ch. III, Sec. 11–16) states that local level disputes and minor crimes which have provision of punishment of less than two years under the Indian Penal Code, 1860 will be redressed by the Gram Sabha and a

Peace Committee formed by the Gram Sabha keeping with community traditions and the spirit of the Constitution of India. On the issues of incidents that breach the peace of the village, matters related to superstition and sorcery (black magic), resolution of disputes, the Peace Committee and the Gram Sabha has the full authority to deliberate and arrive at a decision. Gram Sabha may make a request to the District Collector for presence of an observer to provide factual and scientific information on the matter. When the police receive information on such minor disputes, the officer shall present a detailed report of the matter to the Gram Sabha. As far as possible, the minor conflicts shall be resolved by the Peace Committee in the Gram Sabha. This is a provision well harmonized with the tradition and culture of tribal way of conflict resolution. It is interesting to note the response of the Gujarat elected representatives and the senior government officials. They are of the view that any crime or dispute that attracts Indian Penal Code, 1860, shall not be given in the hands of tradition and culture.

It is the same Bhil tribe who inhabit in Gujarat and Rajasthan. In one state there is openness to restore the tribal culture and tradition and make it functional in the context of modern day, where as in another state there is strong resistance not only from the administration but also from the tribal community and the leaders. In both Gujarat and Rajasthan, there are civil society groups who have been mobilizing the tribal community and interfacing with the government to implement PESA, particularly transferring power to the tribal community to manage their natural resources and management of local conflict and disputes based on their culture and tradition. In many discussions in Gujarat it has been heard that the matters of dispute resolution can only be transferred to Gram Sabha to be redressed keeping in the tradition, after the tradition and culture of the tribals are codified and checked in terms of alignment with Indian Penal Code. One time eminent Civil Service Officer, B.D. Sharma, in the campaign to popularize PESA gave a call to all tribal communities emphasizing that it is a revolutionary Act and they must demand for the implementation of the Act. He wrote a popular booklet in Hindi named *Dole Utha Himalaya – Himalaya is Shaking* !! Sanjay Upadhaya (*EPW*, No. 41, 9–15 October 2010) writes that PESA was enacted with very little debate in the

Parliament and outside. Even today after 20 years of enactment of PESA, there is very little understanding on the key thrust of the Act which primarily offers an opportunity to the tribal community to exercise self-governance on management of natural resources.

The governance process in India has been more conversant with implementation of schemes with an administrative apparatus rather than strengthening decentralized governance. The Gujarat administrative mechanism of tribal development is popularly known as 'Gujarat Pattern' in which the budget of the tribal sub-plan is ploughed back to different departments for implementation of schemes in the tribal area. It also may be stated here that in Gujarat the MGNREGA is being implemented by administration at the taluka level. The gram panchayats only plan and approve the works. Perhaps the years of implementation of schemes by the administration while delivered services, has given inadequate emphasis on decentralized governance, particularly as enshrined in PESA. The scheme-based development without empowerment of tribal communities has created a feeling even among the tribal leaders that mainstreaming of tribal community will only be possible by participating in the implementing schemes and not strengthening governance based on custom and tradition.

To cite an example, the Kotwalias, a tribal community of south Gujarat make a living from bamboo. Arun Patel of Gujarat Vidyapeeth, in an article in *Indian Journal of Traditional Knowledge* (2005), has documented that the Kotwalias produce 22 bamboo products on their own. However, their life depends on the release of bamboo by the forest department. They have no ownership over the bamboo forest. There has been no popular movement in Gujarat to extend community rights over any form of natural resources. The adjoining states of Maharashtra and Rajasthan have many assertions to establish community rights and management of natural resources based on traditional practices. The tribal village of Mendha Lekha in Gadchiroli district of Maharashtra has received the distinction of self-governance based on customary law. The story of self-rule in Mendha Lekha is all over the internet.

In Mendha Lekha all decisions are taken in the Gram Sabha. If any outside agency, government, research organizations, NGOs intends to carry out any work it has to take permission from the Gram Sabha. The village has constituted Van Suraksha Samiti –

VSS (Forest Protection of Committee) comprising Gram Sabha members and forest officials. As it is a Gram Sabha-led institutional framework of forest management the rules are set by the Gram Sabha and VSS. The disputes are settled in the Gram Sabha. They have successfully implemented total ban on procurement of liquor from the market. Gram Sabha controls the production of traditional liquor to be used for ceremonial purposes. The decision-making has a strong participation of women. Women have power to veto on the decision taken by the Gram Sabha. Mendha Lekha has revived the institution of Ghotul as a source of traditional knowledge for the education of the adolescents.

Interestingly, the self-rule of Mendha Lekha has its genesis much before the 73rd Constitutional Amendment and enactment of PESA in 1996. Mendha Lekha has inspired many villages and local leaders. Saigata village in Chandrapur district in Maharashtra, Olavanna in Kozhikode district in Kerala have set up exemplary self-governed system. The water harvesting and management of Olavanna have received both domestic and international recognition. Water management experts from Thailand, Philippines, Sudan, Iran, China and the USA have visited Olavanna. The self-governance of Mendha Lekha can be well understood by its famous slogan – *Dilli Mumbai Amchasarkar, Amache Ganavat Amhich Sarkar* (Delhi and Mumbai is our government, In our village we ourselves are the government). It is not that all the decisions on establishing self-governance came easily. There are many instances when the village and the government came in serious conflict. Mendha Lekha has travelled a long way in establishing self-rule. Currently, it is fixing the rates for forest produce in the Gram Sabha and engaged in open auction. It was reported that the action rate was much higher than the rate fixed by the Forest Department. Mendha Lekha Gram Sabha has PAN card and VAT registration.

Mendha Lekha is an example of a remote village inhabited by Maria Gonds who have been governing their village based on tribal customary law and have very well also adopted the modern management practices. It can be termed as an isolated example and the outcome can be credited to many external organizations like Vrikshmitra (Mohan Hirabai Hiralal), Kalpavrikshaand local leadership of the young tribal Devaji Tofa. Mendha Lekha example may not have replicated widely but gives a clear indication that the tribal community can be governed by their traditional customary law and at same time can integrate in the mainstream society.

In early part of 2015, the author had the privilege to attend 'Adivasi Sammelan' in Kotda block of Udaipur district in Rajasthan. The 'sammelan' was organized by the tribal village associations. (ASTHA, Udaipur-based NGO and partner organizations have promoted the Adivasi People's Organisation). It was said that about 150 villages of Udaipur and Dungarpur districts have declared self-rule under PESA. In their assessment of self-rule, they revealed that there is satisfactory progress in the areas; like: (i) power to enforce prohibition and regulate the sale of intoxicants, (ii) approval of village development plans for implementation of schemes by the Gram Sabha, and (iii) issue of utilization certificate on the government programmes by the Gram Sabha. Some progress has been achieved in the areas like (i) power to exercise control over money lending, (ii) ownership of minor forest produce, and (iii) consultation with the Gram Sabha before making land acquisition in schedule areas for development projects. In the areas where no progress has been made are related to: (i) dispute and conflict resolution as per the tradition keeping in mind the principle of natural justice, (ii) auction of minor mineral; and (iii) control of the local market.

The presentation by the tribal leaders on self-assessment of accomplishment of PESA created many a thought process with regard to achievement of PESA in Gujarat where the author has been working for many years and launched many awareness drives, trained the PRI representatives under PESA through the support of Government of Gujarat and conducted and participated in many official and non-official consultations. Here, the effort has been to arrive at a sense, why the PESA implementation is not effective in Gujarat. Rajasthan has enacted PESA rules in 2011 after prolonged consultations. In Gujarat, there is a PESA guideline and no rules have been notified yet. However, in Gujarat many Acts have been harmonized looking into the PESA Act, 1996. The Gujarat Money Lenders Act, 2011, has provisions for approval from the Gram Sabha with regard to registration and renewal for money lending and rate of interest in the schedule area. The Gujarat Mines and Mineral (Development and

Regulation) Act 1957 issued a notification in August 2010, stating that for the lease for extraction of minor mineral in the PESA area, explicit sanction of the Gram Sabha is required – Ch. II, 4(6). Direct interaction with PRI representatives in PESA area clearly reveals that neither there is any understanding on the harmonization of such Acts in favour of PESA, nor is there any interest for the implementation.

The Gujarat Minor Forest Produce Trade Nationalization Act, 1979 and the Gujarat State Forest Development Corporation Ltd. (Nigam) needs a special mention with regard to harmonization with PESA. It is well known that tribal people depend largely on the forest produce and transfer of management of some of the minor forest produce can contribute in strengthening tribal self-rule. It is learnt that the Forest Nigam fully controls the procurement, storage, value addition and marketing of the minor forest produce and there has been no official discussion on the transfer of management. The Halpatis and the Kotwalias who have subsistence level of production, perhaps benefit a lot if the minor forest produce management and the forest land under community rights developed by growing bamboo is left to the tribals. The Forest Nigam transfers certain amount of the profit from the sale of minor forest produce to the respective panchayats. The PRIs plead ignorance about the transfer of profit.

With regard to regulation and control over the production of traditional use of liquor the Government of Gujarat has issued permits to older tribal people. All the permits expired on 31 March 2015. A senior official reported that the *adivasis* of Gujarat have converted to 'Bhagats' – a lifestyle following the path of 'sanskritization'.

The question that needs to be asked is, whether the tribal community of Gujarat are fully/mostly mainstreamed and they do not need to practice their customary law in their local governance. How deep and wide is this realization. Is it a '*sarkari* articulation' imposed over the people or it is the aspiration of tribal communities in Gujarat to get freed from the tribal tradition, culture and customs. There is a view that not only tribal welfare programmes but also programmes designed for 'Adimjan Jati' – Primitive Tribal Groups (PTG) are top-down programmes with little emphasis on transfer of power to the tribals. To cite the argument on protection of Jarawas in Andaman Islands in pursuing their traditional way of life and need for insulation from the external world to stop the process of extinction, there is also a need to provide medical treatment at instances of outbreak of epidemic. Protection of tribal/indigenous culture and tradition is not in contradiction to adoption of modern living. Both can exist simultaneously. The provisions in PESA are in the direction of protection of tribal culture and customary law through self-governance and making available the provisions of development programmes of a democratic state. The over emphasis on the process of 'bhagatization' (sanskritization), mainstreaming without protection of traditional culture and customary law will lead to erosion of a tribal identity on the altar of development.

Where panchayats did not appear to have addressed this issue at all, the manner of disposal of waste could be a potential source of diseases and unhygienic living environment.

The scenario is no better when one looks at the manner of disposal of liquid waste by the sample households across the 23 tribal talukas. The dominant practice, immensely unhygienic, indicated was throwing the waste on the street. In certain cases, where the homestead was closer to farms liquid waste was made to flow there.

Even the limited discussion on the data collected on hygienic practices affirms the poor living environment in the survey areas. Inaction by the local state in addressing issues in IEC for healthier sanitation practices as well as safe disposal of solid and liquid waste could be pointed out as a key factor in perpetuating the risk of diseases and morbidity in the tribal talukas.

## Functioning of and Views on Water Supply Schemes in Villages

As has been made clear in the previous chapters, the schemes concerning drinking water as designed under the VKY were often indistinguishable from the existing systems or infrastructure. Hence, a series of questions asked about the general awareness about aspects of the drinking water schemes and even opinion about their performance and improvement elicited responses those were likely to be concerning the schemes under the VKY; however, in the absence of adequate information forthcoming from the official sources this was the best that could be done.

*Awareness about Schemes and Their Functioning:* As was surmised from the detailed data collected regarding the awareness of schemes and their functioning, the proportion of respondents knowing that their village and/or household has been served by a state provision of drinking water varied between about 97 per cent in Nasvadi and merely 17 per cent in Bhiloda. This affirmed that the drinking water component under the VKY had not received adequate attention by the villagers. It could be that the initiatives could be no different from the usual efforts made through the GWSSB or WASMO.

Respondents' knowledge, even of a basic nature, regarding the technical aspects of the water supply provision was important to note as that would reflect the efforts made by the concerned government functionaries to familiarize local inhabitants about the possible solutions for handling any minor problems in the system, be it non-functioning of a handpump or leakage in a pipe or broken washers. In certain talukas (as represented by the sample villages), a large proportion of households was familiar with the basic techniques/steps of sorting out a problem with the available drinking water supply infrastructure. For instance, in talukas as Amirgadh, Valia, Tilakwada and Vyara, more than 80 per cent of sample respondents stated to have been familiar with the technical aspects of the drinking water schemes. However, in talukas such as Bhiloda (12%) and Fatepura (20%), the awareness level was very low. This points to the poor or no efforts made to ensure a meaningful participation of the local community in the process of implementing the drinking water schemes/ programmes.

The practice of paying water charges was not quite common in the survey areas. While at one level many respondents were not even aware that a certain water tariff needed to be paid for the use of public facilities, many others had not paid the same for several years. The proportion of respondents having some idea about or actually paid such tariff was generally low across the sample talukas. Importantly, the proportion was below even 10 per cent in Bhiloda, Vijaynagar, Santrampur, Jhagadia, Mangrol, Umbergaon, Vyara, Valod, Chikhli and Bansda. Even when water charges were reported to have been paid, these were mostly those related to use of handpumps. It needs to be emphasized that the payment shown under handpumps related to shared bearing of costs of repair and maintenance as and when the contraption had failed. These payments were made collectively and on voluntary basis and have no reference to formal water tariffs as levied by the state. Practically no attention has been paid regarding the collection of water charges as was originally planned under the VKY.

Quite similar to the respondents, limited involvement in the payment of water charges, there was practically very little awareness amongst the sample households regarding the stages of implementation, including contributions (financial and/or labour, depending upon the system in question) to be made towards using drinking water systems, especially, that under the sector reforms or Swajaldhara (SRS) programme. However, the survey data revealed that most respondents did not have an idea regarding such methods/processes of implementation, which was often construed under the demand driven systems at least, as reflecting popular participation in the use and maintenance of drinking water infrastructure set up in the villages. However, only in case of handpumps, there appeared to be some degree of awareness by a relatively large proportion of sample households in a few talukas, namely Bhiloda, Nasvadi and Fatepura.

When it comes to community participation in maintaining the drinking water supply infrastructure the responses indicating responsibility taken up by sample households presents a mixed picture. While the proportion of responsible respondents was as high as over 95 per cent in talukas as Nasvadi, Tilakvada and Nandod, in Bhiloda the proportion was less than 17 per cent. However, as handpumps remained the ubiquitous source of drinking water in tribal areas, popular concern regarding the maintenance, repair and overall upkeep of the systems could be observed.

*Users Perspectives on the Schemes:* Questions regarding respondents' views about the major aspects of functioning of the drinking water schemes and infrastructure were asked in order to elicit a realistic assessment of the users at the village level. Respondents had expressed their opinion regarding issues in execution of the schemes, quality of work and utilization of funds for the same.

So far as execution of the schemes is concerned the overwhelming response has been positive indicating popular satisfaction over the schemes. While largely favourable response had come forth about their views on the overall quality of work, a few respondents did refer to the deficiencies in the quality of work. These included irregularities in the supply of water, leakages in the water tanks fallen into disrepair, pipelines not connected to the tanks built two years back, defunct motors and broken platforms for handpumps. In certain instances, the respondents felt that these could partly be due to the incompetence of the contractors whom the work was given and also because of the irresponsiveness of functionaries of the local offices in attending to complaints regarding the drinking water infrastructure as problems in handpumps, motors, pipelines or tanks.

However, their knowledge and opinion about fund utilization might not be a reliable basis to judge the efficiency of financial aspects of the schemes. In fact, as may be observed from the responses, in a large number of cases across the talukas, respondents did not have any information about the manner and extent of utilization of funds. Only in certain talukas, for instance, Jhalod and Bardoli, a larger proportion of respondents was aware that the funds for the drinking water schemes were routed through and managed by the gram panchayat. If transparency at the local level was a concern, then there was the need to revamp the information system that could be accessed by the villagers openly and without restrictions of any kind.

As regards the adequacy of water available the proportion of respondents expressing satisfaction varied widely across talukas. However, talukas where only less than one-third of respondents did find the supply adequate were Bhiloda and Vijaynagar. There were seven talukas where over half the respondents reported the availability of water below their minimum requirements. As far as regularity in water supply was concerned the situation appeared better in nine talukas where more than three-fourth of respondents had no issues about the timing of water supply. However, talukas where irregular supply was a serious concern were Bhiloda, Vijaynagar, Dharampur and Ahwa. Responses to the question of access to drinking water varied across talukas although Bhiloda and Vijaynagar emerged as facing a crisis-like situation. Perceptions about the quality of water suggested that most respondents agreed that the water supplied was of good potable quality. However, in the absence of chemical and bacteriological test of water, it would be difficult to establish its quality.

Soliciting popular suggestions towards improving drinking water supply in tribal areas yielded two main actions. One, efforts to provide water on a regular basis and reducing wastage through pipe were considered an important step in addressing the drinking water problem in the talukas. The major suggestion was about meticulous collection of people's contribution and depositing the same with the gram panchayat. The fund thus collected could be of use in the smooth administration of drinking water schemes.

## Concluding Observations

The central objective of this study had been to examine the status, functioning and constraints of policy initiatives in broad-basing access to safe drinking water amongst the tribal regions of Gujarat. As the state government efforts at provisioning drinking water in all parts, that eventually covers tribal tracts, have existed, under the Eleventh Plan, the TDD designed and initiated the VKY for the population to launch a series of special policy measures, include those concerning drinking supply. The initiatives took recourse to the four distinct schemes, namely, the RWSS, mini piped scheme, the handpumps and those under the sector reforms or Swajaldhara programme.

In terms of basic infrastructure in the tribal areas, the ownership of homestead, access to electricity approach-roads and schools by a large number of inhabitants was a positive feature. However, in the entire tribal belt as spread in the northern, central and southern regions of the state RWSS and individual pipe schemes were accessed by about 15 per cent and 35 per cent of the village respectively. Handpumps remained the major source of drinking water in about 37 per cent of villages. If one considers the three specific schemes, namely, handpumps, individual pipe scheme, mini pipe water scheme these account for over 80 per cent of all tribal villages in the northern, central southern regions, in terms of provisioning drinking water supply. It is important to note that all these depend significantly on the groundwater.

As has been consistently recognized, the crucial challenge facing the state efforts at broad-basing access to drinking water remains the governance of groundwater. While geo-hydrological factors could, uncritically, be shown as hindrances to drinking water access across space in the tribal areas, management of available resources in terms of conserving and enhancing supply has been a serious concern. It is well recognized that excessive dependence upon groundwater has implications for sustainability of energy resources and also cost. That both the supply and demand driven approaches have hardly invested efforts towards conservation of water – as through promoting/rejuvenating and modernizing (through scientific means, where required) water harvesting systems – remains a vital issue for policy attention in tribal areas.

The other issue that merits immediate attention is the role of local institutions in contributing to the decision-making processes in drinking water related infrastructure and distribution approaches. The fact that there was very little participation by the local inhabitants of the villages such as Pani Samitis and Gram Sabhas while discussing drinking water problems (and solutions), there is a definite need to review the processes of designing and implementing drinking water schemes in tribal regions. Much needs to be done in addressing the institutional lacunae in ensuring popular participation in all matters concerning drinking water provisioning and access.

Another dimension of drinking water provisioning relates to the dimension of water quality, which, as the field surveys laid bare, had received the least attention in such state interventions. In the absence of scientific testing (both chemical and bacteriological tests) of water supplied popular opinion cannot be accepted as the base to determine the potability of water. This calls for intensive policy efforts at setting up water quality testing facilities in the regions in question and also to ensure that the local people have the wherewithal to actually access the service.

There had been problems regarding group panchayats being a reason for certain villages (away from the village where the panchayat is located) failing to register their voice concerning several constraints facing availability and quality of drinking water. Moreover, within a village, secondary habitations also faced similar challenges as, typically, much of the policy action in drinking water would take place in the main village.

A particularly confounding aspect of the drinking water provisioning in tribal areas relates to the lack of clarity in the role and responsibility of at least the three agencies of the state, namely, the GWSSB, WASMO and TDD. Little systematic data are available even to show the list of villages in these tribal areas where drinking water schemes have been implemented under the VKY 10-Point Programme. Despite claims of transparency and efficiency, it was near impossible to obtain village wise and scheme wise financial information as the TDD, the originator of the VKY, did not possess relevant data on these. It is unclear as to the overlapping of the drinking water schemes in these villages and calls for scrutiny of claims of achievement.

It may be underscored that the governance of the drinking water under the VKY needs to be closely examined before arriving at any definitive view regarding its success or otherwise. It would be premature to speak of replicability of this as a 'model' elsewhere in India.

## Acknowledgements

Sincere thanks are due to the Tribal Development Department, Government of Gujarat, Gandhinagar, for sponsoring this study under its flagship programme the Vanbandhu Kalyan Yojana. The usual disclaimers apply.

## References

Das, Keshab and Memon, Gani. Decentralised Governance and Infirmities: Assessing Interventions in a Tribal Tahika of Gujarat. Report submitted to the Department of Rural Development Government of Gujarat, Gandhinagar. Gujarat Institute of Development Research, Ahmedabad. (Mimeo, unpublished), 2012.

Hirway, Iridira and Mahadevia, Darshini. 'Understanding Status of Drinking Water and Sanitation in Rural Gujarat' [http://www.slideshare. net/pravah/status-orwater-sanitation-in-gujarat-ihsg-final (Accessed 12 May 2015)], 2011.

Ministry of Tribal Affairs. *Statistical Profile of Scheduled Tribes in India 2013,* Statistics Division, Ministry of Tribal Affairs, Government of India, New Delhi, 2013. [http://www.tribal.nic.in/

WriteReadData/userfiles/file/Demographic.pdf (Accessed 5 May 2015)].

Ministry of Tribal Affairs. *Annual Report 2010–11,* Ministry of Tribal Affairs, Government of India, New Delhi, 2011. [http://tribal.nic.in/writereaddata/mainlinkFile/Filel288.pdf (Accessed 10 August 2012)].

Ministry of Tribal Affairs. *Annual Report 2011–12,* Ministry of Tribal Affairs, Government of India, New Delhi, 2012. [http://tribal.nic.in/writereaddata/mainlinkFile/Filel391.pdf (Accessed 10 August 2012)].

National Sample Survey Office (NSSO). *Key Indicators of Household Consumer Expenditure in India, 2009–10. NSS 66th Round (July 2009 – June 2010),* NSSO, Ministry of Statistics and Programme Implementation, Government of India, New Delhi, 2011.

# Appendices

*Tribal Groups*

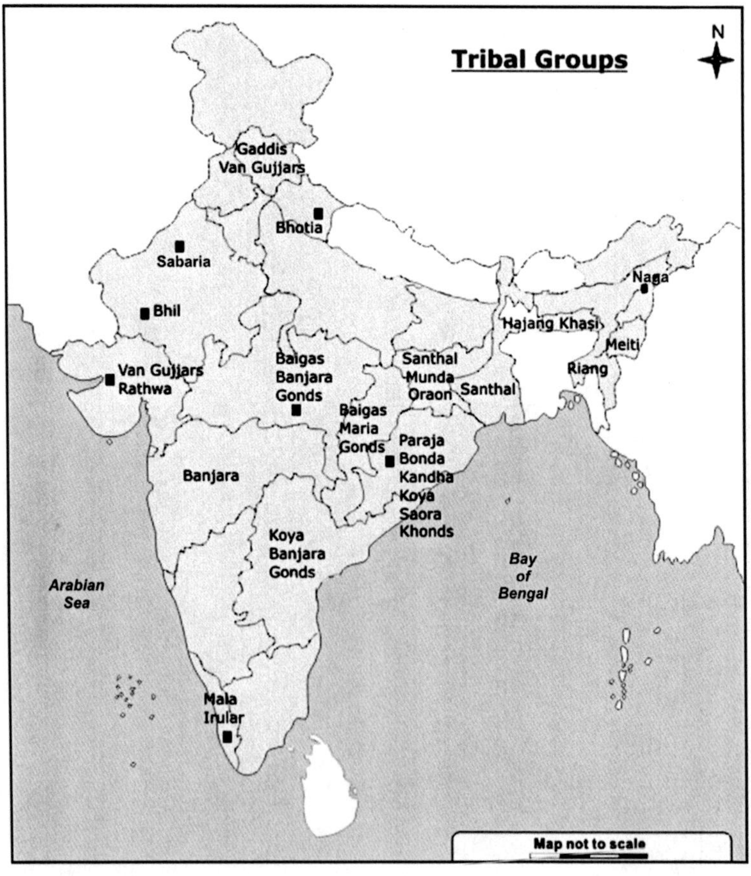

*Some Indian Tribes*

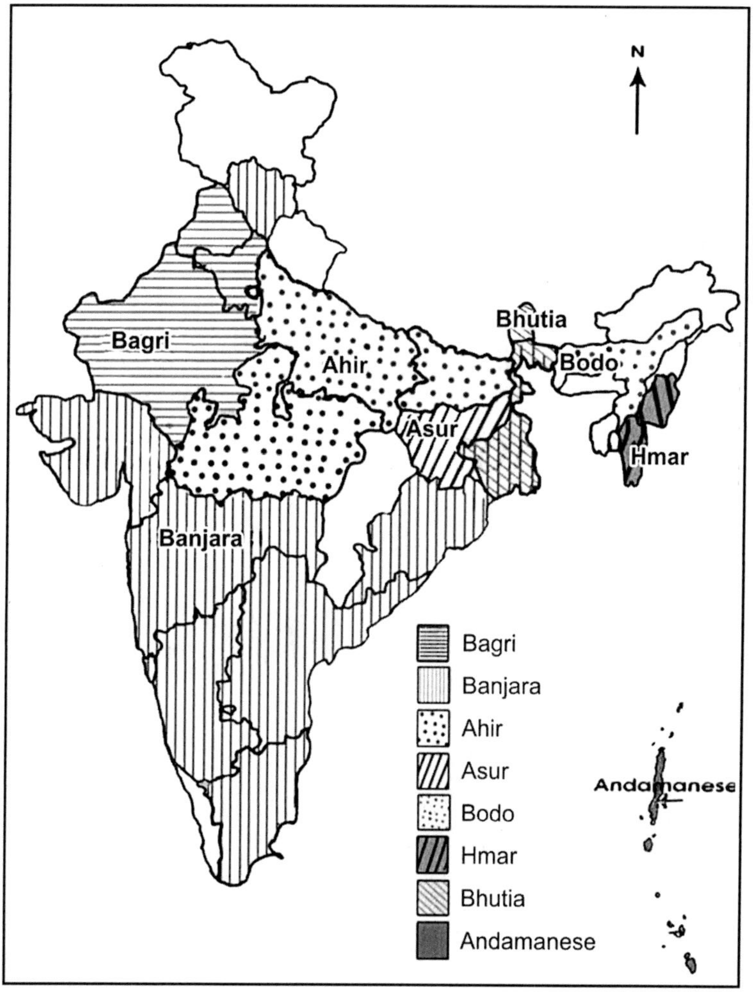


*Source:* indianmirror.com

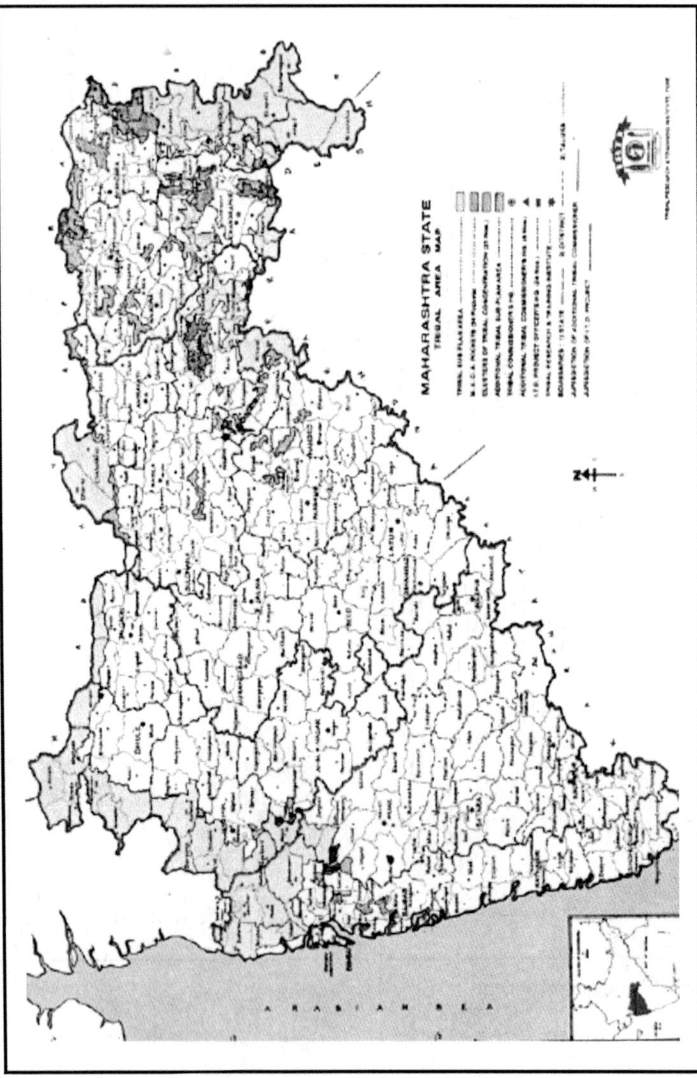


*Map of Maharashtra*

Tribal Concentration Areas in Madhya Pradesh

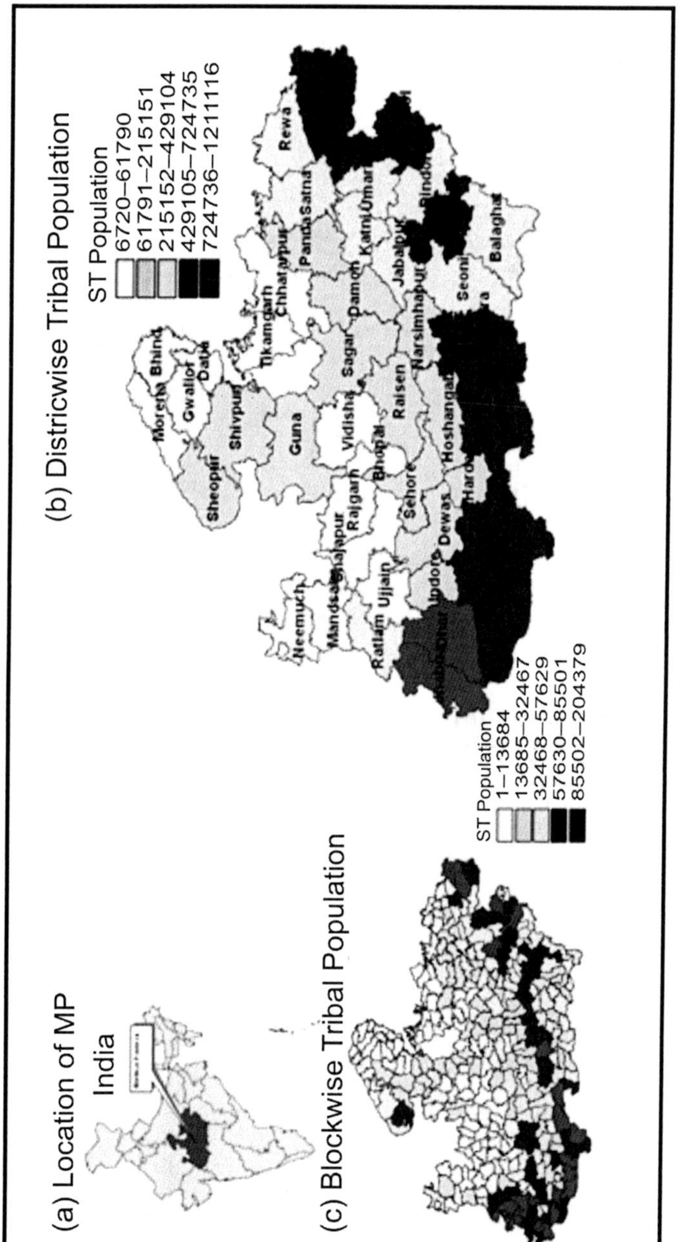

*Tribal Concentration Areas in Rajasthan*

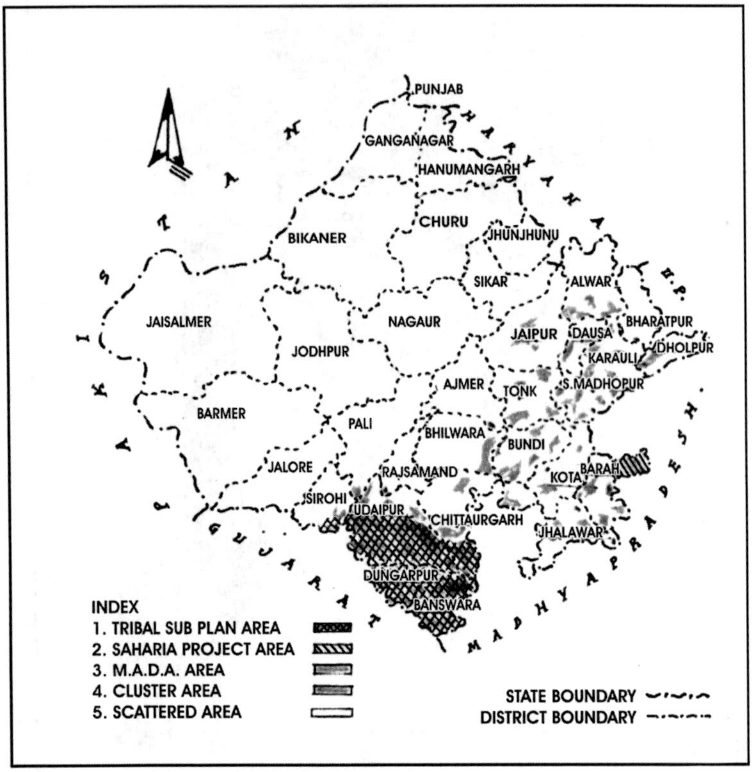

*Tribal Concentration Areas in Gujarat*

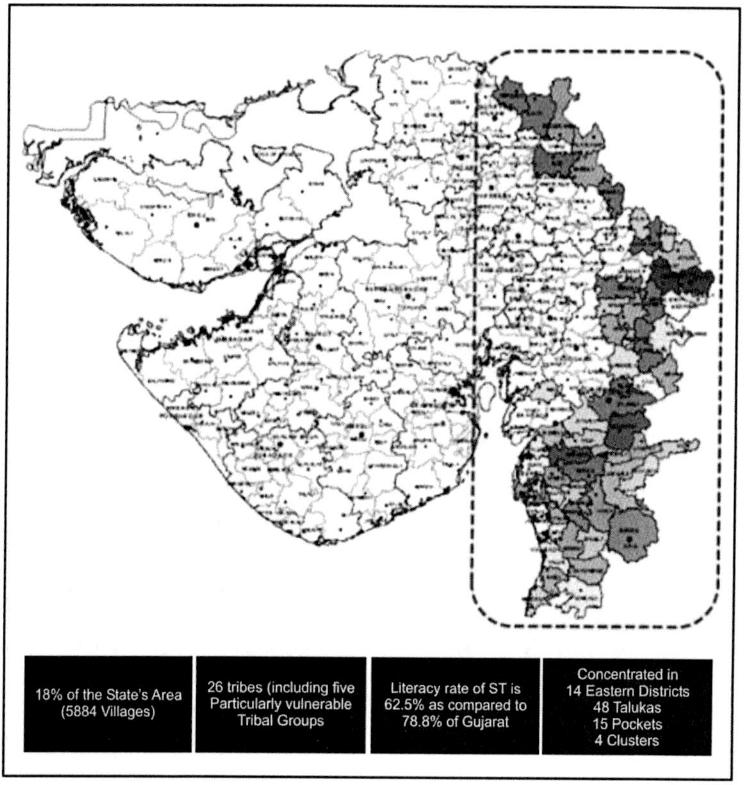

## Appendix Table 1

*State/UT-Wise Literacy Rates of Scheduled Tribes (Census 2011)*

| S. No. | State/UTs | Total | | | Rural | | | Urban | | |
|---|---|---|---|---|---|---|---|---|---|---|
| | | Person | Male | Famale | Person | Male | Female | Person | Male | Female |
| 1. | Andhra Pradesh | 49.2 | 58.3 | 40.1 | 46.9 | 56.1 | 37.7 | 66.8 | 74.7 | 58.7 |
| 2. | Arunachal Pradesh | 64.6 | 71.5 | 58.0 | 60.4 | 67.7 | 53.3 | 84.6 | 90.3 | 79.4 |
| 3. | Assam | 72.1 | 79.0 | 65.1 | 70.9 | 78.0 | 63.8 | 90.0 | 93.7 | 86.3 |
| 4. | Bihar | 51.1 | 61.3 | 40.4 | 50.3 | 60.7 | 39.5 | 65.3 | 72.5 | 57.6 |
| 5. | Chhattisgarh | 59.1 | 69.7 | 48.8 | 57.6 | 68.4 | 47.1 | 76.9 | 84.9 | 69.0 |
| 6. | Goa | 79.1 | 87.2 | 71.5 | 78.4 | 86.4 | 70.7 | 80.2 | 88.3 | 72.7 |
| 7. | Gujarat | 62.5 | 71.7 | 53.2 | 61.3 | 70.7 | 51.8 | 72.7 | 80.0 | 65.1 |
| 8. | Haryana | – | – | – | – | – | – | – | – | – |
| 9. | Himachal Pradesh | 73.6 | 8.32 | 64.2 | 73.0 | 82.7 | 63.4 | 87.4 | 92.5 | 81.9 |
| 10. | Jammu and Kashmir | 50.6 | 60.6 | 39.7 | 49.1 | 59.3 | 38.3 | 71.7 | 79.6 | 62.6 |
| 11. | Jharkhand | 57.1 | 68.2 | 46.2 | 55.2 | 66.6 | 48.9 | 75.4 | 83.2 | 67.8 |
| 12. | Karnataka | 62.1 | 71.1 | 53.0 | 59.0 | 68.5 | 49.4 | 74.8 | 81.9 | 67.7 |
| 13. | Kerala | 75.8 | 80.8 | 71.1 | 74.0 | 79.3 | 69.0 | 90.4 | 92.7 | 88.2 |
| 14. | Madhya Pradesh | 50.6 | 59.6 | 41.5 | 49.3 | 58.4 | 40.1 | 66.7 | 74.0 | 59.2 |
| 15. | Maharashtra | 65.7 | 74.3 | 57.0 | 63.2 | 72.2 | 54.1 | 80.3 | 86.1 | 74.1 |
| 16. | Manipur | 77.4 | 82.1 | 72.7 | 75.9 | 80.8 | 71.1 | 87.7 | 91.6 | 83.9 |
| 17. | Meghalaya | 74.5 | 75.5 | 73.5 | 71.0 | 72.2 | 69.8 | 91.3 | 92.3 | 90.3 |
| 18. | Mizoram | 91.5 | 93.6 | 89.5 | 84.5 | 88.6 | 80.2 | 97.9 | 98.4 | 97.5 |
| 19. | Nagaland | 80.0 | 83.1 | 76.9 | 76.0 | 79.5 | 72.4 | 92.6 | 94.6 | 90.6 |
| 20. | Orissa | 52.2 | 63.7 | 41.2 | 51.1 | 62.7 | 39.9 | 69.1 | 77.7 | 60.5 |
| 21. | Punjab | – | – | – | – | – | – | – | – | – |
| 22. | Rajasthan | 52.8 | 67.6 | 37.3 | 51.7 | 66.7 | 36.1 | 69.0 | 81.0 | 55.6 |
| 23. | Sikkim | 79.7 | 85.0 | 74.3 | 77.5 | 8.32 | 71.4 | 89.2 | 92.9 | 85.6 |
| 24. | Tamil Nadu | 54.3 | 61.8 | 46.8 | 51.3 | 59.0 | 43.6 | 69.1 | 75.4 | 62.7 |
| 25. | Tripura | 79.1 | 86.4 | 71.6 | 78.4 | 86.0 | 70.7 | 92.2 | 94.8 | 89.7 |
| 26. | Uttar Pradesh | 55.7 | 67.1 | 43.7 | 54.5 | 66.2 | 42.3 | 67.0 | 74.8 | 58.0 |
| 27. | Uttarakhand | 73.9 | 83.6 | 63.9 | 72.4 | 82.5 | 62.0 | 88.3 | 93.7 | 82.6 |
| 28. | West Bengal | 57.9 | 68.2 | 47.7 | 56.7 | 67.2 | 46.2 | 71.2 | 78.4 | 64.0 |
| 29. | A and N Islands | 75.6 | 80.9 | 69.9 | 74.2 | 79.8 | 68.2 | 95.2 | 98.0 | 92.6 |
| 30. | Chandigarh | – | – | – | – | – | – | – | – | – |
| 31. | Dadra and Nagar Haveli | 61.9 | 73.9 | 50.3 | 58.5 | 70.8 | 46.3 | 79.5 | 88.0 | 71.1 |
| 32. | Daman and Diu | 78.8 | 86.2 | 71.2 | 79.6 | 87.5 | 71.7 | 78.0 | 85.0 | 70.7 |
| 33. | Delhi | – | – | – | – | – | – | – | – | – |
| 34. | Lakshadweep | 91.7 | 95.7 | 87.8 | 91.5 | 94.7 | 88.3 | 91.8 | 96.0 | 87.6 |
| 35. | Puducherry | – | – | – | – | – | – | – | – | – |
| | India | 59.0 | 68.5 | 49.4 | 56.9 | 66.8 | 46.9 | 76.8 | 83.2 | 70.3 |

*Source:* Registrar General of India, Census, 2011.

## Appendix Table 2

*All Population and ST Population – Total, Male and Female (Census 2011)*

| State | Name of the State/UT | All Population | | | Scheduled Tribe | | |
|---|---|---|---|---|---|---|---|
| | | Total | Male | Female | Total | Male | Female |
| 00 | India (Excl. 3 Sub-divi-sions of Senapati Distt. of Manipur) | 1,21,05,69,573 | 62,31,21,843 | 58,74,47,730 | 10,42,81,034 | 5,24,09,823 | 5,18,71,211 |
| 01 | Jammu & Kashmir | 1,25,41,302 | 66,40,662 | 59,00,640 | 14,93,299 | 7,76,257 | 7,17,042 |
| 02 | Himachal Pradesh | 68,64,602 | 34,81,873 | 33,82,729 | 3,92,126 | 1,96,118 | 1,96,008 |
| 03 | Punjab | 2,77,43,338 | 1,46,39,465 | 1,31,03,873 | 0 | 0 | 0 |
| 04 | Chandigarh | 10,55,450 | 5,80,663 | 4,74,787 | 0 | 0 | 0 |
| 05 | Uttarakhand | 1,00,86,292 | 51,37,773 | 49,48,519 | 2,91,903 | 1,48,669 | 1,43,234 |
| 06 | Haryana | 2,53,51,462 | 1,34,94,734 | 1,18,56,728 | 0 | 0 | 0 |
| 07 | NCT of Delhi | 1,67,87,941 | 89,87,326 | 78,00,615 | 0 | 0 | 0 |
| 08 | Rajasthan | 6,85,48,437 | 3,55,50,997 | 3,29,97,440 | 92,38,534 | 47,42,943 | 44,95,591 |
| 09 | Uttar Pradesh | 19,98,12,341 | 10,44,80,510 | 9,53,31,831 | 11,34,273 | 5,81,083 | 5,53,190 |
| 10 | Bihar | 10,40,99,452 | 5,42,78,157 | 4,98,21,295 | 13,36,573 | 6,82,516 | 6,54,057 |
| 11 | Sikkim | 6,10,577 | 3,23,070 | 2,87,507 | 2,06,360 | 1,05,261 | 1,01,099 |
| 12 | Arunachal Pradesh | 13,83,727 | 7,13,912 | 6,69,815 | 9,51,821 | 4,68,390 | 4,83,431 |
| 13 | Nagaland | 19,78,502 | 10,24,649 | 9,53,853 | 17,10,973 | 8,66,027 | 8,44,946 |
| 14 | Manipur | 25,70,390 | 12,90,171 | 12,80,219 | 9,02,740 | 4,50,887 | 4,51,853 |
| 15 | Mizoram | 10,97,206 | 5,55,339 | 5,41,867 | 10,36,115 | 5,16,294 | 5,19,821 |

Cont'd...

*...Cont'd*

| | | | | | | | |
|---|---|---|---|---|---|---|---|
| 16 | Tripura | 36,73,917 | 18,74,376 | 17,99,541 | 11,66,813 | 5,88,327 | 5,78,486 |
| 17 | Meghalaya | 29,66,889 | 14,91,832 | 14,75,057 | 25,55,861 | 12,69,728 | 12,86,133 |
| 18 | Assam | 3,12,05,576 | 1,59,39,443 | 1,52,66,133 | 38,84,371 | 19,57,005 | 19,27,366 |
| 19 | West Bengal | 9,12,76,115 | 4,68,09,027 | 4,44,67,088 | 52,96,953 | 26,49,974 | 26,46,979 |
| 20 | Jharkhand | 3,29,88,134 | 1,69,30,315 | 1,60,57,819 | 86,45,042 | 43,15,407 | 43,29,635 |
| 21 | Odisha | 4,19,74,218 | 2,12,12,136 | 2,07,62,082 | 95,90,756 | 47,27,732 | 48,63,024 |
| 22 | Chhattisgarh | 2,55,45,198 | 1,28,32,895 | 1,27,12,303 | 78,22,902 | 38,73,191 | 39,49,711 |
| 23 | Madhya Pradesh | 7,26,26,809 | 3,76,12,306 | 3,50,14,503 | 1,53,16,784 | 77,19,404 | 75,97,380 |
| 24 | Gujarat | 6,04,39,692 | 3,14,91,260 | 2,89,48,432 | 89,17,174 | 45,01,389 | 44,15,785 |
| 25 | Daman & Diu | 2,43,247 | 1,50,301 | 92,946 | 15,363 | 7,771 | 7,592 |
| 26 | Dadra & Nagar Haveli | 3,43,709 | 1,93,760 | 1,49,949 | 1,78,564 | 88,844 | 89,720 |
| 27 | Maharashtra | 11,23,74,333 | 5,82,43,056 | 5,41,31,277 | 1,05,10,213 | 53,15,025 | 51,95,188 |
| 28 | Andhra Pradesh | 8,45,80,777 | 4,24,42,146 | 4,21,38,631 | 59,18,073 | 29,69,362 | 29,48,711 |
| 29 | Karnataka | 6,10,95,297 | 30,966,657 | 3,01,28,640 | 42,48,987 | 21,34,754 | 21,14,233 |
| 30 | Goa | 14,58,545 | 7,39,140 | 7,19,405 | 1,49,275 | 72,948 | 76,327 |
| 31 | Lakshadweep | 64,473 | 33,123 | 31,350 | 61,120 | 30,515 | 30,605 |
| 32 | Kerala | 3,34,06,061 | 1,60,27,412 | 1,73,78,649 | 4,84,839 | 2,38,203 | 2,46,636 |
| 33 | Tamil Nadu | 7,21,47,030 | 3,61,37,975 | 3,60,09,055 | 7,94,697 | 4,01,068 | 3,93,629 |
| 34 | Puducherry | 12,47,953 | 6,12,511 | 6,35,442 | 0 | 0 | 0 |
| 35 | Andaman & Nicobar Islands | 3,80,581 | 2,02,871 | 1,77,710 | 28,530 | 14,731 | 13,799 |

*Source:* Census 2011.

## Appendix Table 3

*List of Tribe with more than 5 Lakh of Population and Their Usual Place of Habitation per Census 2001*

| *Tribe Name* | *Population* | | | *Usual Place of Habitation (State Name)* |
|---|---|---|---|---|
| | *Person* | *Male* | *Female* | |
| Bhil | 1,26,89,952 | 64,28,757 | 62,61,195 | Tripura, Andhra Pradesh, Rajasthan, Chhattisgarh, Adhya Pradesh, Gujarat, Maharashtra, Karnataka |
| Gond | 1,08,59,422 | 54,41,476 | 54,17,946 | Bihar, West Bengal, Jharkhand, Orissa, Chhattisgarh, Madhya Pradesh, Gujarat, Andhra Pradesh, Karnataka |
| Santal | 58,38,016 | 29,45,209 | 28,92,807 | Bihar, Tripura, West Bengal, Orissa, Jharkhand |
| Mina | 38,00,002 | 19,76,425 | 18,23,577 | Rajasthan, Madhya Pradesh |
| Naikda etc. | 33,44,954 | 16,96,530 | 16,48,424 | Karnataka, Rajasthan, Gujarat, Daman & Diu, Dadra & Nagar Haveli, Maharashtra, Goa |
| Oraon | 31,42,145 | 15,80,607 | 15,61,538 | Bihar, West Bengal, Jharkhand, Orissa, Chhattisgarh, Madhya Pradesh, Maharashtra |
| Sugalis etc. | 20,77,947 | 10,71,589 | 10,06,358 | Andhra Pradesh |
| Munda | 19,18,218 | 9,66,070 | 9,52,148 | Bihar, West Bengal, Jharkhand, Chhattisgarh, Madhya Pradesh, Tripura, Orissa |
| Naga etc.* | 18,20,965 | 9,37,444 | 8,83,521 | Nagaland, |
| Khond | 13,97,384 | 6,89,330 | 7,08,054 | Bihar, West Bengal, Jharkhand, Orissa |
| Boro etc. | 13,52,771 | 6,82,710 | 6,70,061 | Assam |
| Koli Mahadev etc. | 12,27,562 | 6,25,019 | 6,02,543 | Maharashtra |
| Khasi etc. | 11,38,356 | 5,64,412 | 5,73,944 | Mizoram, Meghalaya, Assam |

*Cont'd...*

*...Cont'd*

| | | | | |
|---|---|---|---|---|
| Kol | 9,91,400 | 5,08,920 | 4,82,480 | Orissa, Chhattisgarh, Madhya Pradesh, Maharashtra |
| Varli | 9,74,916 | 4,84,893 | 4,90,023 | Gujarat, Daman & Diu, Dadra & Nagar Haveli, Maharashtra, Karnataka, Goa |
| Kokna | 9,26,763 | 4,66,087 | 4,60,676 | Dadra & Nagar Haveli, Rajasthan, Gujarat, Maharashtra, Karnataka |
| Kawar | 8,12,770 | 4,05,524 | 4,07,246 | Orissa, Chhattisgarh, Madhya Pradesh, Maharashtra |
| Ho | 8,06,921 | 4,01,913 | 4,05,008 | Bihar, West Bengal, Jharkhand, Orissa |
| Gujjar | 7,99,344 | 4,18,655 | 3,80,689 | Jammu & Kashmir, Himachal Prades |
| Korku etc. | 7,74,196 | 3,95,334 | 3,78,862 | Chhattisgarh, Madhya Pradesh, Maharashtra |
| Bhumij | 7,65,909 | 3,87,336 | 3,78,573 | West Bengal, Jharkhand, Orissa |
| Garo | 7,25,502 | 3,66,629 | 3,58,873 | Nagaland, Mizoram, Meghalaya, Assam, West Bengal, Tripura |
| Koya | 6,92,435 | 3,45,040 | 3,47,395 | Orissa, Maharashtra, Andhra Pradesh, Karnataka |
| Any Mizo (Lushai) Tribes etc. | 6,67,764 | 334983 | 332781 | Manipur, Mizoram, Meghalaya, Assam |
| Halba etc. | 6,39,094 | 3,19,254 | 3,19,840 | Chhattisgarh, Madhya Pradesh, Maharashtra |
| Dharua | 6,30,469 | 3,16,877 | 3,13,592 | Gujarat, Daman & Diu, Dadra & Nagar Haveli, Maharashtra, Karnataka, Goa |
| Dubla etc. | 6,27,599 | 3,16,502 | 3,11,097 | Gujarat, Daman & Diu, Dadra & Nagar Haveli, Maharashtra, Goa |
| Mising/Miri | 5,87,310 | 2,99,790 | 2,87,520 | Assam, Arunachal Pradesh |
| Tripuri etc. | 5,43,848 | 2,75,784 | 2,68,064 | Tripura |
| Rathawa | 5,36,135 | 2,73,754 | 2,62,381 | Gujarat, Maharashtra, Karnataka |
| Saharia etc. | 5,27,015 | 2,71,471 | 2,55,544 | Chhattisgarh, Madhya Pradesh, Rajasthan |

## Appendix Table 4

*List of Gujarat Tribes*

1. Barda
2. Bavacha, Bamcha
3. Bharwad (in the Nesses of the forests of Alech, Barada and Gir)
4. Bhil, Bhil Garasia, Dholi Bhil, Dungri Bhil, Dungri Garasia, Mewasi Bhil, Rawal Bhil, Tadvi Bhil, Bhagalia, Bhilala, Pawra, Vasava, Vasave
5. Charan (in the Nesses of the forests of Alech, Barada and Gir)
6. Chaudhri (in Surat and Valsad districts)
7. Chodhara
8. Dhanka, Tadvi, Tetaria, Valvi
9. Dhodia, Dhodi
10. Dubla, Talavia, Halpati
11. Gamit, Gamta, Gavit, Mavchi, Padvi
12. Gond, Rajgond
13. Kathodi, Katkari, Dhor Kathodi, Dhor Katkari, Son Kathodi, Son Katkari
14. Kokna, Kokni, Kukna
15. Koli Dhor, Tokre Koli, Kolcha, Kolgha
16. Kunbi (in the Dangs district)
17. Naikda, Nayaka, Cholivala Nayaka, Kapadia Nayaka, Mota Nayaka, Nana Nayaka
18. Padhar
19. Pomla
20. Rabari (in the Nesses of the forests of Alech, Barada and Gir)
21. Rathawa
22. Siddi, Siddi- Badshan (in Amreli, Bhavnagar, Jamnagar, Junagadh, Rajkot and Surendranagar districts)
23. Varli
24. Vitola, Kotwalia, Barodia
25. Bhil, Bhilala, Barela, Patelia
26. Tadvi Bhil, Bawra, Vasave
27. Padvi

## Appendix Table 5

*List of Madhya Pradesh Tribes*

| | | | |
|---|---|---|---|
| 1. | Agariya | 17. | Halba,Halbi |
| 2. | Andh | 18. | Kamar |
| 3. | Baiga | 19. | Karku |
| 4. | Bhaina | 20. | Kawar, Kanwar, Kaur, Cherwa, Rathia, Tanwar, Chattri |
| 5. | Bharia Bhumia, Bhuinhar Bhumia, Bhumiya, Bharia, Paliha, Pando | 21. | (Omitted) |
| 6. | Bhattra | 22. | Khairwar, Kondar |
| 7. | Bhil, Bhilala, Barela, Patelia | 23. | Kharia |
| 8. | Bhil Mina | 24. | Kondh, Khond, Kandh |
| 9. | Bhunjia | 25. | Kol |
| 10. | Biar, Biyar | 26. | Kolam |
| 11. | Binjhwar | 27. | Korku, Bopchi, Mouasi, Nihal, Nahul, Bondhi, Bondeya |
| 12. | Birhul, Birhor | 28. | Korwa, Kodaku |
| 13. | Damor, Damaria | 29. | Majhi |
| 14. | Dhanwar | 30. | Majhwar |
| 15. | Gadaba, Gadba | 31. | Mawasi |
| 16. | Gond, Arakh, Arrakh, Agaria, Asur, Badi Maria, Bada Maria, Bhatola, Bhimma, Bhuta, Koilabhuta, Koliabhuti, Bhar, Bisonhorn Maria, Chota Maria, Dandami Maria, Dhuru, Dhurwa, Dhoba, Dhulia, Dorla, Gaiki, Gatta, Gatti, Gaita, Gond Gowari, Hill Maria, Kandra, Kalanga, Khatola, Koitar, Koya, Khirwar, Khirwara, Kucha Maria, Kuchaki Maria, Madia, Maria, Mana, Mannewar, Moghya, Mogia, Monghya, Mudia, Muria, Nagarchi, Nagwanshi, Ojha, Raj, Sonjhari, Jhareka, Thatia, Thotya, Wade Maria, Vade Maria, Daroi | 32. | Omitted |
| | | 33. | Munda |
| | | 34. | Nagesia, Nagasia |
| | | 35. | Oraon, Dhanka, Dhangad |
| | | 36. | Panika [in (i) Chhatar-pur, Panna, Rewa, Satna, Shahdol, Umaria, Sidhi and Tikamgarh districts c, and (ii) Sevda and Datia tehsils of Datia district)] |
| | | 37. | Pao |
| | | 38. | Pardhan, Pathari, Saroti |
| | | 39. | Omitted |

*Cont'd...*

*...Cont'd*

40. Pardhi, Bahelia, Bahellia, Chita Pardhi, Langoli Pardhi, Phans Pardhi, Shikari, Takankar, Takia [in (i) Chhindwara, Mandla, Dindori and Seoni districts, (ii) Baihar tehsil of Balaghat district, (iii) Betul, Bhainsdehi and Shahpur tahsils of Betul district, (iv) Patan tahsil and Sihora and Majholi blocks of Jabalpur disitrict, (v) Katni (Murwara) and Vijaya Raghogarh tahsils and Bahoriband and Dhemerkheda blocks of Katni district, (vi) Hoshangabad, Babai, Sohagpur, Pipariya and Bankhedi tahsils and Kesla block of Hoshangabad district, (vii) Narsinghpur district, and (viii) Harsud tahsil of Khandwa district]
41. Parja
42. Sahariya, Saharia, Seharia, Sehria, Sosia, Sor
43. Saonta, Saunta
44. Saur
45. Sawar, Sawara
46. Sonr

## Appendix Table 6

*List of Maharashtra Tribes*

1. Andh
2. Baiga
3. Barda
4. Bavacha, Bamcha
5. Bhaina
6. Bharia Bhumia, Bhuinhar Bhumia, Pando
7. Bhattra
8. Bhil, Bhil Garasia, Dholi Bhil, Dungri Bhil, Dungri Garasia, Mewasi Bhil, Rawal Bhil, Tadvi Bhil, Bhagalia, Bhilala, Pawra, Vasava, Vasave
9. Bhunjia
10. Binjhwar
11. Birhul, Birhor
12. Omitted
13. Dhanka, Tadvi, Tetaria, Valvi
14. Dhanwar
15. Dhodia
16. Dubla, Talavia, Halpati
17. Gamit, Gamta, Gavit, Mavchi, Padvi
18. Gond, Rajgond, Arakh, Arrakh, Agaria, Asur, Badi Maria, Bada Maria, Bhatola, Bhimma, Bhuta, Koilabhuta, Koilabhuti, Bhar, Bisonhorn Maria, Chota Maria, Dandami Maria, Dhuru, Dhurwa, Dhoba, Dhulia, Dorla, Gaiki, Gatta, Gatti, Gaita, Gond Gowari, Hill Maria, Kandra, Kalanga, Khatola, Koitar, Koya, Khirwar, Khirwara, Kucha Maria, Kuchaki Maria, Madia, Maria, Mana, Mannewar, Moghya, Mogia, Monghya, Mudia, Muria, Nagarchi, Naikpod, Nagwanshi, Ojha, Raj, Sonjhari Jhareka, Thatia, Thotya, Wade Maria, Vade Maria.
19. Halba, Halbi
20. Kamar
21. Kathodi, Katkari, Dhor Kathodi, Dhor Kathkari, Son Kathodi, Son Katkari
22. Kawar, Kanwar, Kaur, Cherwa, Rathia, Tanwar, Chattri
23. Khairwar
24. Kharia
25. Kokna, Kokni, Kukna
26. Kol
27. Kolam, Mannervarlu
28. Koli Dhor, Tokre Koli, Kolcha, Kolgha
29. Koli Mahadev, Don-gar Koli
30. Koli Malhar
31. Kondh, Khond, Kandh
32. Korku, Bopchi, Mouasi, Nihal, Nahul, Bondhi, Bondeya
33. Koya, Bhine Koya, Rajkoya
34. Nagesia, Nagasia
35. Naikda, Nayaka, Cholivala Nayaka, Kapadia Nayaka, Mota Nayaka, Nana Nayaka
36. Oraon, Dhangad
37. Pardhan, Pathari, Saroti
38. Pardhi, Advichincher, Phans Pardhi, Phanse Pardhi, Langoli Pardhi, Bahelia, Bahellia, Chita Pardhi, Shikari, Takankar, Takia
39. Parja

*Cont'd...*

*...Cont'd*

| | | | |
|---|---|---|---|
| 40. | Patelia | 44. | Thakur, Thakar, Ka Thakur, Ka Thakar, Ma Thakur, Ma Thakar |
| 41. | Pomla | 45. | Omitted |
| 42. | Rathawa | 46. | Varli |
| 43. | Sawar, Sawara | 47. | Vitolia, Kotwalia, Barodia |

## Appendix Table 7

*List of Rajasthan Tribes*

| | | | |
|---|---|---|---|
| 1. | Bhil, Bhil Gara sia, Dholi Bhil, Dungri Bhil, Dungri Garasia, Mewasi Bhil, Rawal Bhil, Tadvi Bhil, Bhagalia, Bhilala, Pawra, Vasava, Vasave | 7. | Kokna, Kokni, Kukna |
| 2. | Bhil Mina | 8. | Koli Dhor, Tokre Koli, Kol cha, Kolgha |
| 3. | Damor, Damaria | 9. | Mina |
| 4. | Dhanka, Tadvi, Tetaria, Valvi | 10. | Naikda, Nayaka, Cholivala Nayaka, Kapadia Nayaka, Mota Nayaka, Nana Nayaka |
| 5. | Garasia (excluding Rajput Garasia) | 11. | Patelia |
| 6. | Kathodi, Katkari Dhor Kathodi, Dhor Katkari, Son Kathodi, Son Katkari | 12. | Sehria, Seharia, Sahariya. |

## Appendix Table 8

*Name of the Particularly Vulnerable Tribal Groups (PTGs) (Earlier Called as Primitive Tribal Groups) – State/UT-Wise*

| *Name of the State* | *Name of PTGs* |
|---|---|
| Gujarat | Kathodi |
| | Kotwalia |
| | Padhar |
| | Siddi |
| | Kolgha |
| Madhya Pradesh (including Chhattisgarh) | Abujh Marias |
| | Baigas |
| | Bharias |
| | Hill Korbas |
| | Kamars |
| | Saharias |
| | Birhor |
| Maharashtra | Katkaria (Kathodia) |
| | Kolam |
| | Maria Gond |
| Rajasthan | Seharias |

# Index